Family Circle
CHRISTMAS TREASURY
1 • 9 • 8 • 7

Other Books by Family Circle

The Best of Family Circle Cookbook
1986 Family Circle Cookbook
The Family Circle Christmas Treasury
1987 Family Circle Cookbook

Family Circle Favorite Needlecrafts
(Pub. date: October, 1987)

1988 Family Circle Cookbook
(Pub. date: January, 1988)

To order **FamilyCircle** books, write to Family Circle Special Projects Dept.,
110 Fifth Avenue, New York, NY 10011.

To order **FamilyCircle** magazine, write to Family Circle Subscriptions,
110 Fifth Avenue, New York, NY 10011.

PROJECT STAFF

Project Editor—Ceri E. Hadda
Copy Editor—Jane Glicksman
Project Assistant—Kristen J. Keller
Book Design—Bessen & Tully, Inc.
Typesetting—Angela LaGreca
Illustrations—Maggie Zander, Lauren Jarrett

FAMILY CIRCLE STAFF — EDITORIAL

Editor, Book Development—Carol A. Guasti
How-To Editors: Arlene Gise, Toni Scott

FAMILY CIRCLE STAFF — MARKETING

Manager, Marketing & Development—
Margaret Chan–Yip
Project Coordinator—Karen Wang

Cover Photo—Ralph Bogartman
Photographers—Robert Ander, Ralph Bogartman, John Bonjour,
C. Fleig, David Glomb, Ron Harris, Richard Jefferey, Taylor Lewis,
Mort Mace, Maris/Semel, Bill McGinn, Rudy Muller, Leonard Nones,
Bradley Olman, Bruno Pellegrini, Ron Schwerin, Gordon E. Smith,
Bob Stoller, Theo, René Velez.

Published by The Family Circle, Inc.
110 Fifth Avenue, New York, NY 10011

Copyright© 1987 by The Family Circle, Inc.

Manufactured in the United States of America

10 9 8 7 6 5 4 3 2 1

ISBN 0-933585-04-7
ISSN 0892-3604

FamilyCircle
CHRISTMAS TREASURY
1 • 9 • 8 • 7

TABLE OF CONTENTS

INTRODUCTION

It's the most wonderful time of the year—and we hope this Christmas is your best one ever. For 1987, we're bringing you over 250 craft projects, recipes and ideas to make the season extra-special. There are indoor and outdoor decorations, ornaments for your tree, smart tips and clever hints to make preparations easier. There's even a chapter that combines craft projects and recipes for special Christmas themes! But that's not all: At the beginning of each chapter, you'll find a lovely legend that explains some of the favorite traditions of the season. We also came across some facts about the holidays that were so interesting, we sprinkled them throughout the pages. Look for the boxes marked, "Did You Know..."; they're highlighted with a pretty star.

💲 *Low-Cost* 🔪 *Make-Ahead* 🔪 *Quick and Easy* 📏 *Low-Calorie* 🔪 *Bazaar*

Of course, throughout our Christmas Treasury, we've included symbols to help you identify projects and recipes that suit your skill level and preferences. They're listed above and at the beginning of each chapter. Enjoy the book—and from our "Family" to yours, Merry Christmas!

Shown on our cover: colorful Patchwork Ornaments. For how-to's, see page 55.

Chapter **I**

HOLIDAY HELPER

At Christmas, play and make good cheer,
For Christmas comes but once a year.

That may be true, but *planning* for Christmas sometimes takes weeks—even months! With this in mind, we've gathered our best holiday hints on everything from cleaning and cooking to clever gift ideas. Also in this chapter, you'll find a 1987 Datebook to help pace yourself during the holiday season (and avoid the last-minute rush!) And finally, we offer some sanity-saving guidelines on holiday etiquette. We believe nobody can "do it all"—but a little help can make your life easier, and your holidays alot more enjoyable.

HOLIDAY HINTS AND HELPS

CRAFTY IDEAS

● Save scraps of fabric from various sewing projects. You can make quilt patches, cushion covers, etc. from the prettiest ones. The less pretty bits, such as scraps of pellon, plain muslin and quilt filling, can be sewn together to make potholder padding. Covered with gingham squares and bound with bias strips, these pot holders make attractive Christmas gifts.

● Glass Christmas tree ornaments becoming less attractive with age and use? Wash off the outside paint with a mild mixture of ammonia and water, and spray them with gloss enamel paint. After the ornaments are dry, paint your children's names on them.

● Make your own interesting Christmas tree decorations from old, empty wooden thread spools. Paint them to look like small drums, and they'll make unique additions to your tree.

● Since candles and candlesticks seldom match perfectly, try putting a strip of self-stick foam weather-strip tape around the base of each candle. It will instantly adjust to the candestick opening and remain securely in place. (The narrow foam does not show above the holder either!)

● Satin-covered tree ornaments showing signs of wear, looking rather frayed and shabby? Gently push the loose threads back into place and lightly mist them with hairspray. They'll look good as new!

TRADITIONS

● If you're like many people and you feel the lead up to Christmas necessitates more than one day of celebration, include the day before Christmas as an official part of your family's celebration. Begin with a festive Christmas Eve dinner, but make it a casual buffet so you can enjoy yourself, too. Gather around the tree and open your presents, one at a time. This Christmas Eve priority may seem odd at first, but you'll be surprised at how quickly you'll adjust. Come Christmas morning, you'll still feel all the joy of the holiday, but you can get ready for church and afternoon visiting in leisure.

● If you have extra Christmas cards left over from last season, exchange them with a friend for some of theirs. This way, you'll have all "new" cards for Christmas.

● For a "sweet" countdown to Christmas for the kids, purchase large candy canes wrapped in plastic and hang 24 near the tree. Each evening, just before the kids go to bed, they can move one more cane onto the tree. Then, you can all count the number of ones that are left.

● Try reversing the roles of "playing Santa" in your home. Surprise each grandparent with a large red stocking filled with things the kids have bought for them—small puzzle books, herbal teas, camera film, blank cassette tapes, etc.

PARENT TO PARENT

● To combat the "I want" attitude so prevalent among us, teach your children the true meaning of gift-giving: In January, set aside 25¢ in a special bank made from margarine containers appropriately decorated. Continue adding to the container throughout the year. Come December, let the kids count the money with you and decide what toy to buy for a needy child. Besides learning how to save money, they'll also discover the real spirit of Christmas.

● Cut the colorful smooth panels from last year's Christmas cards into last-minute postcard-size greeting cards. They make perfect cards for the children to send.

● Long trips to visit relatives for the holidays can often be trying. A novel way to make trips more enjoyable is to wrap some inexpensive gifts to be opened by the family every 200 miles or every 3 hours—whichever comes first. It adds excitement to the trip and gives the little ones something to play with as the trip progresses.

● Before gift-wrapping a book for a child, take time to "open" it properly. Place the spine flat on the table and let the covers fall open. Open the first few pages, then run your finger down the seam to gently crease them. Open the last few pages, and crease in the same manner. Continue opening a few pages at a time, alternating front and back, until you reach the middle. Properly "broken in," the binding will last longer, and the book will open more easily for its recipient.

● After the children have opened all their Christmas gifts, pay attention to the toys that they seem to have lost interest in or cast aside. Then make a "rainy day box" to be brought out on bad-weather days only. You will have quite a collection over the year, and the children will be delighted to pick up their "old" toys again.

● A great stocking-stuffer for the college student or anyone who uses a lot of coins is a small drawstring purse filled with quarters, dimes and nickels. Sew the pouch from fabric scraps, using pieces of ribbon or shoelace for the drawstring. Write the recipient's name with felt-tip pens for an easy ID.

CLEANING MADE EASY

● On cold or snowy winter evenings, everyone likes to gather around the glowing warmth of a fireplace. However, cleaning out the ashes the next day is such a messy job. So before you build a fire, remove the grate, line the bottom of the fireplace with a double layer of heavy-duty aluminum foil, then replace the grate. As the fire burns, it not only reflects more heat from the foil but gives a much brighter, cheerier glow. When the ashes are cold, remove the grate again, roll up the foil and dispose of it. This is certainly a time-saver, especially during this hectic, happy season!

● When using a sinkful of hot water to rinse the dishes, add a capful of vinegar to cut any excess grease or soap. This will give your dishes a clean, sparkling look.

● Shorten dusting time by spraying furniture polish on cotton work gloves. Slip the gloves on and simply rub the furniture.

● Give your house a thorough once-over for Christmas. But before you start, try to clean up your cleaning equipment, too. Soak mops, brooms, etc. in a baking soda solution. It will remove dirt and odors, leaving them fresh and clean.

● China or glassware with depressions in the design can often be a catchall for coffee and tea stains, or even invisible germs. To clean the cutwork design, use an old toothbrush dipped in a water and ammonia mixture; follow with soap and water, then give it a good rinse.

● When trimming the outside of your house with Christmas lights, run the lead wire through a piece of old garden hose and lay it on the ground. The wind will not loosen it and it can be walked on without danger. Later, the hose can be rolled and stored with the wires.

GIFT SMARTS

- Wrapping small or odd-shaped stocking stuffers becomes a breeze when you use aluminum foil. It fits any shape, requires no tape, looks festive and can be opened by little ones.

- Every year, make or buy a special ornament for each child in your family. When the children grow up and establish their own homes, each will take along a box filled not only with ornaments, but also with love and memories with which to decorate their first Christmas tree.

- Let older children make gifts for their younger siblings: With colored markers, a few stickers and a lot of love and patience, have them decorate lunch bags with rainbows, unicorns and flowers, incorporating the sibling's name into each design. The youngest will be so delighted and proud to show off big sister's or brother's artwork at school each day.

- Include your own "care labels" with the sweaters you knit as Christmas presents for family and friends. Cut heart-shaped labels, attach the care instructions from the yarn band, some strands of yarn (for repairs) and extra buttons, if applicable. The label also becomes a greeting card.

- To perk up crushed bows, insert a rolled-up paper towel into the loops and, with a warm iron, press each loop. Presto! The bows look brand new.

COOK'S CORNER

- To add a festive touch to the holiday buffet, bake pull-apart rolls in a tube pan. After it cools, place the circle of rolls on the table and add a sprig of holly or a red bow for a wreathlike effect.

- Each time you cook in quantity, increase the proportions to make two more servings to go into the freezer as Christmas gifts for working friends. Choose entrees such as coq au vin, seafood crepes and lasagna. Freeze in foil-covered aluminum pie plates and label each entree on top with instructions for defrosting and reheating, plus a few words to set the mood. (For example, "Toss a simple green salad, uncork a bottle of good burgundy, light the candles and enjoy!") You can also include gift certificates from a pastry shop; so the recipients can add a scrumptious finish to their elegant dinner.

- Type up on individual sheets of paper all the recipes you will be serving at your next holiday buffet and make photocopies of them. Roll them into "scrolls" and tie each with a red or green ribbon for a festive touch, then place them in a basket near the buffet table so that anyone who just *has* to have the recipe for any of the dishes can take home a "scroll."

- If the first batch of candy you make does not turn out quite right, instead of asking the family to eat the "mistakes" or throwing them out, grind the candy in a nut chopper and add it to cookie recipes. It works especially well with oatmeal cookies.

1987 DATEBOOK

LATE SUMMER

● Start your gift list by thinking about people's talents, travel and hobbies. To cut down on returns, update clothing sizes for everyone on your gift list. (Remember that babies will be almost five months bigger by Christmas time!)
● Consider planning a holiday bazaar at your local church or school.
● Start making those gifts that take a bit more effort, such as the Men's Sweater Quartet (*page 87*) Woman's Oversized Vest (*page 82*) Child's Norwegian Cardigan and Hat (*page 111*).

SEPTEMBER

● Send away for holiday mail-order catalogs.
● Put together the items you'll be selling at your bazaar (*see ideas in the* Bazaar Boutique, *in* Chapter 5).

OCTOBER

● Now's the time to make your more intricate decorations, like the Outdoor Crèche (*page 20*), perky Stockings (*pages 37-8*)and the Balsa Wood Ornaments (*page 65*).
● Make a list of the ingredients you'll need for Christmas baking and holiday meals. Check your pantry inventory.

8 WEEKS TILL CHRISTMAS

OCT. 30 - NOV. 5

- It's time to bake the breads, cookies and cakes you plan to freeze. (*See Chapter VII for freezing tips.*)

7 WEEKS TILL CHRISTMAS

NOV. 6 - 12

- Mark all special dates for the season on your calendar—school and church concerts, parties, school vacations, etc.
- Start collecting a basketful of inexpensive stocking-stuffers and small gifts for children and unexpected guests.
- Avoid last-minute searching: Gather your favorite holiday recipes and keep them in an envelope. Make a list, with page numbers, of recipes in books. Note which can be made ahead.

6 WEEKS TILL CHRISTMAS

NOV. 13 - 19

- Order catalog gifts *now*. Most take from 4 to 6 weeks to arrive.
- Buy the Christmas turkey to store in your freezer, if you have space.
- Check your cooking utensils, serving dishes, platters, glasses and china place settings. Do any need replacing?
Tip: Store nonperishable foods to be used during the holidays for one meal in a labeled bag—easy to find when you start cooking.
- Make sure all electrical appliances— including TV, mixer, hot trays—are in good working order.
- Decide what additional holiday decorations you're going to make rather than buy (*see Chapters II-VI*).

5 WEEKS TILL CHRISTMAS

NOV. 20 - 26

- Get some of your gift shopping done early at church bazaars and school fairs.
Tip: Start saving boxes in useful sizes for packing presents.
- Polish silver pieces. Store in airtight plastic bags.
- Make edible gifts to give (*see Chapter VII*).
- Buy Christmas cards and stamps. You should also collect all of your other paper supplies, like napkins, paper cups, wrapping paper and ribbon (or alternative gift-wrapping materials such as fabric, baskets and tins).
- Update your Christmas card list by noting any address or name changes.

4 WEEKS TILL CHRISTMAS

NOV. 27 - DEC. 3

- Mail those Christmas cards.
- Send out invitations for Christmas and holiday parties.
- Bake fruitcakes and plum puddings. Store to mellow (*see page 233*).
- Make sure you have enough cooking pots and stovetop burner space for the dishes you plan to serve.
- Make and freeze hors d'oeuvres and casseroles.
- Plan menus for Christmas Eve, Christmas Day and for parties. (*See menus and countdowns in "Home For the Holidays," Chapter 6.*)
- Special-order goose, game or fresh turkey for Christmas dinner.
- Plan time for a special holiday outing or activity with each of your children, perhaps an afternoon of gift making they can be involved in (*see page 115*).

3 WEEKS TILL CHRISTMAS

DEC. 4 - 10

- Schedule beauty appointments—haircut, perm, manicure, etc.
- Have your kids help you make a Gingerbread House (*see page 41*).
- Stock up on canned and frozen foods, crackers and chips for instant snacks.
- Replenish paper and cleaning supplies (foil, wax paper, food-storage and garbage bags, dish detergent).
- Are your holiday outfits in tip-top shape? (Fix hems and loose buttons; make alterations and get clothing dry-cleaned.)
- Make pie shells and freeze.

Tip: Wrap and tag presents as you buy them. Tag the children's presents with numbers if you don't want them to guess whom the packages are for!

2 WEEKS TILL CHRISTMAS

DEC. 11 -17

- It's time to go to work on those outdoor decorations: Checking and hanging the lights, decorating your door, setting out a crèche.
- Take a look at your tablecloths—do you see any burn holes? Stains? Fix, clean and iron now.
- Arrange to exchange baby-sitting time with another mother so each of you will have free shopping hours.
- Are there any items on your mail-order list that haven't arrived yet?
- Devote an evening or two to any last-minute gifts you want to make.
- Buy batteries for presents that need them.

Tip: Use some of your homemade goodies as hostess gifts at holiday parties you're attending. (*For quick, last-minute food gifts, see page 254*).
- Get out the Christmas stockings!

1 WEEK TILL CHRISTMAS

DEC. 18 -24

- Do your indoor decorating. Remember to put holiday towels in the bathroom and decorations in the kitchen and guest room. (*For easy decorating ideas, see* Night Before Christmas Ideas, *page 51*).
- Start stocking up on ice cubes.
- Buy your tree and store it temporarily in a bucket of water in the garage. (*See page 54 for other tips on Christmas tree care.*)
- Test tree lights. (*See page 54 for Christmas tree light safety tips.*)
- Do you have graham crackers or cookies for Santa's snack?

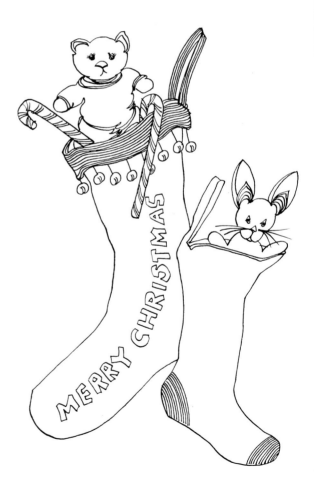

COUNTDOWN
TO A HOLIDAY PARTY

Use this party planner for any of your holiday parties, whether company's coming just for cocktails or for a sumptuous feast. It will help space out your chores so you aren't too exhausted to enjoy your own get-together!

Once you've decided how many people to invite and have planned your menu, it's time to make lists.

List #1: Food Include everything from snacks—mints and nuts—and "real" food (such as casseroles) to ingredients needed for all recipes. Divide the list into two columns: nonperishables and perishables.

List #2: Beverages Liquor, mixers, juice, soda (have planty on hand for nondrinkers), coffee, tea.

List #3: Nonfood items Cocktail napkins, plastic glasses, dripless candles, ice, flowers or centerpieces, paper towels, aluminum foil.

One Week Before
1. Order the ice and flowers and check your beverage inventory against your list.
2. Shop for nonperishable foods.
3. Buy everything on List #3, except ice and flowers.

Four Days Before
4. Select the serving dishes you'll use and set them aside in your cupboard. Need more? Ask a friend now.
5. Check tablecloths, napkins, place mats. Wash and press them if you need to.
6. Make sure you have enough silverware, ashtrays, vases, pitchers, etc.

Three Days Before
7. Do the heavy cleaning, such as floors and walls, and tidy up the house. Let the whole family pitch in.
8. Decide where guests' coats will go. If in a closet, have enough hangers on hand.

Two Days Before
9. Buy the perishables on List #1. Wash and trim the vegetables, then refrigerate them.

One Day Before
10. Make extra ice if needed.
11. Prepare the dishes that can be reheated or served cold.

"The" Day
12. Give the house a once-over in the morning. (If your bedroom is the coat room, neaten it now.)
13. Pick up the flowers and the ice.
14. Use "kid power" to help clean. Set out ashtrays and guest soaps.
15. Arrange the flowers, candles and set up the eating areas and bar.
16. Assemble the ingredients for the dishes that must be cooked that day.

HOLIDAY ETIQUETTE

The holidays present a bevy of sticky situations. Here, etiquette authority Letitia Baldrige gives some helpful answers to often-asked questions.

Q **What is the proper way to seat relatives and friends at a Christmas dinner?**

A Put your father-in-law on your right and the next most important (or oldest) man on your left. Put your mother-in-law on your husband's right and the next most senior woman on his left. Place the other guests in between, alternating men and women whenever you can, and, if possible, avoid seating a husband and wife next to each other.

Q **At a formal dinner party, which pieces of flatware are used for each course?**

A You progress from the outside in, on both sides of the plate. The forks are laid on the table to the left of the plate, and the knives and spoons to the right. If, for example, the first course is a soup, you'll find a soup spoon on the outside right of the place setting. If the next course is fish, you'll find a fish fork on the outside left and a fish knife on the outside right. When the entrée is brought in, you will find a large dinner fork and knife next in line on the left and right. And so on. The dessert implements (most often a fork and spoon) are usually placed in a horizontal position at the top of the plate; leave them there until the dessert course is served.

Q **Is it all right to serve just punch and not offer hard liquor at a holiday party?**

A One punch with alcohol will be fine. And have lots of soft drinks and fruit juices for those who do not drink alcohol.

Q **If you receive a holiday invitation from a friend, isn't it all right to skip the family dinner just once?**

A It's up to you, but there's one element of Christmas that should always come first: your family. Friends come and go, but the family is always there, and I think it's poor judgment to risk offending your relatives.

Q **Is there a subtle way to make sure guests don't bring their children to a party?**

A Don't be subtle. Anyone who has done that to you deserves a special telephone call in which you mention (not casually) that you really don't have the space for anyone's children at this adult party. If they come back to you and say, "But we can't find a babysitter," tell them how sorry you are that they won't be able to make it this time.

Q What kind of gift is appropriate to give to your boss?

A You aren't obligated to give the boss anything at Christmas. If you've been working for your boss for only a short time, a greeting card with a handwritten message of friendship would be appropriate. Or something not too costly—a Christmas tree ornament, a small plant for the office, something good to eat or possibly something you made yourself.

If you have been working for someone a long time and are close to his or her family, you might give something they can all enjoy—such as food, an art book, musical tapes or anything that reflects the family's special interests. But don't overspend; it will embarrass your boss.

Q How—and where—on an invitation should you tell guests not to bring gifts?

A Don't ruin your invitations by putting a negative "No gifts, please" on them. It's far more graceful to say to your best friends that you really don't want any presents.

Q How do you determine how much money to spend on a gift for a friend?

A Friendship should never be based on dollars and cents, and you shouldn't even try to show your gratitude by equating it with a specified sum. Find something you know they will like, something related to their interest or to their taste in food or wine. You might find a useful or decorative item for their home. Such a gift will mean more to them than an expensive one, because you unearthed it on an expedition to find something they would really enjoy. More important than the gift will be the personal note accompanying it—which should be the most carefully planned part of the operation!

Q If a hostess is giving an informal "come as you are" after-work party, is it inappropriate for her to wear an evening skirt?

A As the hostess you may certainly wear a floor-length dress, even if your guests will be dressed much more informally. A simple evening dress, a caftan or a long skirt and blouse are fine for an evening affair.

Q If you thank someone for a gift when you see him or her or talk on the phone, is that sufficient thanks?

A No. A written thank-you is in order for every person who gave you a present, whether or not you have already expressed your thanks in person or on the phone. A thank-you note can be read by several people and enjoyed when reread. It is the only proper kind of thanks.

Q What do you do if your grandchildren never acknowledge the gifts sent to them?

A Announce to all concerned this year that if you don't hear from them in writing after Christmas, you will conclude that they did not receive their gifts. Therefore, "there is no sense in sending you anything, so I will remove your names from my gift list." (And do that if they don't write to you this year!)

SENDING CARDS

Times change, lifestyles change—so sending holiday cards often call for new ground rules. The experts at Hallmark suggest these social and business guidelines.

For Social Correspondence

● When sending a card to a couple with two different last names, address the card to "Mary Smith and John Jones." If there are children, write "Mary Smith, John Jones and Family."

● Remember some divorced women use their maiden name. Make sure you know which last name and courtesy title she prefers.

● If there are children, include their names, too, for family and social friends. Traditionally, family signatures begin with the father's name, then the mother's and finally the children, but this is not a hard and fast rule.

● Keep your signature informal. No courtesy titles, and to close friends and relatives, no last names either.

● Non-Jewish people may send holiday greetings to Jewish friends and vice versa. However, religious Christmas cards or those featuring the word "Christmas" are not appropriate for Jewish friends, nor are Hanukkah cards appropriate for Christians. Choose a non-religious card that says "Happy Holidays" or "Season's Greetings."

● Take special care following a death in a family. Cards are available with messages of sympathy at Christmastime. If the card is to a widow, address her "Mrs. John Jones."

● There is no limit to the number of people you include on your card list, but sending a card to everyone you know is both inappropriate and costly. A Christmas card should be much more than a social gesture—it should be a personal communication to express sincere good wishes.

For Business-Related Correspondence

● Business greeting cards should be more tailored and formal than cards for family and social friends. Messages are brief and usually secular.

● Mail cards for business associates to the office. However, if you are social friends or have met the person's spouse or live-in, send cards to the home. Only you should sign the card (unless your spouse or partner has met the recipient).

● When sending to a married woman who uses her maiden name at work, address the card to "Mr. and Mrs. John Smith." If she prefers to use her maiden name for all occasions, work and social, address the card to "Mr. John Smith and Ms. Susan Jones."

For All Correspondence

● Save yourself holiday hassles by mailing early—any time after Thanksgiving is appropriate.

● Mail cards first class so they will be forwarded or returned to you if the addressee cannot be located.

● Include your return address to comply with the U.S. Postal Service's request and to help your friends keep their mailing lists up to date.

Candy Cane Doorway—A Delectable Way to Say Welcome!

Legend has it…Decking the halls with boughs of holly didn't start off as a Christmas ritual at all. This custom goes back to a Roman festival honoring Saturn, the god of agriculture. During this late December celebration, Romans would fill their homes with greens and give each other holly wreaths as symbols of friendship. The first Christians (who had to practice their new religion in secret) hung holly and greens on their doors to mask their beliefs from the Romans. Later, Christians adopted the custom as their own, and now wreaths, boughs and garlands are a favorite part of Christmas.

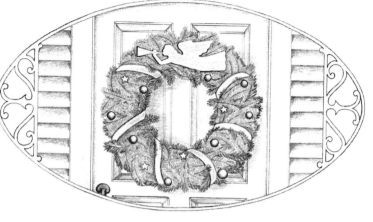

Chapter

II

DECORATIONS: OUTDOORS!

If you've ever driven around your neighborhood to see the holiday displays, you're as much a fan of outdoor decorations as we are. The magic of Christmas *begins* outdoors—with festive doors and windows, twinkling lights, lovely crèches. Here, we bring you some very special decorations: Each adds a touch of holiday cheer; each says "Merry Christmas" to everyone who passes by.

🔲 *Low-Cost*

🔲 *Make-Ahead*

🔲 *Quick and Easy*

🔲 *Low-Calorie*

🔲 *Bazaar*

HOLIDAY DOORS

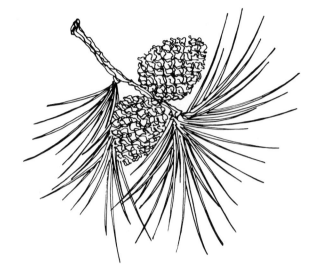

💲
CANDY CANE
(about 15")

EASY: Achievable by anyone.
MATERIALS—for Candy Cane and Basket: Striped fabric (weatherize it with a stain-repellent finish); polyester fiberfill for stuffing; three 5 x 8½" pieces 2"-thick Styrofoam®; carpet thread; sturdy needle; 2½"-wide ribbon; heavy wire.

DIRECTIONS:
1. Enlarge pattern in FIG. 1, following the directions on page 271.
2. Cut one pair of canes (note grainline), with stripes matching.
3. Seam (¼") + right sides together, leaving open between circles.
4. Turn right side out, stuff. Slipstitch opening closed.

FIG. 1   1 SQ. = 2"

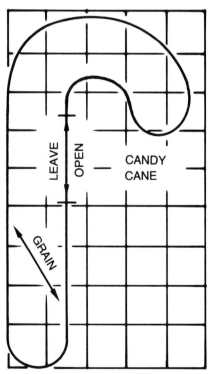

LEAVE OPEN

CANDY CANE

GRAIN

CANDY CANE BASKET
(About 12" deep x 15" x 20")

DIRECTIONS:
1. Stack and glue together Styrofoam pieces. Draw curve from center of one long edge to each end of the opposite edge. Cut along curve.
2. Make 10 canes. Sew them together side by side, taking long stitches through the backs 2" from the bottom using carpet thread. Repeat, near the curved ends.
3. Cut 40" length of ribbon and weave it through the canes, starting 3" from bottom. Repeat just above (*see photo*).
4. Fold ten 12" pieces of wire into U shapes. Hold canes against the foam curve (extending 3" below) and push wire U over each cane (under the ribbon) into the foam. Pull ribbon ends to back of form and fasten with small U's.
5. Push a wire U into top of foam near center back edge. Push thin wire into the back of some canes and tie wire to this central fastener.
6. Wire ribbon bow to "basket" (*see photo*).

LIGHTS! CHRISTMAS! ACTION!

ighted Stairs

LIGHTED STAIRS

EASY: Achievable by anyone.
MATERIALS: Terra cotta pots; sand; tall red candles; gravel; hurricane shades.

DIRECTIONS:
Fill each terra-cotta pot with sand and insert a candle. Top with gravel; add a hurricane shade. Finish the scene by entwining miniature lights in foliage.

WINDOW WONDERLAND

Window Wonderland

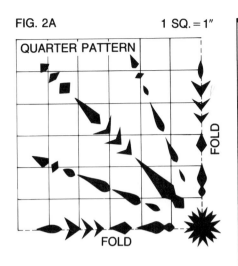

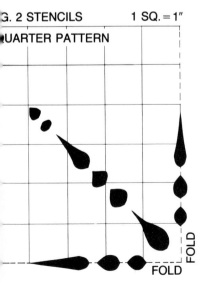

WINDOW WONDERLAND

EASY: Achievable by anyone.

MATERIALS: Lights (*see DIREC-TIONS*); white paper; scissors; masking tape; aerosol snow; paper towels; glass cleaner.

DIRECTIONS:

Lights shown were as follows: clear miniature lights on indoor trees, icicle lights on exterior garland, clear classic lights on the two small trees in outdoor urns.

Enlarge patterns in FIGS. 2 and 2a, following the directions on page 271. Snowflake stencils were made by folding white paper in quarters and then again diagonally and cutting out shapes along the fold lines (the way you made snowflakes when you were kids). Most cutouts were V's or half circles in different sizes and combinations (use FIGS. 2 and 2a or invent your own designs). Since the snowflake is to be used as a stencil or negative, take care not to cut away the edges of the square. The squares are taped to the window with masking tape, and aerosol snow is sprayed on.

FIG. 2A   1 SQ. = 1″

QUARTER PATTERN

FOLD

FOLD

4. After carefully removing the stencils, wipe the areas around them clean with a piece of paper towel dampened with glass cleaner. Do not apply cleaner directly to window, as the snowflakes might run.

FIG. 2 STENCILS   1 SQ. = 1″

QUARTER PATTERN

FOLD

FOLD

SAFETY POINTERS

● *Check your light sets for cracked insulation, frayed wires or damaged sockets. Any one of these could cause short circuits.*

● *Don't overload your string sets. Check instructions on package to find out how many light sets can be connected to each other.*

● *Avoid overloading curcuits. Most home circuits can take 15 amps, or 1,800 watts.*

● *Cover each outdoor plug and connector joint with plastic wrap to protect from rain, sleet and snow; seal with electrical tape.*

● *If you use staples instead of tape to secure lights, be sure that they're insulated staples.*

● *Make sure that decorations pose no danger to children or pets. Don't leave cords dangling or strung loosely on the floor or stairs.*

TIPS ON OUTDOOR LIGHTING

● *Try floodlighting evergreens for drama. Stick to blue, green, clear and deluxe white mercury lamps—these enhance the colors of evergreens. Avoid red, yellow, amber and pink, which turn the trees a muddy brown color.*

● *Illuminate deciduous trees as well as your evergreens. You can flood a tree, to highlight its shape and pattern, with a single spotlight. Or place shiny ornaments in the tree and light it from below with several smaller spots.*

● *Get more sparkle and glitter with transparent bulbs. Unlike color-coated bulbs, they allow the filament to show through.*

● *Set up your display at night, when you can see the effects of your illumination. You can't get the true overall picture in daylight.*

● *Use an adequate number of bulbs for trimming your home.*

● *Use light bulb colors in the same family. Blue and green are "cool colors." Red, orange, yellow and white are "warm."*

● *Choose one major theme.*

● *Place floodlights and spotlights in strategic positions. Your efforts at holiday time can be used year-round for security.*

Outdoor Crèche

OUTDOOR CRÈCHE
(26"Dx65"Hx69"L)

CHALLENGING: Requires more experience in woodworking and craftwork.

MATERIALS: *Plywood*—4 panels of ½" x 4' x 8', one ¼" x 4' x 68", one ¼ x 17" x 68" (AB-EXT grade); *lumber*—1 x 1 x 6', 1 x 2 x 14', 1 x 2 x 16', 1 x 4 x 6'; *hardware*—1",

1¼" F.H. wood screws; 2d, 4d finishing nails; ¾" brads; waterproof glue; four 3" flat corner braces, two 3" "T" braces; one 2' x 7' Mylar (opaque, thin plastic sheet sold in art supply stores for drafting); ⅛" dia. x 10' of copper or aluminum wire or rod; four screw-eyes to fit wire dia.; beige and med. green flat paint.

TOOLS REQUIRED: Power saw; jig or sabre saw; hammer; screwdriver; drill and screwdrill set; staple gun; portable belt sander; "C" clamps.

FIG. 3

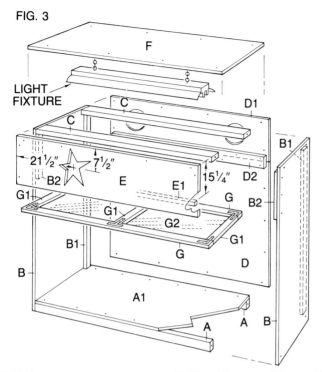

LIGHT
FIXTURE

CUTTING DIRECTIONS FOR STABLE

CODE	PIECES	SIZE
A(2x4)	(2)	$1\frac{1}{2}$" x $3\frac{1}{2}$" x 67" Bottom rails
A1(PLY)	(1)	$\frac{1}{2}$" x 24" x 67" Bottom
B(PLY)	(2)	$\frac{1}{2}$" x 24" x 65" Sides
B1(1x2)	(2)	$\frac{3}{4}$" x $1\frac{1}{2}$" x $61\frac{1}{2}$" Cleat
B2(1x2)	(2)	$\frac{3}{4}$" x $1\frac{1}{2}$" x $61\frac{1}{2}$" Cleat
C(2x4)	(2)	$1\frac{1}{2}$" x $3\frac{1}{2}$" x 67" Top rails
D(PLY)	(1)	$\frac{1}{4}$" x 48" x 68" Back
D1(PLY)	(1)	$\frac{1}{4}$" x 17" x 68" Back
D2(1x4)	(1)	$\frac{3}{4}$" x $3\frac{1}{2}$" x $65\frac{1}{2}$" Back cleat
E(PLY)	(1)	$\frac{1}{2}$" x 18" x 68" Front
E1(1x1)	(1)	$\frac{3}{4}$" x $\frac{3}{4}$" x $65\frac{1}{2}$" Support
F(PLY)	(1)	$\frac{1}{2}$" x $25\frac{3}{4}$" x 69" Top
G(1x2)	(2)	$\frac{3}{4}$" x $1\frac{1}{2}$" x 65" Diffuser
G1(1x2)	(3)	$\frac{3}{4}$" x $1\frac{1}{2}$" x $20\frac{1}{2}$" Diffuser
G2	(1)	$23\frac{1}{2}$" x 65" Diffuser

DIRECTIONS:

Start with the stable that will contain the crèche figures.

Bottom (A1) is cut from one sheet plywood, the sides (B) from a second and front (E), top (F) from a third sheet; the plywood that remains is for the figures and palm trees.

Bottom: Cut the 2 x 4 rails (A) to length. Stand the rails on edge ($1\frac{1}{2}$") 4" apart on the floor. Glue/nail (4d) bottom (A1) to top edge of rails (A), flush all around (see FIG. 3).

Sides: Place sides (B) face down on flat surface. Glue/nail (2d) a 1 x 2 cleat (B1) to and flush with a long edge (the back) and 4" from bottom edge. Glue/nail cleat (B2) to the opposite side $1\frac{1}{2}$" from top edge. Repeat for opposite side (B) (see FIG. 3).

Back: Cut a 5"-dia. hole in each end of back (D1), 12" from the ends and $8\frac{1}{2}$" from one long edge. Cut back cleat (D2) to $65\frac{1}{2}$". Place plywood D/D1 on a flat surface, face down, and butt the edges to form a piece 65" x 68". Glue/nail (2d) cleat (D2), centered over the joint, $1\frac{1}{4}$" from each end of D/D1 (see FIG. 3).

5. Top: Place top (F) on a flat surface, face down. Glue/clamp top rails (C), flat-side down, to top (F), 1" from both end edges and one long edge, and $\frac{3}{4}$" from the opposite long edge. When the glue has dried, turn the top over, remove clamps and nail (4d) through top (F) into rails (C).

6. Front: Enlarge (see page 271) the star pattern in FIG. 3F. Trace it on front (E) as shown in FIG. 3. Drill a starter hole and cut out star with a sabre saw. Sand the cutout. Place the front on a flat surface, face down. Glue/nail (1") diffuser support (E1) to the back of front (E), $1\frac{1}{4}$" from each end and $15\frac{1}{4}$" from the top edge (see FIG. 3). Cut a piece of Mylar large enough to cover the star cutout in front (E). Staple the Mylar to the back of E, covering the star.

7. To assemble: With the aid of a helper, place the sides on end, butted against bottom rails (A) and flush at side edges. Screw ($1\frac{1}{2}$") one screw through side (B) into the center of rails (A). Repeat for opposite side. Screw (1") back (D/D/D2) to cleats (B2) on sides (B), back flush with side edges.

Screw ($1\frac{1}{2}$") front (E/E1) to front cleats (B2) on sides (B), flush at top and sides of B. Place top (F/C) on top of the assembly. Rails (C) should fit between sides (B), butted against front and back inner top sides. Screw ($1\frac{1}{2}$") front (E) to front rail (C). Screw (1") back (D1) to the back rail (C).

8. Light diffuser: Cut the frame 1 x 2's (G/G1) to size, lay on a flat surface and attach to each other with corner braces at corners and "T" braces at center. When complete, turn over, staple Mylar to the frame.

9. Lighting: A 48" shop-light fluorescent fixture can be hung from the underside of the top, or bulbs or floodlight bulbs can be used, depending on what you have and what you are willing to spend.

10. The figures: We painted the $\frac{1}{2}$" plywood, then lightly belt-sanded to give an antique look to the wood. Stain can be used and wiped to give a similar effect. Enlarge the patterns in FIGS. 1 A to F. Trace on the $\frac{1}{2}$" plywood and cut out with a jig or sabre saw. The figures are assembled like a jigsaw puzzle (see photo).

11. Shepherd: Glue/nail (¾″) lamb's straight legs to the shepherd, then (2d) the lamb to the legs, lamb's ear to his head. Glue/nail (¾″) shepherd's arm, hair and crook, then hand to crook and headband to hair.

12. The Holy Family—Joseph's body: #2 is glued/nailed to body. #1. His arm, hair, face and beard are glued/nailed. Mary's body is glued/nailed (¾″) to Joseph's body #1, butted against part #2 (*see photo*). Next, add Mary's robe and face, Joseph's hand to his arm, then Mary's robe. Glue/nail (1″) cradle inner legs to Mary, then the cradle to the inner legs. Glue/nail (¾″) the halo to baby's head at the back. Glue/nail (1″) the head to Mary, butted against the cradle edge.

13. The Wise Men: The second Wise Man is glued/nailed (¾″) to the first, the third to the second. Glue/nail arms, beard, hat, hands, crown, etc., in turn.

14. The palm tree trunks are nailed (not glued) to the front side edges of the stable. Palm leaves are nailed to the front, with a center leaf nailed to the center.

15. The figure groups are held in place with a screw-eye halfway up the back of the figure; a corresponding screw-eye is screwed into the stable back. The hook is made from the ⅛″-dia. wire running between the screw-eyes.

16. To take apart: Knock off the palm tree and leaves. Unscrew the top, front, sides and back for storage.

FIG. 3A SHEPHERD

1 SQ. = 2½″

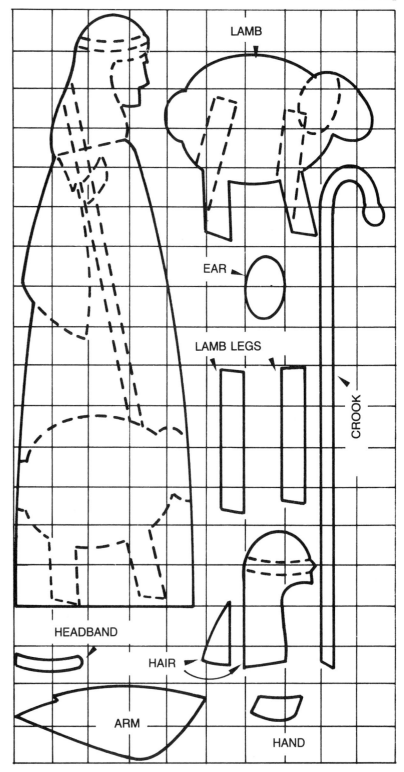

3B

1 SQ. = $2\frac{1}{2}$″

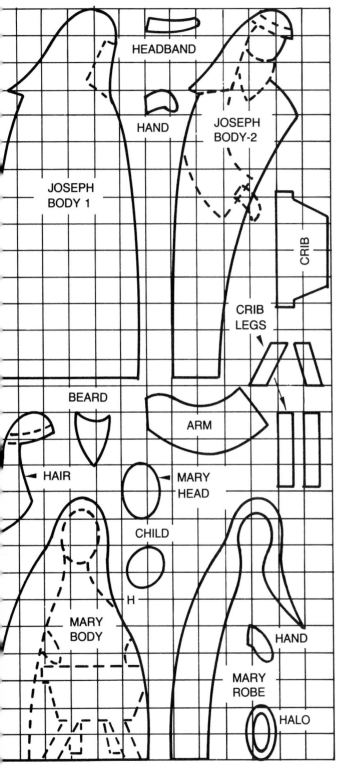

HEADBAND

HAND

JOSEPH BODY-2

JOSEPH BODY 1

CRIB

CRIB LEGS

BEARD

ARM

HAIR

MARY HEAD

CHILD

H

MARY BODY

HAND

MARY ROBE

HALO

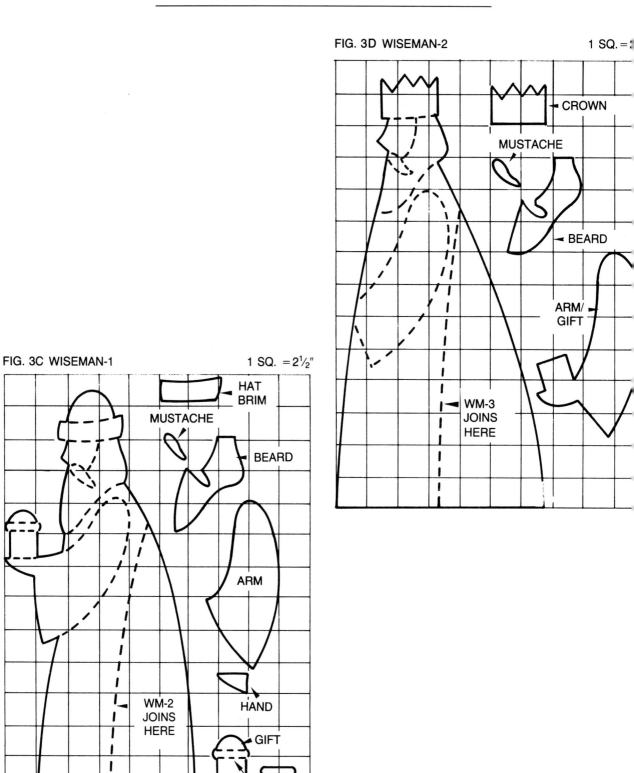

FIG. 3D WISEMAN-2   1 SQ. = 2

CROWN

MUSTACHE

BEARD

ARM/
GIFT

WM-3
JOINS
HERE

FIG. 3C WISEMAN-1   1 SQ. = 2½"

HAT
BRIM

MUSTACHE

BEARD

ARM

WM-2
JOINS
HERE

HAND

GIFT

GIFT RIM

i. 3E   WISEMAN-3   1 SQ. = 2½"

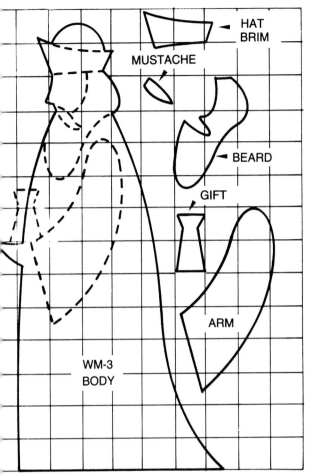

HAT
BRIM

MUSTACHE

BEARD

GIFT

ARM

WM-3
BODY

FIG. 3F   PALM TREES

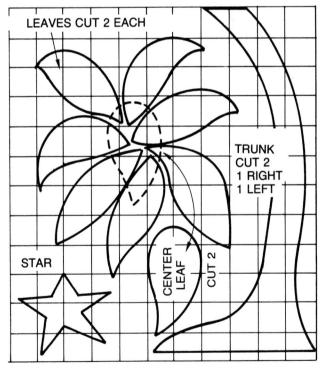

LEAVES CUT 2 EACH

TRUNK
CUT 2
1 RIGHT
1 LEFT

STAR

CENTER
LEAF

CUT 2

Basket Door Decoration

Boxwood Wreath

BOXWOOD WREATH

EASY: Achievable by anyone.
MATERIALS: Styrofoam® or str[a]
wreath form; boxwood; varigated h[o]
ly; red pyracantha berries.

DIRECTIONS:
On the form, insert the boxwo[d]
spacing it evenly throughout. Then [fill]
in the spaces with the varigated ho[ly]
and berries.

BASKET DOOR DECORATION

EASY: Achievable by anyone.
MATERIALS: Small to medium-size
wicker basket; block of florist's foam
(small enough to fit into the basket);
various holiday greens (spruce, pine,
balsam, etc.); holly berries; bright red
ribbon.

DIRECTIONS:
Wet the florist's foam and place it into
the wicker basket. Insert the holly
greens and berries into the foam, ar-
ranging as you go. Tie the ribbon into a
large bow and attach to the basket.

NEAPPLE PLAQUE-
OOR WREATH

SY: Achievable by anyone.
ATERIALS: 2"-thick green Styro-
m®; U-shaped "greening" or fern
s; leaves; green pineapple; paraffin;
avy-gauge wire; floral sticks; red pa-
r "ribbon"; about 28 lady apples.

RECTIONS:

Plaque: From Styrofoam, cut a
que of desired size and shape. Using
shaped fern pins, cover the plaque
th leaves. Spread or twist the wires
back to keep greens in place. Add
l "ribbon," holding loops in place
th U-shaped pins (*see photo*).

Pineapple: Cut a green pineapple in
lf vertically. Dip the cut side in par-
in. Let it dry and dip it again, two
nes or more, drying between dips.
rap a "noose" of heavy-gauge wire
low the foliage.

Hanger: At center back of plaque,
ar the top, stick several floral sticks
angles into the foam (*see* FIG. 4). Cut
any part of the sticks that protrude
m the foam. Cut a hanger wire and
nd it in half. Push both wire ends at
angle through the block to emerge
top (*see* FIG. 4). Bend the U loop
ward to make a back hanger. Twist
re ends together to make a loop for a
p hanger.

Push the ends of the wire "noose"
n the pineapple) through the plaque
d attach them to the back of the
nger.

Push one end of floral sticks through
ple and other end into Styrofoam.
peat with each apple, surrounding
e pineapple (*see photo*).

Pineapple Plaque-Door Wreath

FIG. 4 HANGER.

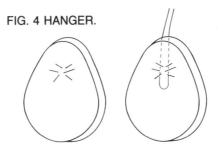

A warm mantel arrangement: Flowering Garlands; Vase Arrangement.

Legend has it... The poinsettia plant has its origins in Christmas history. According to a Mexican story, villagers placed gifts before the crèche in a certain church on Christmas Eve. A small boy, having nothing to give, knelt in prayer in the snow outside. In the spot where he knelt, the legend goes, a beautiful plant with scarlet leaves immediately grew, and he presented it as his gift to the Christ child. Mexicans call this plant "Flor de la Noche Buena" (flower of the Holy Night), believing that the leaves resemble the Star of Bethlehem.

Chapter

III

DECORATIONS: INDOORS!

Christmas isn't *just* trimming the tree! We think half the holiday fun is spreading the Christmas spirit all through the house: hearth and stairway, tables and windows. Because time is always tight during the holidays, many of our projects are super-easy to do. And no one says decorating has to be done on one weekend—why not start after December 1 and work at your leisure? Whether you spruce up one room or every nook and cranny in your home, our ideas can offer inspiration. They'll help you celebrate this year—and create memories for years to come.

Low-Cost

Make-Ahead

Quick and Easy

Low-Calorie

Bazaar

FLOWERING GARLANDS

EASY: Achievable by anyone.

DIRECTIONS:
1. Glue a gold marble (or tiny Christmas ball) to the center of an artificial carnation, then the carnation to the center of a poinsettia. Glue 3 plastic apples together. Repeat.
2. With 3 carnations, some gold marbles and white velvet ribbon, make two nosegays (*see photo*).
3. Glue poinsettias, carnations, birds (or other ornaments) and ribbon to an artificial garland and drape it along the mantel. Tie ribbons around it, where needed, and fasten ribbon ends to mantel top with strong tape. Tie in the apples and nosegays (*see photo*).

VASE ARRANGEMENT

EASY: Achievable by anyone.

DIRECTIONS:
1. Fill a vase with floral foam to inch above the lip. Push the stems small red artificial flowers into oppos sides of the vase. Bend them tow the center, twisting together at the t to make a wreath shape. Twist wh flowers into top of wreath.
2. Push leaves (plucked from flow stems) and small white flowers in foam at mouth of vase. Twist son leaves onto a piece of wire to make spray; push one end into foam and the other drape down the vase.

Did You Know...

That one of the most famous Christmas poems was written by a New York minister in 1822? It was "A Visit From St. Nicholas," ("'Twas the Night Before Christmas") by Dr. Clement Clarke Moore.

WINDOWS ON FESTIVITY

Stenciled Muslin Curtains; Wooden Wreath

STENCILED MUSLIN CURTAINS

AVERAGE: For those with some experience in sewing.

MATERIALS: Muslin; red and green acrylic paints; 7"-square of transparent stencil paper, single-edged razor blade and black pencil; stencil brush.

DIRECTIONS:
1. Curtain: Measure from curtain rod to sill. Cut two muslin pieces that depth and the full window width. Stitch ¼". Hem at side edges, 1½" hem at bottom. Cut top facing strip 3" wide x width of curtain.

2. Tabs: Cut twelve tabs each 5 x 2½". Fold each in half (5 x 1¼") and stitch ¼" from long raw edges. Turn right side out and press. Fold each tab in half and pin to top edge of curtain, right sides together and raw edges even, placing one tab flush with

FIG. 1 STENCILS 1 SQ. = 1"

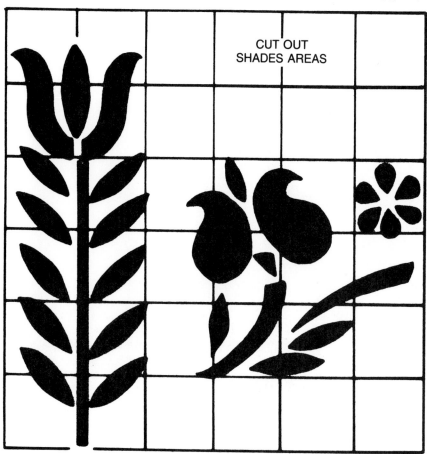

CUT OUT
SHADES AREAS

FIG 2. WOODEN WREATH 1 SQ. = 1

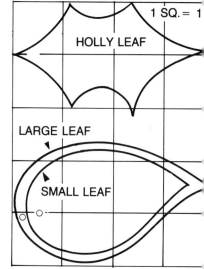

HOLLY LEAF

LARGE LEAF

SMALL LEAF

each side edge and four (equally spaced) between. Pin facing on top and stitch ½″ from top edge of curtain (over tab ends). Turn facing to wrong side and tabs upward; turn under lower edges of facing and slipstitch.

3. Enlarge pattern in FIG. 1. in black pencil, following the directions on page 271. Tape pattern under stencil paper. Over a cutting board, cut out design carefully with a razor blade.

4. Cover flowers with masking tape when painting green leaves; cover leaves when painting red flowers. Tape stencil to muslin, placing motifs as desired (*see photo*). Don't dilute the paint. Pick up a small amount with your brush and tap off the excess on newspaper; then paint, holding brush straight up.

WOODEN WREATH

AVERAGE: For those with some experience in woodworking and crafts.
MATERIALS: Lattice (⅛ x 3″-wide) or, strips (⅛ x 3 x 24″) of "Midwest" Micro-cut cherry wood (at art supply or craft stores); flat latex paint in red and three greens; about a hundred ½″ wooden beads; 8 ft. heavy (⅛″) wire; flexible tie wire; green floral tape, #20 wire.

DIRECTIONS:

1. Wire Wreath: Cut the heavy wire in half. Overlap ends of one piece to make a 15″ dia. circle; fasten overlap with tie wire. Repeat; then tape the two circles together with floral tape.

2. Enlarge pattern in FIG. 2, followin the directions on page 271. Trace pa terns to wood and cut out about 2 do en each of the three leaves. Sand edg and drill a small hole near the base each. Insert 6″ piece of #20 wire an twist ends together tightly to mak "stems." Wrap wire with floral tape.

3. Paint the leaves green, using darke shade for holly. Paint beads red. Inse wire through beads and twist tightly Twist 5 or 6 berries together to make clump. Make 18 clumps.

4. Wrap leaf "stems" around half the wreath; then, changing directior wrap the other half. Wire berry clump to wreath. Cover wreath with flora tape. Add a loop of wire for hanging

Bells

CALICO BELLS
(about 18″ long)

EASY: Achievable by anyone.
MATERIALS: ½ yd. calico; synthetic stuffing; optional trim; ribbon bow.

DIRECTIONS *(¼″ seams allowed)*:
1. Enlarge the bell pattern in FIG. 3, following directions on page 271. Cut two, from fabric, for each bell, and also two clappers *(see broken lines)*.
2. Seam two bells, right sides together, leaving open at bottom edge between circles. Seam clappers together leaving open at straight, top edge. Turn right side out. Stuff bell.
3. Sew gathering row ¼″ from top edge of clapper. Pull up gathering over stuffing and insert at center of bell at lower edge, turning under raw edges of bell and slipstitching closed.
4. Hang from window; add ribbon bow and greens.

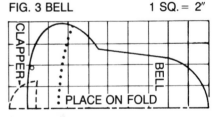

FIG. 3 BELL   1 SQ. = 2″

CLAPPER · · BELL · PLACE ON FOLD

WREATH IDEAS

● *Although they are usually hung from the door, wreaths can be placed in other strategic spots around the house. They make simple mantel decorations (watch out for fire; either use a fireproof wreath or don't light the fire at all).*
● *They can also be the base for punch bowls and vases, small trays for serving food, etc.*
● *Also try hanging wreaths along the rungs of the staircase, as well as against the entryway mirror.*

ENTRANCING ENTRYWAY

Candy Mold Garland and Wreath

ANDY MOLD REATH (12" dia.)

SY: Achievable by anyone.
ATERIALS: 12" dia. BASIC ARTIFI-
L WREATH; *(directions follow)*; sili-
ie glue; tin candy molds.

RECTIONS:
Assemble wreath, following direc-
ns for the BASIC ARTIFICIAL WREATH.
Glue candy molds to greenery *(see
to)*.

ANDY MOLD ARLAND

SY: Achievable by anyone.
ATERIALS: Postal twine; artificial
enery; flexible wire. **For each bow:**
d. each of four widths of red polka-
t ribbon and 3 yds. 2"-wide red rib-
n; silicone glue; tin candy molds.

RECTIONS:
Cut postal twine the desired length
d wrap artificial greenery to twine
th flexible wire.
For bows, cut ribbon into various
igths *(see photo)* following directions
Basic Bows and Streamers *(direc-
ns follow)*. Glue candy mold in mid-
e of 6" piece narrow ribbon and tie
und center of bow to cover wire.
it several lengths of narrow ribbon
d glue candy molds near ends. At-
ch to bow. Cut 2"-wide ribbon for
eamers.

BASIC ARTIFICIAL WREATH

EASY: Achievable by anyone.
1. Wrap a Styrofoam wreath form with
green floral tape.
2. Insert sprays of greens into the form
at a slight angle, covering the top and
sides. If it is necessary to divide the
greens, cut #16 wire into 7" lengths,
bend into a hairpin shape and use them
to secure the greenery to the wreath.

BASIC BOWS AND STREAMERS

EASY: Achievable by anyone.
Note: All wrapping is done with thin
flexible wire.
BOWS: Cut ribbon into 18" lengths,
unless otherwise indicated. Fold the
ribbon into loops so the ends meet at
center back. Wrap 2 or 3 looped ribbons together at a time, gradually enlarging the loops until the desired bow
is achieved.
Assembling: Cut 5" lengths of #16
wire for each bow and streamer, and
tape the bow and streamers to them.
Wire-wrap a bow and streamer together, and insert into the wreath.
Streamers: Cut lengths of ribbon and
fold the lengths in half; wrap together
with wire.

*Centerpieces can be used in other
places besides the dining room table.
Make them the focal point of the
mantel, or place them in a setting on
the windowsill.*

STOCKINGS TO HANG

Noël Stocking

·OËL STOCKING

FIG. 4 NOËL   1SQ. = 1"

·VERAGE: Requires some experi-
·ce in sewing.

·ATERIALS: ³⁄₈ yd. each, red
·oadcloth, white piqué fabric; ¹⁄₈ yd.
·ch, red stripe, red calico, green cali-
·, holly print, candy cane print, red/
·een stripe; ³⁄₈ yd. muslin; ³⁄₈ yd. bat-
·g; ¹⁄₂ yd. cluny lace (¹⁄₂" wide);
· yd. eyelet beading (1" wide, with ¹⁄₄"
·ts for ribbon); 1 yd. red satin ribbon
·⁄₄" wide); thread.

·IRECTIONS:

·Cutting: Red broadcloth—Cut one
·ece using stocking back; Piqué—Cut
·ie 9x16¹⁄₂" cuff; Remaining fabrics—
·ut all fabrics into 2x4" strips (total of
· strips); Muslin—Cut two pieces us-
·g pattern; Batting—Cut two pieces
·ing pattern; one 4¹⁄₂x16¹⁄₂" for cuff.

·Construction: (Note: *All seams*
·".) **Patchwork:** Following photo-
·aph, make 17 rows of five strips each.
·:am strips together at short ends.
·:ess all seams open. Seam rows to-
·:ther so that the short seams of one
·w meet the center of the strips on the
·:xt row. Press seams open. Note that
·:rtical edges of the patchwork piece
·ill not be even.

· Enlarge stocking pattern in FIG. 4,
·llowing the directions on page 271.
·se stocking pattern to cut out stock-
·g front.

· Quilting: Layer batting between
·atchwork front and one muslin piece.
·aste layers together at edges and
·:ross front. Using 8-10 stitches per
·ich, machine quilt on top of all
·:ams.

· Stocking back: Layer batting be-
·ween stocking back and remaining
·uslin piece. Baste together at edges.
·Quilt if desired.

· Cuff: Baste batting to wrong side of
·uff. Stitch 9" edges of cuff together
·rming a ring. Press seam open.
·Vrong sides together, fold cuff in half,
·atching raw edges, and crease the
·ld line. Open out cuff. Baste cluny
·ice to cuff along crease. Stitch eyelet
·eading on top of edge of cluny lace.

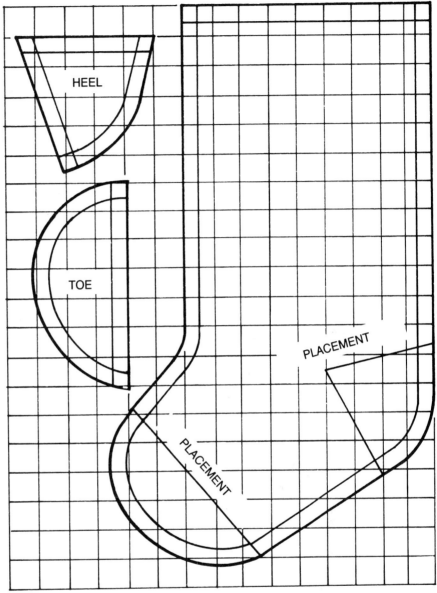

(labels: HEEL, TOE, PLACEMENT, PLACEMENT)

Refold cuff and baste the raw edges
together.

7. FINISHING: Right sides together,
stitch front to back, leaving top
straight edge open. Trim and overcast
seam. Turn right side out and lightly
press edges flat. Cut a 7" piece of ribbon, fold in half and baste cut edges
together, forming a loop. Position loop
and stitch cuff, right side, to wrong
side of stocking at top edge, encasing
loop in seam. Trim and overcast seam.
Turn cuff to outside of stocking.

CHICKEN SCRATCH CHRISTMAS STOCKING

AVERAGE: For those with some experience in embroidery.

MATERIALS: ½ yd. tan/white ⅛" check gingham; ½ yd. lightweight lining fabric; six-strand embroidery floss, 1 skein *each* coffee, toast, scarlet, blue, lavender, light emerald, chartreuse, emerald, fuchsia, peach; #7 embroidery needle; embroidery hoop; scissors; pins.

DIRECTIONS: Note: The gingham checks are used as the guide for embroidery stitches. Each square on the diagram represents one check on gingham. All embroidery shown is worked with 2 single strands of the floss *except* French Knots and Straight Stitches, which use 4 strands. (*Refer to the Embroidery Stich Guide on page 269.*) The gingham has 3 shades of tan as checks, dark, medium and light plus white.

1. Hold fabric so the lines of dark and medium-color tan run vertically. Cut one piece 12x20" for stocking front with 20" length placed vertically. Cut another piece the same size for backing.

2. With basting thread, outline the stocking on one piece of fabric, allowing a 2" margin of fabric around edges. Place fabric in embroidery hoop.

3. Refer to FIG. 5 and stitch details. Embroider design starting with girl and boy. Center them on upper part of stocking outline 2" below upper edge of fabric. Starting with Star Stitches indicated by black arrows on diagram, work these stitches over a *white* check on gingham. Work *all* Star Stitches first using symbols in Key to indicate color. Follow Key for symbols for Wheels and Spokes and French Knots and also for color of these stitches. (Some symbols have been used several times to indicate the same stitch but in different colors.) Finish embroidery. Press piece.

Chicken Scratch Christmas Stocking

4. Cut out stocking shape leaving an excess of free, unworked fabric at least 1" wide on all but top edge. Top edge has 2" excess. Using this piece as a guide cut out backing piece and 2 lining pieces.

5. Baste a lining piece to wrong side of each stocking piece. Pin stocking pieces, right sides together, and sew (½" seam) along all but top edge. Turn down 1¼" on top edge, turn under ½ at raw edge and hem. Slash seams to ease curves and turn stocking to right side.

6. For hanger, cut one 2x6"-piece gingham. Fold lengthwise. Fold both long raw edges to center fold. Sew together to secure.

7. Make loop. Sew to stocking.

5 CHICKEN SCRATCH STOCKING

1 sq. = 1 Gingham Check

BOY
- Emerald Fr. Knots
- Scarlet Fr. Knots
- Coffee Stars
- Emerald Stars
- Coffee Wheel/Spokes
- Fuschia
- Lt. Emerald Wheel/Spokes

KYLAND
- Coffee Stars
- Scarlet Stars
- Sky Blue Stars
- Emerald Stars
- Fuschia Stars
- Peach Stars
- Lt. Emerald Stars

RTS
- Coffee Stars
- Coffee Fr. Knots
- Sky Blue Stars
- Fuschia Stars
- Peach Wheels/Spokes
- Lt. Emerald Wheel/Spokes
- Scarlet Wheels/Spokes
- Coffee Fr. Knots
- Lavender Stars

SE
- Coffee Stars
- Emerald Fr. Knots
- Nectarine Stars
- Scarlet Fr. Knots
- Peach Stars, Wheels/Spokes
- Scarlet Stars

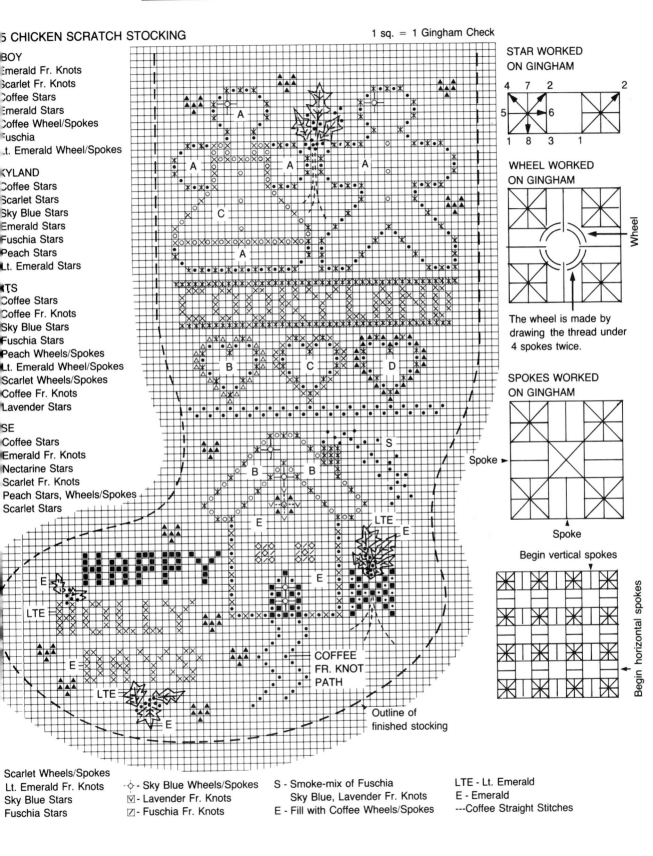

STAR WORKED ON GINGHAM

WHEEL WORKED ON GINGHAM

Wheel

The wheel is made by drawing the thread under 4 spokes twice.

SPOKES WORKED ON GINGHAM

Spoke ►

Spoke

Begin vertical spokes

Begin horizontal spokes

S

LTE

E

E

E

E

E

LTE

LTE

COFFEE FR. KNOT PATH

Outline of finished stocking

- Scarlet Wheels/Spokes
- Lt. Emerald Fr. Knots
- Sky Blue Stars
- Fuschia Stars
- ⋄ - Sky Blue Wheels/Spokes
- ☑ - Lavender Fr. Knots
- ☑ - Fuschia Fr. Knots
- S - Smoke-mix of Fuschia Sky Blue, Lavender Fr. Knots
- E - Fill with Coffee Wheels/Spokes
- LTE - Lt. Emerald
- E - Emerald
- ---Coffee Straight Stitches

Hansel and Gretel Gingerbread House

Be creative when thinking of centerpieces. As shown on these pages, a centerpiece can be a gingerbread house, a special grouping of candles or a lavishly filled basket.

◄◄

Hansel And Gretel
Gingerbread House

AVERAGE: For those with some experience in cake decorating.

Gingerbread House Dough (about 5 batches will be used; make dough as needed; recipe follows)
Extra-wide, heavy-duty aluminum foil
Ruler
Pencil
Lightweight glossy cardboard
Scissors
Paper (graph or typing paper are best)
Hansel, Gretel and Witch Patterns (see page 43)
Carbon paper
2-inch gingerbread boy and girl cookie cutters
Sharp-pointed paring knife
Tiny heart-shaped aspic cutter (optional)
1 Package (30 tablet-size) menthol drops or other pale-colored cough drops
Decorator Frosting (about 5 batches will be used; make each batch as needed; recipe follows)
Food paste colorings; red, green, brown, pink, yellow and black
Pastry bag and tips; medium writing tip, medium leaf tip and large leaf tip
24x20-inch piece plywood, $\frac{1}{4}$ to $\frac{1}{2}$ inch thick, for base
6 candy sticks (5-inch)
2 to 3 bags ($6\frac{1}{2}$ ounces each) sliced unblanched almonds
1 bag (8 ounces) red cinnamon jelly disks
35 red-and-white peppermint swirl candies (approximately)
1 box ($7\frac{1}{2}$) pumpernickel snack sticks OR: plain bread sticks broken into $2\frac{1}{2}$-inch pieces
1 container (4 ounces) small red cinnamon candies
1 box (4 ounces) sugar ice cream comes
Fine-tipped watercolor paintbrush

1. Prepare a batch of Gingerbread House Dough.
2. Line two $15\frac{1}{2}$ x 12-inch cookie sheets with the extra-wide, heavy-duty aluminum foil, wrapping the edges under. Place the cookie sheets on a damp cloth to prevent them from sliding when rolling out the dough.
3. Place one-half of the dough on each cookie sheet. Shape the first half of the dough into a rectangle with your hands and flatten slightly. Roll out to a $14\frac{1}{2}$ x $11\frac{1}{2}$-inch rectangle, about $\frac{1}{4}$-inch thick. Cover with plastic wrap; refrigerate for at least 30 minutes. Repeat with the second half.
4. Meanwhile, use ruler and pencil to make patterns for house on lightweight glossy cardboard. Label each piece and cut out. All directions for right and left sides given assume that you are looking at the front of the house.
House Back: Draw rectangle, 12 x $11\frac{1}{2}$ inches. Label one 12-inch side **Top.** On **Top,** mark 6 inches from side for center. Mark $4\frac{1}{2}$ inches down from **Top** corner on each side. Draw lines from top mark to marks on each side to form roof peak; each line should be $7\frac{1}{2}$ inches long. Cut out pointed roof.
House Front: Trace **House Back** on cardboard. Cut out. For door, mark 1 inch from left side on bottom. Make another mark $4\frac{3}{4}$ inches from left side at bottom. Mark point $2\frac{1}{2}$ inches up from bottom and 1 inch over from left side, and another point $4\frac{3}{4}$ inches from left. Draw lines between marks to make $2\frac{1}{2}$ x $3\frac{3}{4}$-inch rectangle. Mark center of door by measuring $1\frac{7}{8}$ inches in from either side on top and bottom line. Place ruler on marks and draw 5-inch line from house bottom upward. Draw 2 curved lines to connect top point with left and right sides of door to form a rounded door top. Carefully cut out door in one piece. Label piece **Door** and reserve as pattern for front door sections and fireplace. For **Front Window,** make a $2\frac{1}{2}$ x2-inch rectangle on graph paper; cut out. Place on house front 2 inches from right side and $2\frac{1}{2}$ inches from house bottom. Trace and cut out window, reserving pattern piece for side window.
House Left Side: Cut out $9\frac{1}{2}$ x 7-inch rectangle from cardboard. Label one $9\frac{1}{2}$-inch side **Bottom.**

Center **Front Window** pattern $2\frac{1}{2}$ inches from **Bottom.** Trace and cut out.

House Right Side: Cut out another $9\frac{1}{2}$ x 7-inch rectangle from cardboard. Label one $9\frac{1}{2}$-inch side **Top.** For **Window,** cut out 2x$1\frac{1}{2}$-inch rectangle from graph paper. Position pattern on upper left corner of house side with short side $1\frac{1}{4}$ inches from **Top** and long side $1\frac{1}{4}$ inches from left side. Trace and cut out.

Roof: Cut out two $11\frac{1}{4}$ x 9-inch rectangles from cardboard. Label one **Right Roof** and the other **Left Roof.** Label a long side of Right Roof, **Bottom.** Cut out $3\frac{1}{4}$ x $2\frac{1}{2}$-inch rectangle from graph paper. Place a short side $1\frac{3}{4}$ inches from right edge of **Right Roof** with a long side of pattern even with roof **Bottom** edge. Trace and cut out 3 sides from roof for chimney to fit.

Fireplace Chimney: Cut out 12 x 6-inch rectangle from graph paper. Fold in half lengthwise. Label 2 short sides **Top** and **Bottom.** Keeping paper folded and starting at **Top,** draw 8-inch line $1\frac{1}{4}$ inches from and parallel to center fold. Mark point on side opposite fold, $3\frac{1}{4}$ inches from **Bottom.** Draw line to connect point with lower end of 8-inch line; you should have drawn a 2-inch line. Cut along lines through both thicknesses of paper. Unfold; trace on cardboard. Cut out and label **Fireplace Chimney.** Cut out 2 rectangles, 8 x 2 inches, from cardboard; label each **Chimney Side.** Cut out 2 rectangles, $3\frac{1}{4}$ x 2 inches from cardboard; label each **Fireplace Side.** Cut out 2 squares, 2 x 2 inches; label each **Fireplace Top Side.** Cut out rectangle, 4 x $2\frac{1}{2}$ inches; label it **Chimney Back.** Using reserved front door piece, trace top curved half on cardboard. Cut out and label **Fireplace Oven Doors.**

Balcony: Cut out 12 x $1\frac{3}{4}$-inch rectangle from cardboard. Label a long side **Top Balcony Front.**

Measure and mark 1 inch up from a bottom corner. Measure and mark 1 inch over from top corner of same side. Draw line between two marks. Cut along line to remove corner. Repeat with other top side corner. Draw and cut out 2 rectangles, 1 x $\frac{1}{2}$ inch from cardboard; label each **Balcony Side.** Draw and cut out 12 x 1-inch rectangle; label **Balcony Base.**

Front Door Piece: Trim $\frac{1}{4}$ inch all around from reserved **Door** pattern. Door piece must be smaller than door opening as cookie dough spreads slightly when baked. New **Front Door Piece** pattern should be $4\frac{1}{2}$ inches high, $3\frac{1}{4}$ inches wide.

Shutters: Make rectangle 2 x $\frac{3}{4}$ inch. (You will need to make 8 gingerbread shutters.)

Large Flower Boxes: Fold small piece of paper in half. Draw $1\frac{1}{2}$-inch line perpendicular to center fold. Measure down $\frac{3}{4}$ inch from line and draw $1\frac{1}{4}$-inch line from center fold, parallel to first line. Connect the ends of the 2 lines. Cut out. Unfold and trace on cardboard for flower box. (You will need to make 2 large gingerbread flower boxes.)

Small Flower Box: Proceed as above, making top line 1 inch and bottom line $\frac{3}{4}$ inch. (You will only make one small gingerbread flower box.)

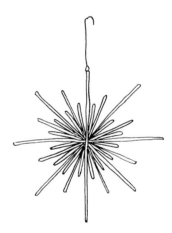

Left Roof Front Trim: On graph paper, draw rectangle, $7\frac{1}{2}$ x $6\frac{1}{2}$ inches. Label a $7\frac{1}{2}$-inch side **Top.** On left side, measure down $5\frac{1}{4}$ inches from **Top** and mark. Draw line from mark to top right corner. You should have 9-inch diagonal line. On right side, measure $1\frac{1}{4}$ inches down from **Top** and mark. Draw line from mark to bottom left corner. You should have 9-inch line parallel and about 1 inch away from first. Draw

Gingerbread Figures

scallop border between the 2 parallel lines, with scallop resting on bottom line (*see photo for scallop design*). Cut out pattern piece. Trace onto cardboard and cut out.

Right Roof Front Trim: Reverse **Left Roof Front Trim** pattern on cardboard. Trace and cut out.

Figures: Trace **Hansel, Gretel** and **Witch,** using carbon paper on cardboard. Cut out. Trace **Boy** and **Girl Fence** figures if you do not have 2-inch boy and girl cookie cutters. Cut out all figures.

5. Preheat the oven to moderate (350⁰). Dust the cardboard cottage pattern pieces lightly with flour: **House Back; House Front; House Left** and **Right Sides; Right** and **Left Roofs; Fireplace Chimney Front, Sides** and **Back; Fireplace Oven Door; Balcony Front, Sides** and **Base; Front Door Piece; Shutters; Flower Boxes; Left** and **Right Roof Front Trim.**

6. Remove the cookie sheets of dough from the refrigerator. Arrange as many cottage pattern pieces as possible on the dough, leaving ½ inch between pieces.

7. Using a sharp-pointed paring knife and a ruler edge as a guide, carefully cut out each piece. Carefully remove the cardboard patterns and all excess dough, leaving the foil on the cookie sheets. Press all excess dough together and refrigerate in plastic wrap. Reserve the excess dough to use for figures, fence and bricks.

8. With a sharp-pointed paring knife, score the upper half of the **House Front, Balcony Front** and **Front Door Piece** to look like wood planking (*see photo*). Use a tiny aspic cutter to cut heart

shapes out of the **Balcony Front,** if you wish.

9. Cut out the windows on the **House Front** and **House Side** pieces, being careful not to cut into foil. Add to excess dough. Fill window openings with crushed cough drops.

10. Bake house pieces in preheated moderate oven (350⁰) for 15 minutes or until edges of dough begin to brown and cookies are set. Remove trays to wire racks; cool completely before removing pieces from foil.

11. Continue making dough as needed, rolling out on foil-lined cookie sheets, cutting out and baking until all house pieces are completed. Store baked pieces at room temperature, loosely covered. Do *not* refrigerate.

12. Let excess dough warm to room temperature, 1 hour. Roll out on foil-covered baking sheets to ⅛-inch thickness. Refrigerate dough, covered with plastic wrap, at least 30 minutes.

13. Lightly dust **Hansel, Gretel** and **Witch** patterns with flour. Place on dough, ½ inch apart. Cut

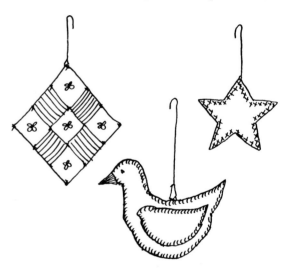

out with sharp-pointed paring knife. Use 2-inch boy and girl cookie cutters or patterns to cut out 20 of each for **Boy** and **Girl Fence.** Cut out 1 heart using aspic cutter or ½-inch heart patten, if you wish.

14. Bake in the preheated moderate oven (350⁰) for 6 minutes.

15. Again gather excess scraps. Roll very thin (¹⁄₁₆ inch) on foil-covered baking sheet. Refrigerate for 30 minutes.

16. Cut about 20 rectangles, 1x¼ inch, for bricks.

17. Bake in the preheated moderate oven (350⁰) for 2 minutes. Cool all pieces as above.

18. Make one batch of Decorator Frosting (make each new batch as needed). Always keep frosting covered with plastic wrap or damp paper toweling. Frost lower half of house front to resemble stucco. To indicate **Balcony Base** placement, mark point on right side in frosting 1 inch below where roof starts slanting. Repeat on left side. Draw line to connect two marks. Spread frosting on back edge of **Balcony Base;** press firmly in place on line in "stucco." Let dry overnight.

19. Tint about 1 cup of frosting red, using red paste food coloring. Spoon into pastry bag fitted with medium writing tip. Use to outline bottom edge of **Left** and **Right Roof Front Trim, Boy** and **Girl Fence** cookies, **Shutters** and **Fireplace Oven Door.** Decorate each **Fireplace Oven Door** with heart in the center and 2 hinges on right and left curved sides. Outline heart cutouts on **Balcony Front.**(Or pipe hearts on every other scored line if a cutter was not used.) Pipe 2 diamonds on each scored line that doesn't have a heart. Pipe heart in center of each **Shutter.** Pipe a tiny heart on center front of each **Flower Box.**

20. Fill pastry bag fitted with medium writing tip with 1 cup white Decorator Frosting. Make fleur-de-lis design above and below heart on each **Shutter** and at either side of heart on each **Flower Box.** Outline each **Window** and pipe in pane dividers, using 2 horizontal lines and 3 vertical lines for **Front** and **Left Side Windows.** Use 2 horizontal and 1 vertical line for **Right**

Side Window. Using frosting for glue, attach a **Shutter** on each side of every window. Two **Shutters** should be left for closed window above balcony. Attach large **Flower Box** under **Front** and **Left Side Windows.** Attach small **Flower Box** under **Right Side Window.** Let dry overnight.

21. Use white Decorator Frosting to "glue" **House Front, Right Side, Back** and **Left Side** together. If necessary, use soup cans to hold walls in position. Let dry overnight.

22. Assemble **Fireplace Chimney:** Place **Fireplace Chimney Front** face down on table. Spread frosting along edge of right side. Press edge of 8 x 2-inch **Chimney Side,** then a 2 x 2-inch **Fireplace Top Side** and finally $3\frac{1}{4}$ x 2-inch **Fireplace Side** into place. Repeat with other side. Use soup cans to hold pieces in place, if necessary. Let dry. Attach **Chimney Back** with frosting to upper portion of chimney, making all edges even at the top. Let dry. Frost entire fireplace and chimney to look like stucco. Attach decorated **Fireplace Oven Doors** to **Fireplace Front,** centering them along the bottom, before stucco dries. Let dry.

23. Place house on base and secure with frosting. Slide **Chimney** of **Fireplace** into cutout of **Right Roof** to check for fitting. If chimney is too large to fit, carefully enlarge opening in roof, using serrated knife. Chimney should fit loosely; almond roof shingles will cover any gaps. Frost all top edges of house and fit **Right** and **Left Roof**

24. Frost back edges of **Chimnney** and fit into place on **Right Side** of house, sliding into roof section.

25. Frost two 1-inch side edges and ½-inch bottoms of 2 **Balcony Side** pieces. Attach to either side of **Balcony Base**, 1-inch side against house and ½-inch side against base. Frost bottom edge and side edges of decorated **Balcony Front** and press into place on **Balcony Base** and against **Balcony Sides**. **Balcony Base** should extend beyond **Balcony Front** for flowers.

26. Frost backs of remaining 2 **Shutters** and attach in closed position to center of upper half of house front (above and behind the balcony front).

27. Use frosting to attach a candy stick to house corner; stick will not reach roof. Repeat with other corners. Gently cut remaining sticks into 4 pieces long enough to fit in between top of candy sticks and roof; line up swirls in candy sticks when possible. Using pastry bag fitted with medium writing tip, pipe decorative edge along each side of all candy sticks to finish corners.

28. Frost front edge of **Right Roof**. Place scalloped **Right Roof Front Trim** against frosting. Repeat with left side. Brace underside seam with a little extra frosting if necessary. Let dry.

29. **Shingle Roof:** Starting at roof bottom on one side and working up, frost a small section of roof and gently press sliced almonds into frosting for shingles. Continue working up roof, overlapping rows slightly to look like shingles. Repeat with other side of roof.

30. Frost entire base with white Decorator Frosting to look like snow. When the section in front of door is frosted, immediately press red cinnamon disks into frosting in rows of 4 to make path. Unwrap red-and-white peppermint swirl candies, apply dab of frosting to backs and attach around base of **House Front** and **House Left Side**.

31. Use pumpernickel snack sticks to make a **Log Pile** under **Right Side Window.** Use dab of frosting to secure each log to base and each other. Frost **Brick** backs and place in random pattern on stucco **Fireplace, Chimney** and **House Front**.

32. Add green food paste coloring to a batch of Decorator Frosting to make a light green color. Place about ½ cup in pastry bag fitted with medium leaf tip. Pipe leaves in the 3 window boxes and along balcony ledge. Squeeze remaining frosting back into bowl and cover with plastic wrap and reserve. Use a dab of white frosting to attach small red cinnamon candies to leaves. Using a little white frosting in pastry bag fitted with medium writing tip, pipe little white berries in groups of 2 or 3 near red cinnamon candies.

33. Make **Trees:** To reserved green frosting, add more green food coloring paste and just a very little black food coloring paste to make dark green frosting. Place in pastry bag fitted with large leaf tip. To make 2 large trees, stack 3 sugar ice-cream cones for each, using a little frosting to hold firmly together. Pipe row of leaves (tips downward) around bottom of cones. Continue piping rows above, slightly overlapping each row to resemble evergreen branches. Let dry. For 4 smaller trees, cut with serrated knife ¼ to ½ inch from open end of each cone. Pipe branches on as with larger trees. Let dry.

34. Attach little **Boy** and **Girl Fence** cookies, alternately, to base with dab of frosting to make fence around house.
35. Thin about 2 cups white Decorator Frosting with a little water. With a spoon, carefully drizzle frosting over peak and front roof edges, wood pile and trees for snow and icicle effect. Let dry.
36. Add a little more water to frosting. Use to frost **Hansel, Gretel** and **Witch.** (Frosting should be a thin, smooth glaze on figures.) Let dry.

37. Color ³/₄ cup white Decorator Frosting brown. Place in pastry bag fitted with medium writing tip. Outline all figures. Thin red, yellow, brown and pale pink food color paste with a little water. With fine-tipped watercolor paintbrush, paint clothing, skin coloring and features. You may want to practice painting on paper first. Attach small gingerbread heart to **Gretel's** hands and 3 small red cinnamon candies to **Hansel's** hands.
38. Check to be sure **Front Door Piece** fits into door opening. Trim door with serrated knife to fit, if necessary. Cut door into 4 parts, 2 upper doors and 2 bottom doors. Frost bottom of **Witch** figure; press against top back side of lower left door. Let dry. Frost outside edges of lower right, left and upper right doors. Place in doorway. Let dry. Frost edges of bottom left corner of upper left door and place in doorway in open position so **Witch** can be seen; door should partially rest on lower door. Hold up with small can or box. Let dry. Remove can or box.
39. Position trees around house. Use dollops of white frosting to position **Hansel** and **Gretel.**
40. **To Preserve House for Another Year:** Wrap tightly in plastic wrap and store in cool, dry place. Or spray with semigloss polyurethane spray. Let dry completely and store tightly covered in cool, dark place.

Gingerbread House Dough

Bake cottage pieces at 350⁰ for 15 minutes; figures for 6 minutes; bricks for 2 minutes.

5 cups unsifted all-purpose flour
1¹/₂ teaspoons ground cinnamon
1 teaspoon ground ginger
¹/₄ teaspoon ground nutmeg
1 cup dark corn syrup
³/₄ cup (1¹/₂ sticks) margarine
³/₄ cup firmly packed dark brown sugar

1. Stir together the flour, cinnamon, ginger and nutmeg in a large bowl.
2. Heat together the corn syrup, margarine and brown sugar in a 2-quart saucepan over medium heat, stirring occasionally. Let cool.
3. Stir the cooled syrup mixture into the flour mixture until well blended. Knead the dough with hands until pliable, smooth and an even color. (Do not refrigerate dough before rolling it out.)

Decorator Frosting

Makes 2¹/₂ cups.

1 box (1 pound) 10X (confectioners') sugar
3 egg whites
¹/₂ teaspoon cream of tartar

Beat together the 10X (confectioners') sugar, egg whites and cream of tartar in a medium-size bowl until blended with an electric mixer at low speed. Beat at high speed for 7 minutes or until a knife drawn through the mixture leaves a path. Keep unused frosting covered with a damp cloth.

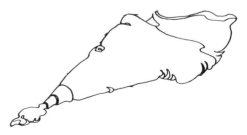

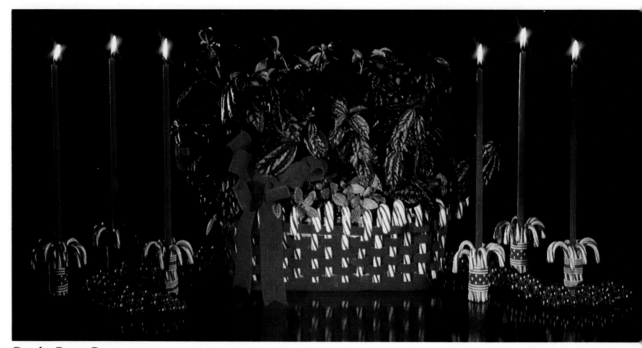

Candy Cane Centerpiece

💲

CANDY CANE CENTERPIECE

EASY: Achievable by anyone.
MATERIALS: Large basket (we used a mushroom basket); heavy-duty aluminum foil; double-stick tape or floral adhesive (available in florist's shops); 6 lengths of red velvet ribbon slightly longer than the circumference of the basket; small and medium candy canes; 6 red tapers; short lengths of striped or plain ribbon; clusters of red balls; 1 or 2 each of *Fittonia* (nerve plant) and *Pilea* (aluminum plant), depending on the basket size.

DIRECTIONS:

1. To weave ribbon and medium canes: Set basket on its side. With dou-

ble-edged tape, attach **4** lengths of ribbon evenly spaced **across** the height the basket. Place a candy cane und first ribbon, over second, under th and over fourth. Continue with oth canes, weaving ribbons as you go, ur entire basket is covered. Place o length of ribbon around top and around bottom of basket, over can to finish; secure with tape or strai pin stuck into basket.

2. Line basket with heavy–duty alum num foil; place plants, potted or ca fully unpotted, in basket. Place a do ble or triple red velvet bow amo plants.

3. To make holders for candles, wr double-edged tape around taper a press on small candy canes all aroun making sure they're level on the be tom. Tie or tape lengths of ribb around canes.

4. Cut pieces of foil the size of bask bottom and cane-held candles; pla under each to prevent any stickin from marring table.

5. Arrange a serpentine line of red b clusters or red balls around candles a basket.

...able Wreath

⧉N

...ABLE WREATH

...ASY: Achievable by anyone.

DIRECTIONS:

1. Cover a Styrofoam® wreath with felt so it won't scratch the table. Glue a dried green frond over the top; glue silk leaves to inside and outside surface.

2. Make a braid of gold ribbon and glue it on top. Glue gold centers (marbles, buttons or beads) to white artificial flowers and tuck them into the braid (*see photograph*). Glue red flowers at each side with a cluster of tiny white flowers.

Glowing Greens and Oranges

GLOWING GREENS AND ORANGES

EASY: Achievable by anyone.
MATERIALS: Round basket (without handles); 17 oranges (approx.); 17 white votive candles; real or artificial greenery.

DIRECTIONS:
1. Hollow out oranges from the top, leaving as much of the white part (pith) as possible.
2. Place one votive candle in each orange.
3. Arrange candles in a "star" formation (*see photo*); fill with greenery.

OTHER CENTERPIECE HOUSEPLANT IDEAS

Houseplants, dressed up with bright ribbons and candles, make easy arrangements that work well on a dining room table or buffet.

● Fill a wooden bowl with an old tea towel, then arrange small pots of herbs in the bowls. Fill in the spaces between the pots with curly moss (available in florist supply shops), or with bunches of fresh parsley. Surround with groupings of metal balls and a long candle on either side of the centerpiece. The balls will reflect the light of the candles and contrast nicely with the herbs' greenery.

● Combine pots of cacti with small bud vases of varying heights on a round or rectangular mirror. You can also use succulents or jade plants for this arrangement. For the flowers, choose red roses or chrysanthemums.

● Make a pyramid of Styrofoam, cutting it low; cut out a hole at the top to accommodate a pot of Christmas pepper plant. Place 3 or 4 more pepper plants on each side and in back, to make a continuous mass of plants. Pile fresh fruit around and cascading down from the pots, using double-edged tape or florist's wire to anchor the fruit. Set two 3-inch-wide green or red candles in among the fruit.

● Houseplant cuttings can also be used as the greenery for a centerpiece. Anchor with florist's foam in a pretty bowl or dish. Add flowers, if you wish.

NIGHT BEFORE CHRISTMAS IDEAS

● Fill your home with lots of brightly colored candles, especially the scented varieties (make sure they are on fireproof trays, away from flammable materials).

● Quickly jazz up a table by entwining sweet-smelling cedar cuttings around different-colored candles. Complement with country-print napkins and mats in gingham, muslin, calico, etc.

● For the bathroom, set out guest soaps in red and green. Bring in a flowering plant, perhaps a Christmas cactus or a small poinsettia.

● Fill a glass vase or bowl with greens and a dripless candle; add a festive plaid ribbon outside. Perfect for displaying on a coffee table or tucking among books or plants.

● For an instant holiday setting, place red candles on the mantel (or anywhere else you need a punch of color). Take down a picture and replace it with a wreath instead. Hang up a Christmas stocking in a prominent spot. Then bring out the mulled cider and cookies!

● When a room needs cheering up, think RED. Use red plaid tablecloths on the dining room table and lamp table, replace a lamp shade with a red one, use red ribbon to hang up wall decorations.

● Fill baskets with sweet-smelling pomander balls.

● For a sparkling centerpiece or accent piece, fill a vase with pine cones and white Christmas tree lights buried in the center (just let wire trail outside, under mats and down to the outlet).

● Fill a large glass vase with sprays of evergreens; place on the coffee table. Or, tuck sprays of holly or evergreen in picture frames, along the mantel, anywhere you want a touch of green.

Beautiful Patchwork Ornament tree, brimming with color.

Legend has it... The first Christmas tree was an evergreen that sprang from the center of an oak cut down by St. Boniface in Germany, in the 8th century. The oak was sacred to the pagan religion practiced then; chopping it down symbolized the end of the old beliefs. As the tree reached up to the sky, St. Boniface told the crowd: "This...shall be your Holy tree. It is the sign of endless life, for its leaves are evergreen and point toward heaven. Let this be called the tree of the Christ Child; gather about it in your homes and surround it with gifts and rites of kindness."

Chapter

IV

COME TRIM THE TREE

Remember the magic of the Christmas tree when you were a child? The excitement of hanging each special ornament, the thrill when you stepped back and saw the tree fully decorated? That's what this chapter is all about: wonderful ornaments that bring back those special feelings, from plush velvet patchwork to homemade wooden collectibles. And because no tree is complete without a skirt, we have some pretty ones that set the stage for gifts—as well as catch pine needles! Then, once you look through these pages, flip to Chapter VI (Home For The Holidays) for more beautiful trees and decorations.

BUYING A CHRISTMAS TREE

● *Determine where in your home you will display your tree. You should select a tree that is the right height for the space you have chosen for it. Cutting large portions off either end will alter the natural taper of the tree. If you're planning to place your tree in a corner, keep in mind that it doesn't have to be perfectly shaped.*
● *Freshness is the key when selecting your tree. The needles should be resilient, not brittle. Shake or bounce the tree on the ground lightly to see that the needles are firmly atttached. If only a few drop off, the tree is fresh, and with proper care, should retain its freshness indoors throughout the holiday season.*
● *The limbs should be strong enough to hold ornaments and strings of electric lights, and the tree should have a strong fragrance and good green color.*
● *Be sure it displays the best qualities for that particular species:*

Douglas firs are the most popular trees. Dark green to bluish-green in color, they are noted for graceful branching and excellent needle retention. They are also the most fragrant.
Norway spruces, the second favorite, are dark green with somewhat pendulous branches. Their needles have moderate retention.
Scotch pine trees are blue- or gray-green with needles up to three inches long and have excellent retention.
Colorado blue spruces are green to silvery-blue with inch-long needles and good retention.
White pine trees are green or bluish green with flexible branches and excellent needle retention.

WANT A TREE YOU CAN PLANT?

● *Choose a tree that isn't more than 4 feet tall and has fresh, not brittle, needles with signs of new growth. Also be sure you have a pot or sturdy box in which you can place it in your home.*
● *Keep the tree well watered while in the house. Try not to keep it indoors for more than 4 or 5 days.*
● *Before planting, place the tree in a garage or cold basement for a day or two to gradually accustom it to the cold.*
● *Remember to dig a hole for it before the ground freezes and cover the hole with insulating material, such as straw or leaves.*
● *If you can't plant it until spring because the ground is frozen, place it oudoors, surrounded by a 6- to 12-inch layer of mulch. It should be located near the house or in the shelter of other trees. Be sure to plant it when the ground thaws.*

CHRISTMAS TREE SAFETY

● *Make sure the tree stand you use is large enough to support your tree, or else it may topple over.*
● *Use only fire-resistant ornaments.*
● *Never put lit candles on a tree.*
● *To reduce risk of fire, choose a fresh tree that has no evidence of drying—brown needles or needles that fall off easily.*
● *More fire prevention: Spray the tree with fire retardant before you decorate it; keep it well watered and away from heat sources.*
● *Dispose of the tree when it becomes so dry that large amounts of needles fall off.*
● *Avoid angel hair; it's made of spun glass, a skin irritant to some people.*

CHRISTMAS TREE CARE

● *If you buy your tree several days before it will be set up and decorated, store it outside. Cut the butt of the tree at a diagonal about one inch above the original cut—this opens the pores and aids in the absorption of water. Place the butt end in a container of water.*
● *When you bring it into the house, saw the butt again, squaring off the diagonal. This facilitates placing the tree in a stand as well as aiding absorption.*
● *Keep the butt end of the tree in a container of water the entire time it is in the house. Refill the container daily. To enhance the tree's freshness, replenish the water level with aluminum sulfate or calcium chloride (from hardware or garden-supply stores). Combine 1 pound of either chemical with 1 quart water. Add a little daily to tree stand, along with additional lukewarm water.*
● *Sprinkling water on the branches and needles before you decorate the tree will help retain freshness.*
● *Be sure that the base of the tree is well supported and the tree is placed away from fireplaces, radiators, electric heaters, televisions or any other source of heat.*
● *Open flames, such as lighted candles, should never be used on or near the tree. In addition, never leave your home with the Christmas tree lights still on.*

FIG. 1 PATCHWORK ORNAMENTS   1 SQ. = 1″

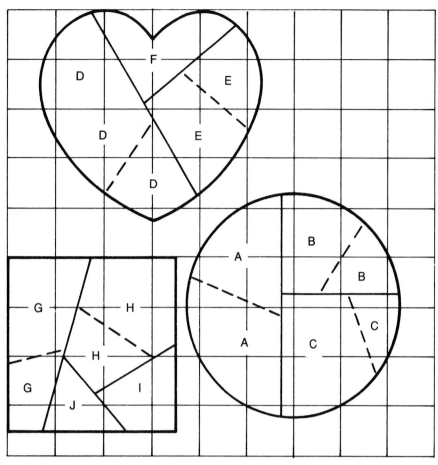

PATCHWORK ORNAMENTS

AVERAGE: For those with some experience in embroidery and sewing.

MATERIALS: Scraps of fabric; 6-strand embroidery cotton; small beads; lace edging; ½″-wide ribbon; synthetic stuffing; crisp cardboard; tracing paper.

DIRECTIONS:

Patterns: Draw a 3½″ square, a 4½″ circle and a heart from patterns in Fig. 1 onto cardboard, following the enlarging directions on page 271. Draw patch seams across them, spaced like ours. Letter each patch and trace each cardboard on tracing paper to keep for a permanent record. Cut cardboards apart on drawn lines to make patterns.

Cutting: Trace patterns to wrong side of fabric and cut ¼″ *outside the traced lines.*

Patchwork: Seam matching letters together, in alphabetical order. Then using tracings as a guide, seam the 3 or 4 sections together on the solid lines. Press seams open. Cut a single back piece same size as front.

4. Trimming: Embroider across the seams in stitches of your choice, incorporating small beads if you wish. (We used Chain, French Knot, Fly, Cross, Feather and Blanket stitches—*see Embroidery Stitch Guide, page 269*). Add tiny appliqués or more embroidery on some of the patches.

5. Edging: With right sides together, seam lace edging to edge of patchwork ornament front. Pin the back piece on top, right sides together, and stitch ¼″ from edges, leaving an opening for turning. Turn right side out.

6. Finishing: Stuff ornament. Turn in open edges and slipstitch. Tie ribbon bow (takes 15″-18″ of ribbon) and sew or glue it to the ornament (*see photo*). Fold a 7″ piece of ribbon in half and glue ends behind bow, for a hanger.

Did You Know . . .

The United States has a National Christmas tree? It's located in General Grant National Park near Fresno, California. The tree is 267 feet high.

Snowflake Tree Skirt

SNOWFLAKE TREE SKIRT

EASY: Achievable by anyone.
MATERIALS: 19″ piece 72″-wide red felt, $\frac{1}{4}$ yd. white felt, or piece 18 x 45″; $3\frac{1}{3}$ yds. white ball fringe; white glue (optional, not necessary if sewn); paper for pattern pieces.

DIRECTIONS:
1. Enlarge patterns in Fig. 2 on paper, following the directions on page 271. Arrange the patterns on the white felt and cut out six 18″ lengths of trim and 6 snowflakes.
2. Cut out the circle halves from red felt as illustrated in Fig. 2A. Lap the straight cut edges about $\frac{1}{2}$″; pin and sew ONLY ONE of the edges together. (The other edge is to be left open to allow you to slip the skirt around your tree.)
3. Lay out the trim strips evenly on the red felt circle, as shown in the photo-graph, radiating them from the cent hole and being sure to center one sti along the open length in order to cov the overlap. Baste, then sew by ha or machine **or** glue to the circle.
4. Arrange the 6 snowflakes betwe the trim strips. Baste and sew (or glue
5. Put the tape of ball fringe arou the underside edge of the tree ski starting at one opening and ending the other, so that just the balls sho Sew (or glue) in place, being sure tuck in the raw edges of the fringe prevent raveling.

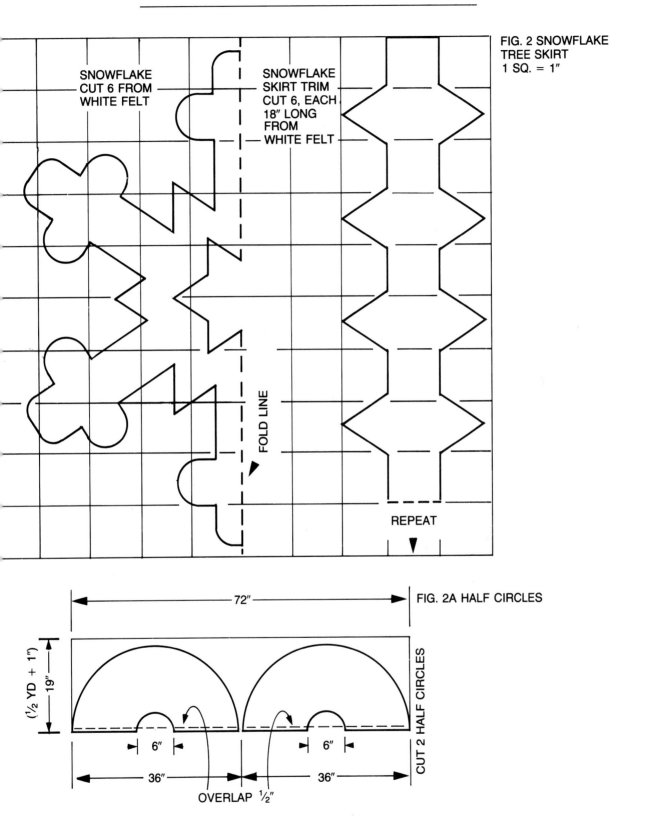

SNOWFLAKE
CUT 6 FROM
WHITE FELT

SNOWFLAKE
SKIRT TRIM
CUT 6, EACH
18" LONG
FROM
WHITE FELT

FIG. 2 SNOWFLAKE
TREE SKIRT
1 SQ. = 1"

FOLD LINE

REPEAT

FIG. 2A HALF CIRCLES

72"

(½ YD + 1")
19"

6"

6"

CUT 2 HALF CIRCLES

36"

36"

OVERLAP ½"

Christmas Tree Skirt

CHRISTMAS TREE SKIRT

AVERAGE: For those with some
perience in embroidery.

MATERIALS: 1⅜ yds. 52"-wide white burlap, 1⅜ yds. 52"-wide backing fabric; 5¼ yds. red covered cording; 4 snap fasteners; worsted-weight yarn in the following colors and amount: 95 yds. scarlet, 60 yds. emerald, 16 yds. gold, 12 yds. black, 12 yds. topaz, 28 yds. dark green, 4 yds. cinnamon; sewing thread; tapestry needle; scissors; tailor's chalk.

DIRECTIONS:

1. Cut a 3" strip from one selvage; cut in half widthwise. Cut a slit from center of burlap to center of one side edge. Stitch half of 3" strip to one side of slit. Stay-stitch all edges of burlap to prevent raveling.

2. Enlarge the pattern in Fig. 3 and trace it onto burlap with tailor's chalk, following the directions on page 271.

3. To embroider, use the cross stitch (see *Embroidery Stitch Guide*, page 269) and the photo as a guide for color. The crosses are worked over three threads of burlap. Embroider around the work, being careful not to miscount threads. Work all crosses in the same direction, with all underneath stitches going in one direction and all top stitches going in the opposite direction. To begin and end strands, catch yarn under stitches on back of work.

4. When embroidery is completed, place the skirt face down and iron, using a damp pressing cloth. Round the corners.

5. On outside, baste or stitch cording along seam line on outer edge, allowing ½" seam allowance.

6. Prepare backing fabric the same way you prepared the burlap. With right sides together, pin backing to burlap. Sew together, allowing ½" seam allowance. Leave underneath side of slit open.

7. To form opening for trunk, cut a 3½" square in center of burlap. Clip corners; turn. Turn edges in between layers. Topstitch burlap and backing together along the slit and around trunk opening. Sew on snap fasteners. Press.

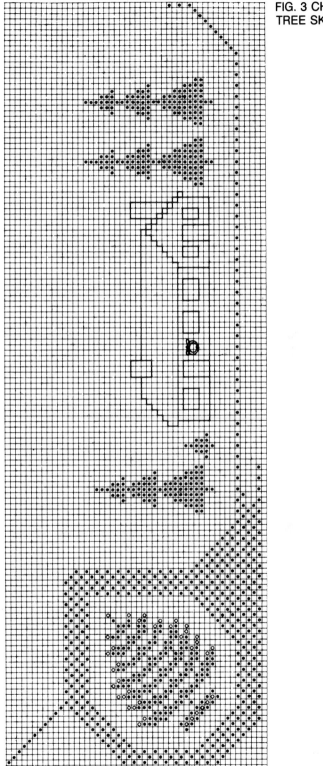

FIG. 3 CHRISTMAS TREE SKIRT

ORNAMENTS

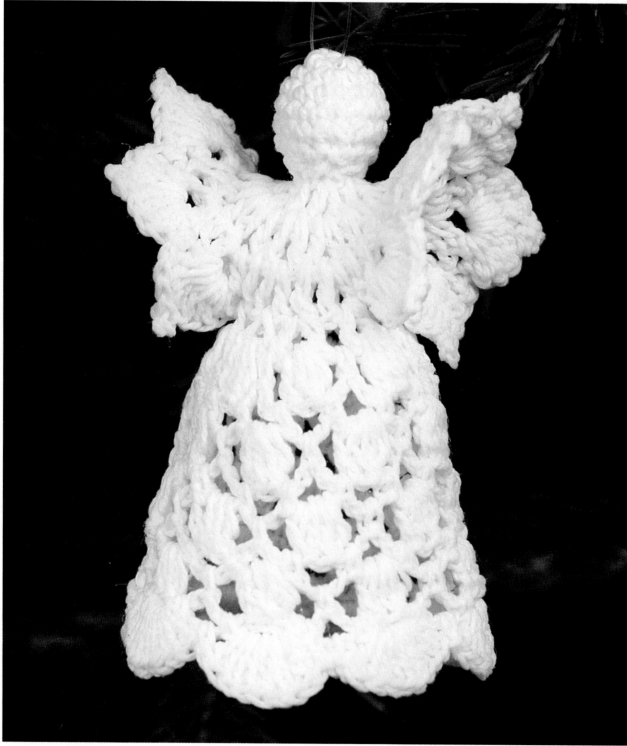

Crocheted Angel

ROCHETED ANGEL
(¼" high)

VERAGE: For those with some ex-
rience in crocheting.

ATERIALS: Medium-weight cot-
n thread 100% mercerized cotton 1
75 yd.) ball No. 1 White; steel cro-
et hook, No. 7; one cotton ball for
ffing head; wax paper; laundry
rch; plastic thread for hanging.

RECTIONS:

Head: Starting at top of head, ch 3.
in with sl st to form ring. **Rnd 1:**
ork 6 sc in ring. **Do not join rnds.
ark beg of rnds unless otherwise
ated. Rnds 2 and 3:** ˙ *2 sc in next sc—
c made;* sc in next sc; rep from ˙
ound—14 sc. **Rnd 4:** Sc around, in-
easing 4 sc evenly spaced—18 sc.
nd 5: Sc in each sc around. **Rnd 6:** ˙
: in next sc, *draw up a lp in each of next
sc, yo and draw through all 3 lps on
ok—dec made;* rep from ˙ around—
: sc. **Rnd 7:** Work in the same way as
 last rnd until 7 sc remain. Stuff
ead. **Rnd 8:** Sc in each sc around—7
. Join with sl st to first sc. **Do not
sten off.**

Bodice: Rnd 9: Ch 4, dc in same st
 sl st, ˙ *(dc, ch 1, dc) in next sc—**V-st
ade;** rep from ˙ around—7 V-sts.

Join with sl st to 3rd ch of beg ch-4.
Rnd 10: Sl st in first ch-1 sp, ch 4, dc
in same sp, ˙ work a V-st in sp between
next 2 dc, V-st in next ch-1 sp; rep
from ˙ around—14 V-sts. Join. **Rnd
11:** Sl st in first ch-1 sp, ch 4, dc in
same sp, ˙ dc in sp between next 2 dc,
V-st in next V-st; rep from ˙ around—
14 V-sts with single dc between each.
Join. **Do not** fasten off.

3. Skirt—Rnd 12: Sl st across first V-
st and next single dc, ch 4, dc in same
st as last sl st, V-st in next V-st, V-st in
next single dc, V-st in next V-st—**4-
sts made;** sk next 5 single dc and 5 V-
sts for one Wing opening, (V-st in next
single dc, V-st in next V-st) 2 times—
4 V-sts made; sk next 5 single dc and
4-sts for other Wing opening—**8 V-
sts.** Join with sl st to 3rd ch of beg ch-
4. **Rnd 13:** Working on the 8 V-sts
only of Rnd 12, sl st in ch-1 sp of first
V-st, ch 3, *holding last lp on hook of each
dc, work 3 dc in same sp, yo and draw
through all 4 lps on hook—**cluster (cl)
made;** ch3, sk next st, sc in sp between
next 2 V-sts, ˙ ch 3, cl in next V-st, ch
3, sc in sp between next 2 V-sts; rep
from ˙ around, ending with ch 3, sc in
sp between next 2 V-sts—8 clusters.
Join to top of beg ch-3. **Rnd 14:** Sl st
across to center ch of ch-3 sp, sc in
same sp, ˙ ch 3, sc in next ch-3 sp; rep
from ˙ around, ending with ch 3—16
ch-3 sps. Join with sl st to beg-sc. **Rnd**

15: Sl st across to center ch of ch-3 sp,
ch 3, cl in same sp, ˙ ch 3, sc in next
ch-3 sp, ch 3, cl in next ch-3 sp; rep
from ˙ around, ending with ch 3, sc in
next sp, ch 3. Join with sl st to top of
beg ch-3. **Rnds 16-20:** Rep Rnds 14
and 15 two times more, then rep Rnd
14 once. **Rnd 21:** Sl st across to center
ch of ch-3, sc in same sp, ˙ work 9 *dc in
next sp*—**shell made;** sc in next sp; rep
from ˙ around—8 shells. Join with sl st
to beg-sc. Fasten off.

4. First Wing: With right side facing
you, working on the skipped sts of Rnd
12, join thread to first free single dc, sc
in same dc, ˙ in next V-st (work 4 dc,
ch 3, sl st in top of last dc for picot,
4 dc), sc in next single dc; rep from ˙
around—5 shells. Join with sl st to beg-
sc. Fasten off.

5. Secong Wing: Work same as First
Wing.

6. To hang: Weave plastic thread
through top of Head; tie ends tog to
form a loop.

7. To starch: Mix three tablespoons
laundry starch with six tablespoons tap
water. Wet Angel with tap water and
squeeze out excess. Dip Angel in starch
solution. Stuff and shape Skirt and
Body with wax paper. Suspend from
wire hanger with a clothespin at hanging loop, smoothing and shaping as it
dries. When hard and dry (about 8
hrs.), remove wax paper.

SEQUINED AND BEADED BELL

AVERAGE: For those with some experience in crafts.

MATERIALS: $2\frac{1}{2}$"-high Styrofoam® bell; 1 yd. $\frac{1}{4}$" gold ribbon trim; 5mm faceted sequins in orange, blue, green, gold, red, pale turquoise, pink and purple; glass rocaille beads in the same colors plus silver; 13, $2\frac{1}{2}$mm pearl beads; one 4mm pearl; one 6mm faceted bead; two 8mm faceted beads; one 8mm sequin; one 10mm sequin; one pearl-headed corsage pin; $\frac{3}{4}$" sequin pins; straight pin.

DIRECTIONS:

1. Starting at bottom and using sequin pin, bring gold trim up side, pinning as necessary, making a 4" loop at top (for hanger), then bringing trim down opposite side; cut/pin at bottom.

2. To divide bell into fourths, pin second strip trim to top, then around bell and cut/pin at top.

3. Using straight pin, place $2\frac{1}{2}$mm pearl, 6mm faceted bead and 8mm sequin on pin; push into top of bell inside hanger loop.

4. Pin trim around bell, $1\frac{1}{8}$" from top, then another strip below it. Push pearl on pin into each strip where it overlaps the vertical trim. Repeat with one more strip at bottom flange of bell. The bell is now divided into 12 segments.

5. Separate sequins and rocaille beads by color in egg cartons. Using sequin pins, place bead and matching sequin (cup up) in pin and push into a bell segment row by row. Work different color in each segment. (We used silver sequins to back one red and one orange segment.)

6. Clapper: On corsage pin, place 8mm bead, 4mm pearl, last 8mm bead and 10mm sequin; push into bottom of the bell.

Sequined and Beaded Bell

'ine Cone "Stars"

PINE CONE "STARS"

EASY: Achievable by anyone.

MATERIALS: Assorted pine cones of varied sizes and shapes; small artificial sprigs of holly, holly berries and tiny painted pine cones; silver and gold metallic cord; ⅛″ satin ribbon in red and green; artificial snow spray; aluminum foil; hot-glue gun or carpenter's wood glue.

DIRECTIONS: (*Note:* Use aluminum foil to cover work surface.)

1. Place 6 slender cones in a circle with bottom ends together and glue to form a 6 pointed star. Cover the center where they meet with a larger cone and surround that cone with smaller ones. Glue cord for hanging on back.

2. Vary decorations using artificial snow, holly sprigs, and red and green ribbons tied into tiny bows.

STORING ORNAMENTS

● *Wrap strings of tree lights around cardboard paper towel tubes. Taping down the ends prevents the wires from unraveling.*

● *Use the divided boxes from wine or soda to store your other fragile ornaments.*

● *Store tiny ornaments in egg cartons to prevent loss or breakage.*

● *When packing your decorations away in boxes, store your heavier ornaments on the bottom and the lighter ones on top. Place layers of paper towels or newspapers in between to cushion ornaments..*

TREE-TRIMMING GUIDELINES

Tree Height	No. of Miniature Light Bulbs	Garland	Ornaments
2′	35-40	24′x2″	15
3′	70-80	30′x2″	24
4′	100-120	48′x2-3″	36
6′	200-240	72′x3″	48
7′	240-320	84′x3-4″	72
8′	320-360	96′x3-4″	96

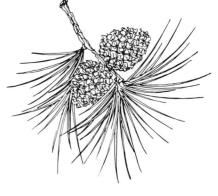

Pine Cone Bluebird

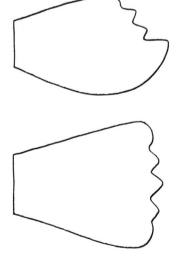

💲
PINE CONE BLUEBIRD

AVERAGE: For those with some experience in crafts.

MATERIALS: One 3″-long pine cone; one ½″ Styrofoam® ball for head; unlined white recipe card; yellow plastic dishwasher detergent bottle; flat acrylic paints in white and pastel colors; white glue; silver glitter; silver elastic thread; black felt-tip marker; tracing paper.

DIRECTIONS:

1. On tracing paper, trace tail a wing at left; cut out. Trace two wir and one tail on recipe card; cut ou

2. Beak: Cut top and bottom from d tergent bottle. Cut 1½″ strip fro sides. Fold in half lengthwise to ma flat ¾″ strip. Cut out a triangul piece, ½″ wide at base (fold) and ¹ deep at sides.

3. Using tip of blunt dinner kni gouge opening in Styrofoam b enough to insert beak at fold. Pla glue in opening and insert beak fold edge.

Hold the pine cone up in front of ⟨y⟩ou in profile, with the bottom wide ⟨par⟩t at left. Place head on cone body ⟨al⟩so in profile) near same end where it ⟨loo⟩ks natural (*see photo*). Press down ⟨har⟩d to get a deep impression, then ⟨rai⟩se; add glue at impression and re⟨pla⟩ce head on body. Dry.

⟨Spread a large plastic bag on your ⟨wo⟩rk surface. Paint bird's head and ⟨wh⟩ile wet, sprinkle with silver glitter. ⟨Ca⟩refully pour stray glitter into a sau⟨ce⟩r to use again. Now paint edges of ⟨th⟩e cone body with a brush and sprin⟨kl⟩e with glitter all over, shake off the ⟨ex⟩cess and again save the remainder.

⟨Paint/sprinkle wings and tail the ⟨sa⟩me way. Glue into cone. Loop 10″ ⟨pl⟩astic thread around body behind ⟨he⟩ad and tie ends in overhand knot to ⟨us⟩e as hanger.

⟨B⟩ALSA WOOD ⟨O⟩RNAMENTS

⟨CO⟩VERAGE: For those with some ex⟨pe⟩rience in woodworking and crafts.
⟨M⟩ATERIALS: Balsa, white glue; ⟨br⟩ass brads; white poster paint; food ⟨co⟩loring (*see* Step 2); string; varnish; ⟨br⟩ass wire; wire nipper; craft knife; fine ⟨sa⟩ndpaper; water color brush.

⟨D⟩IRECTIONS:

⟨1.⟩ Cutting: Enlarge the patterns in ⟨Fi⟩gs. 4a-4c following the directions on ⟨pa⟩ge 271. Trace each piece separately ⟨th⟩rough carbon paper onto balsa. (Un⟨de⟩rlapping portions are indicated with ⟨br⟩oken lines.) Cut the pieces out with ⟨a⟩ sharp-pointed craft knife and sand ⟨th⟩em to remove traces of carbon. For ⟨sm⟩all round holes, cut a hole a little ⟨sm⟩aller than it is drawn. Then turn a ⟨ta⟩pered object (like a pencil) in the ⟨ho⟩le until it is smooth and round. For a ⟨lar⟩ger hole like that in the lute, turn a ⟨do⟩wel wrapped with sandpaper.

⟨2.⟩ Coloring: For white, use poster ⟨pa⟩int. For purple, use liquid water

Balsa Wood Ornaments: Lute, Harp and Viol

FIG. 4A LUTE

FIG. 4B VIOL

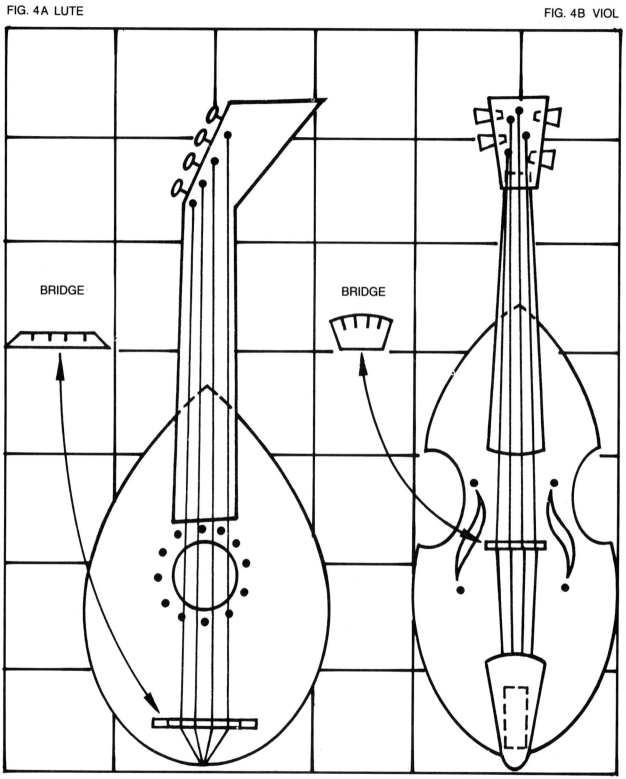

BRIDGE

BRIDGE

1 SQ. = 1"

r. For other colors, use diluted coloring. Brush color on each e and allow to dry before assem-g. (*See photo for color suggestions.*)

ssembly: Glue the pieces togeth-nderlying layers first, as shown in 4a-4c (*except Viol, see* Step 4). brass brads at black dots. Glue a l balsa patch behind the top of the ment and into it push a 2″ piece of s wire, bending the extending end a round loop for hanging. Varnish finished piece.

dditional Detail: Lute: Make a dbox under the soundhole in the as follows: Glue a 1¼″ square of

balsa (painted purple) over two ¼″ deep sides so the purple piece sets about ¼″ behind the lute.

At the four black circles (*see* FIG. 4a) make small holes with a darning needle. On the bridge cut four evenly spaced slits to hold the strings. Cut four 9″ pieces of fine string and thread them through the holes. Glue the ends (1 or 2 inches) to the back of the lute along the neck. Glue a scrap of balsa (behind the holes and over the string ends) to the back of the lute. Into it nail four brads for tuning pegs. (*See photo.*) Stretch the strings down the lute over the bridge, and onto the back

of the soundbox. Glue or tape them in place.

Viol: Assemble in the following order. Cut two curved slits in viol (*see* FIG. 4b) and glue a patch of balsa behind them. Make small holes on the peg-board at the black circles. Glue little triangles of balsa (pegs) to back of peg-board. Glue pegboard to neck. Glue the support (*dotted line on* FIG. 4b) at the lower end of viol. Glue bridge and neck to viol. Cut four 8″ pieces of fine string. Glue the ends to the back of the tailpiece, then glue it over the support. Stretch the strings over the bridge, up the viol through the holes and down to the back of the instrument. Glue strings in place and cover with small scrap of balsa.

Harp: On the back of the harp, place a ruler across the two curved pieces and mark each end of string positions, parallel and about ¼″ apart. Push a push-pin through each position to mark the front. Nail brass brad into each pin-mark (from the front).

Cut about a yard of fine string and wind it up and down the back of the harp from brad to brad, gluing first and last ends. Trim away excess string. Clip brads, if desired, about ¼″ beyond the harp back.

4C HARP   1 SQ. = 1″

IDEAS FOR GARLANDS

Use any of the following for gar-lands on the tree:
- *Freshly popped popcorn (remove from heat and let it steam with the lid on, so the corn will soften and be easier to thread)*
- *Cranberries*
- *Beads, especially pastel and me-tallic pearls*
- *Pasta such as elbow macaroni, wagon wheels, penne*
- *Lengths of lace trim*
- *Felt or fabric loops, strung or glued together*
- *Yards of ribbon, adorned with ribbon bows*

Even Santa has gotten some great gift ideas from this chapter!

Chapter

V

FILLING THE GIFT LIST

"Yes Virginia, there is a Santa Claus. He exists as certainly as love and generosity and devotion exist..." That now-famous 1897 newspaper editorial still rings true today. It's the joy of giving, of caring and of kindness that reaffirms the spirit of Christmas in each of us. And since we all get to "play Santa Claus" during the holidays, this collection of gifts can help you along. There's something for all your favorite people—whether you choose a hand-knit sweater or a simple arts-and-crafts project. *Note:* Many items are also perfect as bazaar best-sellers–look for the ◆ symbol above the projects!

◆ *Low-Cost*

◀ *Make-Ahead*

◀ *Quick and Easy*

◀ *Low-Calorie*

◥ *Bazaar*

BAZAAR BOUTIQUE

Rainbow Napkin Rings

[RA]INBOW NAPKIN [RI]NGS

[COV]ERAGE: For those with some ex-
[peri]ence in needlepoint.

[MA]TERIALS: (To make 4 rings) ½
[shee]t #7 plastic needlepoint canvas; 4-
[ply polyester yarn: 8 yds. *each* yellow,
[red,] green, blue; 16 yds. white; tapes-
[try n]eedle; scissors.

[DI]RECTIONS:

[1. C]ut four strips of canvas, each
[48 x] 12 holes.

[2. U]sing FIG. 1 as guide, work yellow
[sec]tions of design. *Leave 4 holes at each
[end] of each strip unworked.* Remove
[nee]dle and leave remaining yarn at-
[tach]ed to work. Work all colors but
[whi]te, allowing excess yarn to remain
[atta]ched.

[3. R]oll each strip into a ring. Rethread
[nee]dle with one color of yarn and con-
[tinu]e pattern. Work through both lay-
[ers] of canvas. Continue until all colors
[are] used.

[4. W]ith white, backstitch a "fence"
[bet]ween the yellow and green sections
[of d]esign. Repeat between blue and red
[sec]tions.

[5. O]vercast edges of each ring with
[whi]te yarn.

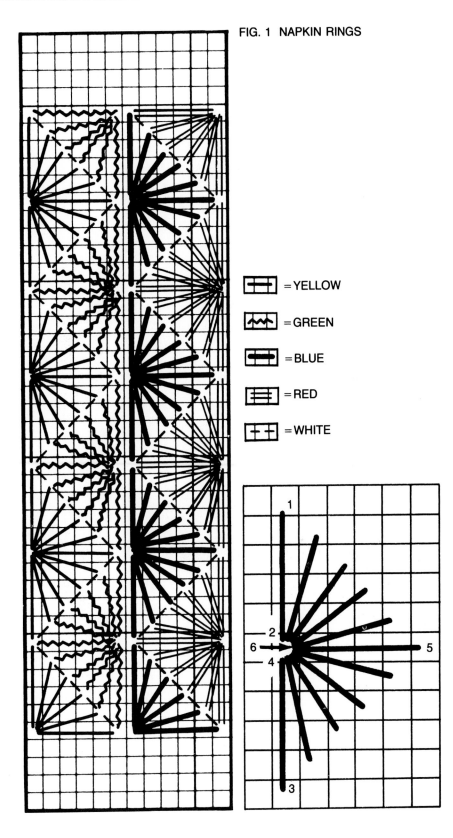

FIG. 1 NAPKIN RINGS

⊞ = YELLOW

⋀⋀ = GREEN

⊟ = BLUE

⊞ = RED

⊞ = WHITE

Starburst Napkin Holder

STARBURST NAPKIN HOLDER

AVERAGE: For those with some e[x]perience in needlepoint.
MATERIALS: 2 sheets #7 plast[ic] needlepoint canvas; rug or craft yar[n] red, yellow, orange, blue; two 9 x 1[2] pieces light blue felt; thread to mat[ch] felt; scissors; tapestry needle.

DIRECTIONS:

1. Using FIG. 2 as guide, cut 2 square[s,] 2 side pieces and 1 bottom piece [of] plastic canvas.
2. Use FIG. 2 as guide for colors an[d] stitching. Work front and back piec[es] beginning at center. Finish all piece[s.]
3. Cut matching pieces of felt. Sew [to] wrong side of each embroidered piec[e.]
4. With blue yarn, join front and bac[k] pieces to side pieces, using overca[st] stitch. Side pieces reach only midpoi[nt] of front and back pieces.
5. Attach bottom. Overcast all r[e]maining edges.

G. 2 STARBURST NAPKIN HOLDER

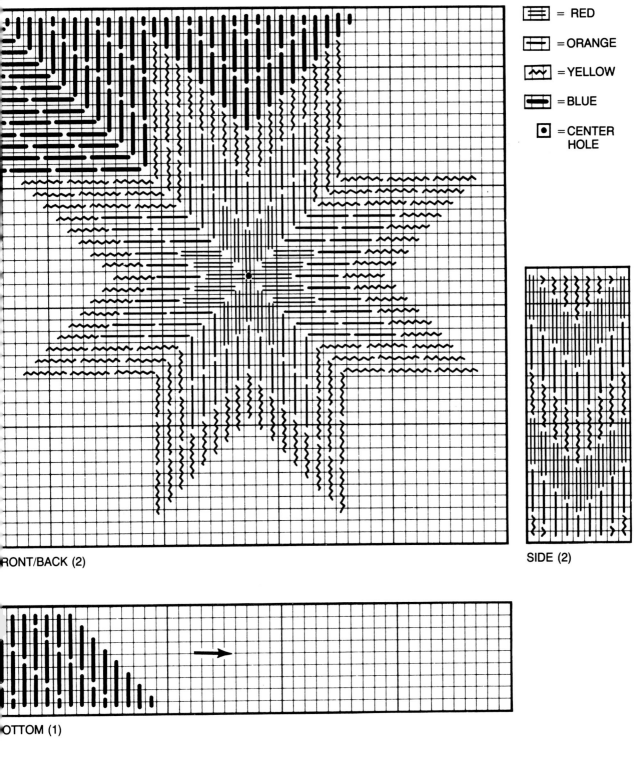

☰ = RED

☰ = ORANGE

〰 = YELLOW

▬ = BLUE

⊡ = CENTER HOLE

RONT/BACK (2)

SIDE (2)

OTTOM (1)

NEEDLEPOINT PINCUSHIONS

(Finished cushions are about 2¼"-square.)

AVERAGE: For those with some experience in needlepoint.

MATERIALS: Four 4¼"-square pieces (12-mesh-per-inch) interlock needlepoint canvas; tapestry needle; 3-ply Persian yarn in 56" strands: 24 white, 9 green, 2 rose, 2 pink, 1 blue, 3 purple, 2 yellow, 2 orange, 1 gold, 1 rust, 1 salmon, 4 lavender; bits of yarn, fabric or fiberfill for stuffing.

DIRECTIONS:

1. For each square, fold back an crease a hem of 3 threads on all 4 sid for a working surface of 41 intersetions (42 holes). Work yarn throug turned-under canvas (4 layers at co ners) as you stitch. Turned-und threads are not shown on charts.

2. Working in continental stitch (s Embroidery Stitch Guide, page 269) ar with 2-ply yarn, follow diagram ar color key in FIGS. 3-3c for each patter Work center motifs and borders firs then fill in white background. Wo outermost borders in slanting gobeli stitch (see Stitch Guide).

FIG. 3 FLOWER POT

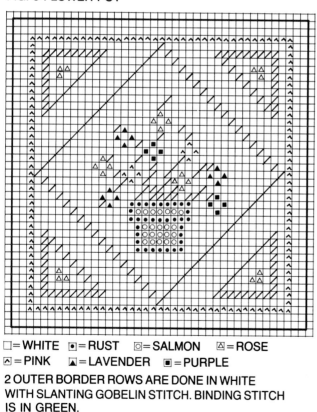

☐ = WHITE ▣ = RUST ◎ = SALMON △ = ROSE
⬙ = PINK ▲ = LAVENDER ■ = PURPLE

2 OUTER BORDER ROWS ARE DONE IN WHITE
WITH SLANTING GOBELIN STITCH. BINDING STITCH
IS IN GREEN.

FIG. 3A FIVE FLOWERS

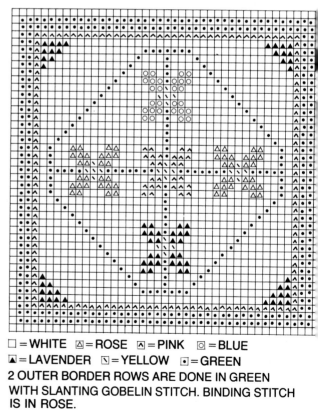

☐ = WHITE △ = ROSE ⬙ = PINK ◎ = BLUE
▲ = LAVENDER ◣ = YELLOW ● = GREEN

2 OUTER BORDER ROWS ARE DONE IN GREEN
WITH SLANTING GOBELIN STITCH. BINDING STITCH
IS IN ROSE.

hen pattern is complete, fold
re in half, wrong sides together.
ends using binding stitch (see
h Guide). Flatten joined ends to
t at center. Join remaining edges
binding stitch halfway.
tuff cushion, then finish binding.

DON'T FORGET QUILTS!

*See "Home For The Holidays"
(Chapter VI) for a variety of special
quilt designs. A quilt is always a
popular first prize for the raffle at
your holiday bazaar.*

---

*See "Come Trim The Tree"
(Chapter IV) and "Home For The
Holidays" (Chapter VI) for beautiful ornaments; they make fast-
selling bazaar items, too!*

3B TULIPS

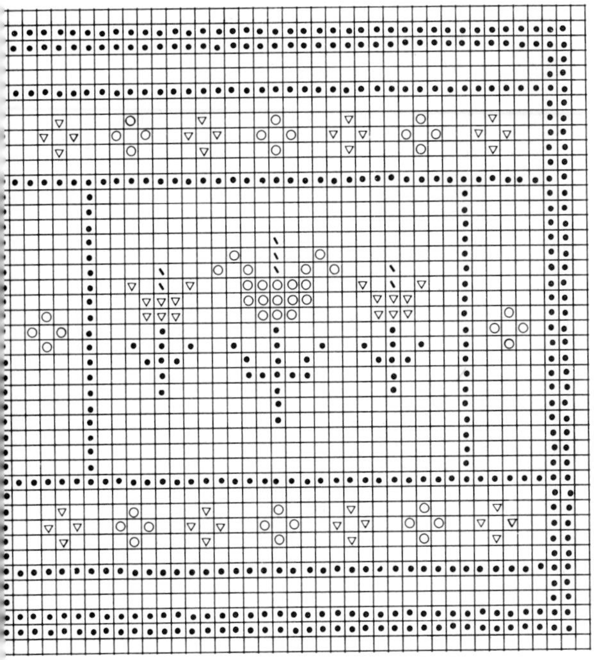

FIG. 3C VIOLETS

WHITE ⊡=ORANGE ▽=GOLD ⊠=YELLOW
GREEN
UTER BORDER ROWS ARE DONE IN GREEN
H SLANTING GOBELIN STITCH. BINDING STITCH
N ORANGE.

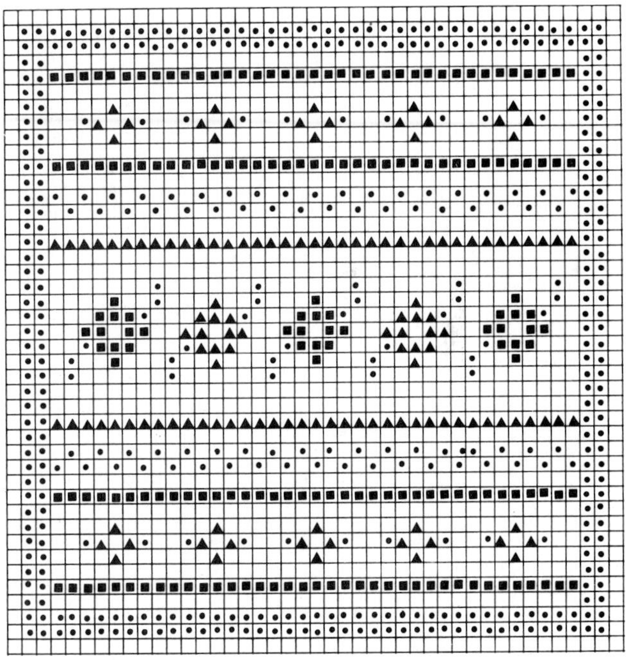

□=WHITE ■=PURPLE ▲=LAVENDER ⊡=GREEN

2 OUTER BORDER ROWS ARE DONE IN GREEN
WITH SLANTING GOBELIN STITCH. BINDING STITCH
IS IN LAVENDER.

Pull-on Baby Bib

PULL-ON BABY'S BIB

AVERAGE: For those with some experience in sewing.
Note: Use premade appliqués or cut your own from printed fabric.
MATERIALS—*Note: This project requires a machine capable of zigzag stitching.* One 10 x 17" terry cloth towel; one 5½" to 6" appliqué with desired Christmas figure; one 3½ x 14" strip of jersey-type material for collar.

DIRECTIONS:
1. Appliqué Christmas figure to center bottom of towel using a medium-wide zigzag stitch and a 12-to-the-inch stitch length.
2. To make neck opening, cut a circle 7" in diameter about 1½" down from center top of towel.
3. Cut a 3½ x 14" piece of jersey material for collar. Fold jersey in half with right sides together so that the 3½" edges meet, and sew a ½" seam. This will form a circle to be used for the collar. Fold the circle so that wrong

sides are together and pin to ne[ck] opening with raw edges matchin[g.] Make sure collar seam is at center t[op] of towel.
4. Using the widest zigzag and a 16-t[o-] the-inch stitch length, sew the coll[ar] to the towel, stretching the jersey [so] that it fits the neck opening.

CROSS-STITCH JAR COVERS

AVERAGE: Requires some experience in embroidery.

MATERIALS: 20-mesh-to-the-inch Aida cloth; 1¼"-wide lightweight beaded (for ribbon) edging; 6-strand embroidery floss; scraps of thin fabric for lining; ¾ yd. silk macramé cord.

DIRECTIONS:

1. Draw 6"-dia. circles on Aida cloth. With 2 strands in needle, work the cross stitch (*see Embroidery Stitch Guide, page 269 and charts in* FIG. 4), centered on the circle. Press. When all embroidery is finished, cut out the circles.

2. Cut same-size circles from lining fabric. With right sides together, seam (¼") Aida to lining, leaving an opening. Turn right side out. Turn in open edges and slipstitch closed.

3. Lap the beaded part of the edging over the Aida cloth and slipstitch the inner edge in place, holding it in slightly so edging lies flat. Seam raw ends together and slipstitch again, near the cloth edge.

4. Thread the cord through the beading and knot each end. Place the cover over a jar top; draw up the cord and tie.

Cross-Stitch Jar Covers

FIG. 4 JAR COVERS

■=PURPLE ▲=ROSE ◮=SALMON ▨=LIME ⊠=YELLOW ▣=DK. BLUE ▣=GREEN ▢=OLIVE ◨=LT. BLUE

SAFE, INEXPENSIVE TOYS FOR YOUR FAVORITE CAT OR DOG

PETS ARE NEVER *too young, or too old, to need and enjoy toys. The right toy can entertain a puppy or kitten for hours, keep him out of mischief and provide needed exercise for young muscles and teeth; and a few minutes chasing a ball or romping with a chew-toy will do wonders to keep an older animal feeling young.*

Playthings for pets need not be expensive or elaborate, but they must be selected carefully. All toys for pets, whether bought or made, must be too large to swallow and too hard to chew into pieces. Toys designed for children won't withstand an animal's sharp teeth. Neither will toys made of hard plastic, wood, Styrofoam, or soft rubber—dangerous small pieces can be chewed off and swallowed. Avoid anything with a squeaker in it; and, of course, never give an animal anything painted with lead paint or with hard, sharp edges.

Toys For Puppies And Dogs
● *Leather toys are excellent and virtually indestructible—straps to tug on, knotted "bones" and other objects. Avoid those with fringe.*
● *Hard rubber balls. Tennis balls and heavy sponge-rubber balls are usually safe for older dogs.*
● *Hard, solid, natural rubber toys—straps to play tug-of-war with, toys to fetch and carry around.*
● *Large knuckle or shin bones that can't splinter or be chewed into bits.*
● *One of the best and simplest toys to make for a puppy or dog is one that can be chewed, tossed or used as a tug-of-war exerciser. It's made by simply knotting a clean old pair of socks or nylon hose several times to form a large, lumpy ball with two ends. If you're making this plaything*

as a gift, you can use new, white tennis socks or a small terry towel and decorate the finished toy with nontoxic paints or food dye. (Dogs, however, are colorblind, and won't know the difference, but the gift will look more festive to human eyes.)
● *Another easy and versatile toy to make is a burlap roll to be hauled around by a puppy or tossed to an older dog. Use a rectangular scrap of burlap and fold it in thirds lengthwise. Stitch the edges firmly with heavy button thread. Then place the stitched burlap on a flat surface and roll from the bottom as tightly as possible, making sure that the stitched lengthwise edges are inside. When the roll is completed, stitch together tightly, over and over. If you're making this toy for a small dog or puppy, be sure that the finished product is small and light enough for him to carry.*

Toys For Kittens And Cats
● *Large, light whiffle balls.*
● *Small, hard rubber balls—not small enough to swallow, but not so big that they're too heavy to be rolled by a small cat or kitten.*
● *Catnip toys made out of soft felt or pliable plastic. Avoid those with bells in them, which might be swallowed.*
● *Dangling objects—avoid bells.*
● *Toys on springs that can be attached firmly to the top of a scratching post.*
● *You can make a simple catnip toy by sewing a small "pillow" out of a scrap of felt or other heavy fabric and stuffing it with catnip.*
● *Spools and corks make excellent dangling toys when strung together and hung on a doorknob. They can be decorated with nontoxic paints or food dye. Be sure that they can be*

attached firmly and that the string can't be pulled loose and swallowed.

Cats will enjoy chasing this toy as it's pulled along the floor or batting it when it's tied to a doorknob.

Glitter Rattle:
1. *Measure the outside circumference of a small empty orange juice can and add $1/4$ inch for a narrow overlap. Measure the length of the can and add $2\frac{1}{2}$ inches. Cut felt to these measurements.*
2. *Lay felt flat and trace circles on it with a dime. Cut out circles. Stitch ($1/4$-inch overlapped seam) the felt down the long edges to form a cylinder. Fringe ends with pinking shears.*
3. *Remove one end of the can and save. Punch a small hole in the remaining end of the empty can. Firmly knot the end of a 2- to 3-foot length of elastic cord and pull through the hole, leaving the knot inside the can. Put a few small stones or a handful of uncooked rice in the can. Tape the loose end back on tightly.*
4. *Cover the can with silver aluminum foil and slip the felt cylinder over it. Gather the ends of the felt tightly with firm and repeated handstitching.*

FOR HIM, FOR HER

Mohair Cable Sweater

MOHAIR CABLE SWEATER

CHALLENGING: Requires more experience in knitting.

Note: This is an oversized sweater. Directions are for Small (8-10). Changes for Medium (12-14) and Large (16-18) are in parentheses.

MATERIALS: Kid mohair: 80% mohair, 20% acrylic (40 gr. balls) 8 (9-10) Green; Size 7 and 11 knitting needles, OR ANY SIZE NEEDLES TO OBTAIN STITCH GAUGE BELOW; 1 double point needle (dpn); 1 stitch holder; 2 buttons.

GAUGE: St st on larger needles: 5 sts = 2"; 4 rows = 2". Pat on larger needles: 4 sts = 1". TO SAVE TIME, TAKE TIME TO CHECK GAUGE.

FINISHED MEASUREMENTS:

Sizes:	Small	Medium	Large
Bust:	46"	49"	52"
Back width at underarm:			
	23"	24½"	26"
Sleeve width at upperarm (approx):			
	19"	20"	21"

DIRECTIONS:

1. PAT I (4 st Cable called - C 4):
Rows 1 and 3 (right side): K 4. **Rows 2, 4 and 6:** P 4. **Row 5:** Sl 2 sts to a dpn, hold in front of work, k 2, k 2 off dpn. Rep these 6 rows for Pat I.

2. PAT II: (Sl st worked over 1 st):
Row 1 (right side): Wyib sl 1. **Row 2:** P 1. Rep these 2 rows for Pat II.

3. PAT III (8 st cable called - C 8):
Rows 1, 3, 7, 9, 11, 13 and 15: K 8. **Row 2 and all even number rows thru 18:** P8. **Row 5 and 17:** Sl 4 sts to a dpn, hold in front of work, k 4, k 4 off dpn. Rep these 18 rows for Pat III.

4. BACK: With smaller needles cast on 66 (70-74) sts. **Row 1 (wrong side):** P 2, • k 2, p 2, rep from • across. **Row 2:** K 2, • p 2, k 2, rep • from across. Rep these 2 rows for rib pat for 3", end with Row 2. Work Row 1 inc 16 sts evenly across - 82 (86-90) sts. Change to larger needles and pat. **Row 1 (right side):** + P 3, Pat I over 4 sts, p 2, Pat II over 1 st, p 2, Pat III over 8

sts, p 2, Pat II over 1 st, p 2, Pat I over 4 sts p 3, + k 18 (22-26); rep between + once more. Keeping to pats as established, working center 18 (22-26) sts in St st, work to 17" from beg, end with a right side row.

5. Shape Upper Sleeves: With a separate strand of yarn cast on 24 sts, break off strand, work across 82 (86-90) sts, cast on 24 sts - 130 (134-138) sts. **Next Row (right side):** P 1, Pat II over 1 st, p 2, Pat I over 4 sts, p 2, Pat II over 1 st, p 2, Pat III over 8 sts, p 2, Pat II over 1 st, keeping to pats as established work - 82 (86-90) sts, Pat II over 1 st, p 2, Pat III over 8 sts, p 2 Pat II over 1 st, p 2, Pat III over 8 sts, p 2, Pat II over 1 st, p 2, Pat I over 4 sts, p 2, Pat II over 1 st, p 1. Being sure that cable twist rows of Pat I and III on sleeve correspond to cable twist rows of back work in pat. Work until sleeve cast-on measures 8 (8½-9)" end with a wrong side row.

6. Shape neck: Row 1: Keeping to pats work 61 (62-63) sts, sl these sts to a holder, bind off center 8 (10-12) sts complete row. **Row 2:** Keeping to pat, complete row. **Row 3:** Bind off 3 sts, complete row. Rep Rows 2 and 3 once more, then rep Row 2 - 55 (56-57) sts. Bind off. Sl sts from holder to a larger needle. Work as other side, reversing shaping.

7. FRONT: As back until cast-on row for sleeves has been completed - 130 (134-138) sts. Working sleeve sts in to pat as on back, work in pat for 63 (65-67) sts, sl to a holder, bind off center 4 sts, complete row. Working one side only, work until sleeve measures 4½ (5-5½)", end at front edge.

8. Shape Neck: Keeping to pats bind off 3 (4-5) sts once, then dec 1 st at neck edge every other row 5 times - 55 (56-57) sts. Work even until sleeve measures same as back to top. Bind off. Sl sts from holder to a larger needle. Work as other side, reversing shaping.

9. SLEEVES: With smaller needles cast on 26 (30-34) sts. Work in ribbing as on lower back for 2", end with row 2. Work Row 1 inc 10 sts evenly across - 36 (40-44) sts. Change to larger nee-

dles and St st, inc 1 st each end ev[ery] 4th row 6 times - 48 (52-56) sts. W[ork] to 9" from beg. Bind off.

10. FINISHING: Sew shoul[der] seams. **Neckband:** From right s[ide] with smaller needles, beg at right fr[ont] opening, pick up and k 58 (62-66) around neck. Work in ribbing as [on] lower back for 6 rows. Bind off in [rib]bing. **Left Front Band:** From right s[ide] with smaller needles, beg at top [of] neckband pick up and k 22 (26-26) along left front opening. Working [in] k 2 ribbing for 7 rows. Bind off in [rib]bing. Along band mark places fo[r] buttons, having top button at cente[r of] neckband and bottom button 2" ab[ove] lower edge. **Right Front Band:** Beg [at] lower edge work as left band for 3 r[ows] after pick-up row. **Buttonhole Row** [Rib to opposite marker, bind off 1 twice, complete row. **Row 2:** Keep [ing] to ribbing cast on 1 st over bound of[f]. Complete as left band. Sew left fr[ont] band to 4 st bindoff at front. Over[lap] right front band at base and sew ne[at] over left front band. Sew lower sle[eve] to cast-on sleeve edges as shown. S[ew] undersleeve and side seams. Sew buttons.

TURTLENECK SWEATER

AVERAGE: For those with some [ex]perience in knitting. *Note:* This is [an] oversized sweater.

Directions are given for Size Small [(8-] 10). Changes for Sizes Medium ([12-] 14) and Large (16) are in parenthes[es].
MATERIALS: Bulky mohair: 45[%] Kid Mohair, 44% Cotton, 11% Acr[yl]ic (50-gr. ball): 18 (19, 20) balls White; knitting needles, one pair ea[ch] No. 9 and No. 10, OR ANY SIZE NEED[LES]

chsia Oversized Vest and Nubby White Turtleneck

TO OBTAIN STITCH GAUGE BELOW; one stitch holder.

GAUGE: In Stockinette Stitch (k 1 row, p 1 row) using larger needles —13 sts = 4"; 9 rows = 2". BE SURE TO CHECK YOUR GAUGE.

Sizes:	Small (8-10)	Medium (12-14)	Large (16)
Body			
Bust:	32½"	36"	38"
Finished			
Bust:	39"	41½"	44"

Width across back or front at underarm:
19½"   20¾"   22"

Width across sleeve at upper arm:
18½"   19¾"   20¾"

DIRECTIONS:

1. BACK: Starting at lower edge with smaller needles, cast on 61 (65, 69) sts. **Row 1** (*wrong side*):P 1, * k 1, p 1; rep from * across. **Row 2:** K 1, * p 1, k 1; rep from * across. Rep these 2 rows for rib pat to 3", ending with Row 1. Change to larger needles and stockinette stitch (st st), inc 4 sts evenly spaced across last row — 65 (69, 73) sts. Work to 14" from beg, ending with a p row.

2. Armhole Shaping: Bind off 2 sts at beg of next 2 rows — 61 (65, 69) sts. Work even until armholes are 9½ (10, 10½)", end with a p row.

3. Neck and Shoulder Shaping: K 25 (26, 27) sts, sl remaining sts to a st holder. Work one side *only*. **Row 1:** At neck edge, bind off 4 sts, complete row. **Row 2:** Bind off 10 sts, work to 2 sts before neck edge and dec one st. **Row 3:** Work even across row. **Row 4:** Bind off remaining 10 (11, 12) sts. Sl sts from st holder onto larger needles. Bind off center 11 (13, 15) sts, complete row. Work as for other side, reversing shaping.

4. FRONT: Work same as Back until armholes measure 7½ (8, 8½)", ending with a p row — 61 (65, 69) sts.

5. Neck Shaping: Work 27 (28, 29) sts, sl remaining sts to a st holder. Working one side *only*, at neck edge

bind off 2 sts every other row twice. Dec one st every row twice, every other row once — 20 (21, 22) sts. Work until armhole measures same as Back to shoulders; ending at armhole edge.

6. Shoulder Shaping: Bind off 10 sts once. Work 1 row. Bind off remaining 10 (11, 12) sts. Sl sts from st holder to larger needles. Bind off center 7 (9, 11) sts, complete row. Work as for other side, reversing shaping.

7. SLEEVES: Starting at lower edge with smaller needles, cast on 39 (40, 43) sts. Work in k 1, p 1 ribbing as on lower Back to 2½". Change to larger needles and st st, inc 4 sts evenly spaced across last row — 43 (45, 47) sts. Work 7 rows. Inc one st each end of next row, then every 7th row 9 (10, 10) times — 63 (67, 69) sts. Work to 20" from beg. Bind off all sts.

8. FINISHING: Sew left shoulder seam.

9. Turtleneck: With right side facing you and smaller needles, beg at right-back neck edge, pick up and k 68 (72, 76) sts around neck edge. Work in k 1, p 1 ribbing for 11¾". Bind off loosely in ribbing. Sew right shoulder and turtleneck tog. Sew in sleeves. Sew upper side edges of sleeves to bound-off sts at underarms. Sew side and sleeve seams.

OVERSIZED VEST

AVERAGE: For those with some experience in knitting.
Directions are given for Size Petite (6). Changes for Sizes Small (8-10), Medium (12-14) and Large (16-18) are in parentheses.

MATERIALS: Worsted weight (100-gr. ball): 5 (6, 7, 8) balls of fuschia; knitting needles, one pair each No. 6 and No. 9, OR ANY SIZE NEEDLES TO OBTAIN STITCH GAUGE BELOW; one circular needle, No. 6 (24" length); three stitch markers; 4 safety pins; one stitch holder.

GAUGE: In Stockinette Stitch (k 1, row, p 1 row) using larger needles — 4 sts = 1"; 5 rows = 1". BE SURE TO CHECK YOUR GAUGE.

Sizes:	Petite (6)	Small (8-10)	Medium (12-14)	La (16
Body				
Bust:	30½"	32½"	36"	4
Finished measurements:				
Bust:	37"	39"	43"	4

Width across back or front at ur arms:
18½"   19½"   21½"   23

DIRECTIONS:

1. BACK: Starting at lower edge smaller needles, cast on 67 (71, 79 sts. Work in k 1, p 1 ribbing for 2" 6 sts evenly spaced across last ro 74 (78, 86, 94) sts. Change to l needles and p across next row. beg pattern st as follows: **Row 1** (side): K 4 (2,2,2), * skip next st o hand needle, k the next st throug back, then k the skipped st through fr **twisted st made;** k 6; rep from * ac ending last rep with k 4 (2, 2, 2). **2, 4, 6, 8:** P across. **Rows 3 and** across. **Row 5:** K 6, * twisted st next 2 sts, k 6; rep from * endin rep with k 2 (6, 6, 6). Rep Rows 1 for pattern st until total length (23, 24, 24½)" from beg, ending a wrong-side row.

2. Neck Shaping: Work in pat a first 25 (27, 31, 35) sts, sl center 2 onto a st holder for back neck; jc 2nd ball of yarn and complete Working both sides at the same t dec one st at each neck edge *every* 5 times — 20 (22, 26, 30) sts side. Work even in pat until length is 25 (26, 27, 27½)" from Bind off 20 (22, 26, 30) sts on side for shoulders. **Mark each side of Back with safety pins** 9½ 10½, 10½)" **down from shou edge.**

3. FRONT: Work same as Back t total length is 8 (9, 10, 10½)" f beg, ending with a wrong-side rov

4. Neck Shaping: Work in pat ac first 36 (38, 42, 46) sts; join 2nd ba yarn and bind off center 2 sts; comp row. Working both sides at the s time, dec one st at each neck

ery 4th row until 20 (22, 26, 30) sts
n. Work even in pat until total
gth is 25 (26, 27, 27½)" from beg.
nd off 20 (22, 26, 30) sts on each
le for shoulder. **Mark each side edge
Front with safety pins 9½ (10,**
½, 10½)" down from shoulder.
FINISHING: Sew shoulder seams.
Armhole Bands: With right side
:ing you and smaller needles, pick up
(82, 86, 86) sts evenly spaced along
mhole edge, from marker to marker.
ork in k 1, p 1, ribbing for 1". Bind
f loosely in ribbing.
Neckband: With right side facing
u and circular needle, beg at right-
.ck shoulder seam, pick up and k 8 (8,
:, 12) sts along right-back neck edge,
24 sts from back st holder, pick up
.d k 8 (8, 12, 12) sts along left-back
·ck edge, pick up and k 64 sts along
·t-front neck edge, place a marker,
.ck up 2 sts from center front, place a
.arker, pick up 64 sts along right-front
·ck edge, place a marker — 170
70, 178, 178) sts. Join. Work around
k 1, p 1 ribbing to within 2 sts of
.arker, k 2 tog, k 2 sts between mark-
·s, k 2 tog directly after marker, work
k 1, p 1 ribbing to end of rnd. Con-
·nue to work in k 1, p 1 ribbing, dec
·e st before and after markers as be-
·re until 2" from beg of ribbing. Bind
·f in ribbing. Sew side/armhole band
·ams.

SHAVE KIT
(about 6 x 7 x 12")

AVERAGE: For those with some experience in sewing.
MATERIALS: 13 x 21" piece blue
print fabric; 7 x 22" piece solid blue
fabric; ½-yd. 45"-wide waterproof lining fabric; iron-on interfacing; 12" zipper; 6 x 12" stiff cardboard.

DIRECTIONS *(½" seams allowed)*:
1. Cutting: From blue fabric, cut two
7" square end pieces and one 3 x 7"
strip; from lining, cut one 13 x 21"
body, two 7" square ends, one 13¼"
square.
2. Pleats and Tabs: Fuse interfacing to
print body and blue end pieces. Baste a
2" box pleat at center top of each end
piece (bag and lining). Fold a 3 x 7"
strip of blue fabric lengthwise; seam,
turn and cut in half. Fold in half for
tabs. Baste on, centered, over each
pleat, matching raw edges.
3. Assembly: With right sides together, stitch zipper (¼") to 13" edges of
body. Seam blue end pieces to body,
right sides together, with zipper centered over tabs and pivoting at corners.
4. Lining: With right sides together
and edges even, pin lining to wrong
side of zipper tapes. Stitch over previous stitching up to ½" from end
pieces, leaving an opening. Turn, then
stitch closed.
5. Fold 13¼" square in half and stitch
any two edges, turn right side out and
press, turning in raw edges. Insert cardboard and stitch opening. Put into bag.

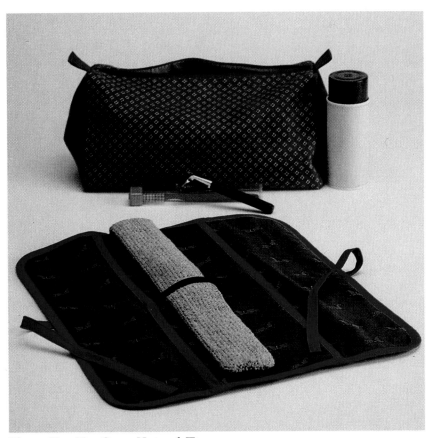

Shave Kit; Tie Case; Knitted Tie

TIE CASE
(14 x 16")

AVERAGE: For those with some experience in sewing.
MATERIALS: ½ yd. 45"-wide green print; ½ yd. interfacing; 1 pkg. each maroon single-fold bias tape and wide bias tape; ½"-wide black elastic, 4⅞ x 15" piece cardboard.

DIRECTIONS:
1. Cut two 14 x 16" rectangles from green print and one from interfacing, rounding corners.
2. With right sides up, baste one print piece (lining) over interfacing. Centered and 5" apart, pin two 16" lengths of the narrower tape across lining to make a slot for cardboard. Slide ends of 6" pieces of elastic under the tapes, ⅝" and 7" from top (14") edge (*see photo*). Edgestitch the tapes catching elastic tie holders. Slide cardboard into slot.
3. With right sides out, baste the two print pieces together. Fold 1 yd. of wide tape lengthwise and edgestitch for a tie; turn over 13" and pin the fold to center of one long edge of outside piece. Bind edges, catching tie.

KNITTED TIE
(2 x 48")

AVERAGE: For those with some experience in knitting.
MATERIALS: One (2-oz.) skein 2-ply 70% Wool/30% Rayon yarn in Beige or the color of your choice; one set of four double-pointed (dp) needles, Size 7, 7" long; OR ANY SIZE NEEDLES TO OBTAIN THE STITCH GAUGE BELOW.
GAUGE: In Stockinette Stitch (st st) with two strands held together throughout — 6 sts = 1"; 8 rows = 1". BE SURE TO CHECK YOUR GAUGE.
Note: Tie is worked with two strands of yarn held together throughout (use front and back ends of one skein). It is worked in tubular form, from the right side on four double-pointed needles.

DIRECTIONS:
TIE: Starting at lower edge with two strands of yarn and one dp needle, cast on 26 sts. Divide stitches on three dp needles as follows: Place 8 sts on first two needles and 10 sts on the third needle. With fourth dp needle, work around in st st (k every rnd) until tube measures 14". Now knit around until the fifth st on the third needle has been completed. Turn the tube to the wrong side and lay the work flat, using the fifth st as the center back. Weave the bottom ends neatly together. Turn the tube to the right side and place a marker after the fifth st for the center back. Continue around in st st as follows: Dec on st before and after the marker on the next rnd, then every 2" 3 times more—18 sts. Work even for 5". Dec one st before and after the marker on the next rnd, then every 2" once more—14 sts. Work even for 13". Inc one st before and after the marker on the next rnd—16 sts. Work even 8" more.
FINISHING: To complete, lay Tie flat, making sure the center back dec's are well centered; weave ends together. Remove all markers; darn in loose ends. Pin Tie to shape and measurements 2" x 48" on a padded surface and cover with a damp cloth; allow to dry. Do not press.

Tobacco Box

TOBACCO BOX
(8 x 8 x 10")

AVERAGE: For those with some [ex]perience in woodworking.
MATERIALS: ¼ x 18 x 12", [ ] 18 x 15" pieces of birch plyw[ood] ½ x ¾ x 36", ½ x ½ x 26" strip[s] pine; ½", ¾", 1" brads; one 3" chro[me] wire pull with short bolts; glue; g[ ] white polyurethane.

CUTTING DIRECTIONS:

PART	PIECES	SIZE	
A (PLY)	2	¼" x 6" x 7"	Sides
A1 (PLY)	2	½" x 2" x 6"	Pipe r[ ]
A2 (PLY)	2	½" x 3½" x 6"	End[ ]
B (PLY)	1	½" x 7" x 9"	Botto[m]
B1	2	½" x ¾" x 7"	Trim
B2	2	½" x ¾" x 10"	Tri[m]
C (PLY)	1	¼" x 5" x 8"	Top
C1	2	½" x ½" x 8"	Trim
C2	2	½" x ½" x 4¼"	Tr[im]
C3	1	3"	Handle

DIRECTIONS:

Cut the plywood pieces; see FIG. 5 pipe rack (A1) pattern. Drill $\frac{7}{8}"$ holes for pipes. Drill top for handles as required.

Glue/nail ($\frac{3}{4}"$ brads) pipe racks (A1) to sides (A). Glue/nail ($\frac{3}{4}"$) sides to ends (A2), flush at edges, see FIG. 5.

Glue/nail trim (B1, B2) to bottom with 1" brads, flush at bottom. Sand and round corners.

Invert, glue/nail (1") the bottom B assembly to the A assembly through bottom (B) into ends (A2), centered on bottom (B) 3" from each end and flush with inner edges of trim (B2), see FIG. 5.

Glue/nail ($\frac{1}{2}"$) top (C) to trim (C1), then trim (C2) flush at all edges, see FIG. 5.

Fill nail holes, sand and paint gloss white. Fasten handle.

FIG. 5 TOBACCO BOX

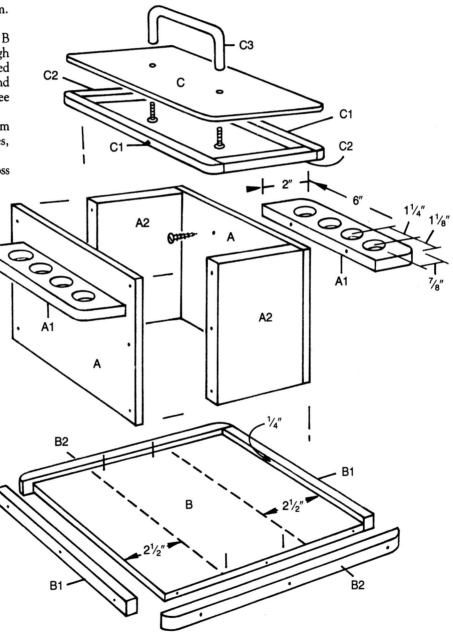

Men's Sweater Quartet (left to right): Fair Isle Pullover; "Crest" Motif Crewneck; Log Cabin Pullover; Cable V-Neck Sweater

MAN'S FAIR ISLE PULLOVER

CHALLENGING: Requires more experience in knitting.

Note: This is a loose-fitting sweater. Directions are for Small (36-38). Changes for Medium (40-42) and Large (44-46) are in parentheses.

MATERIALS: Worsted weight 96% wool, 4% polyester yarn (50 gr. skeins): 9 (10-11) Black (MC), 8 (8-9) Grey (A). 1 Magenta (B). Size 7 and 9 knitting needles, OR ANY SIZE NEEDLES TO OBTAIN STITCH GAUGE BELOW; 1 stitch holder.

GAUGE: Knit in pat on larger needles: 4 sts = 1"; 4 rows = 1": TO SAVE TIME, TAKE TIME TO CHECK GAUGE.

FINISHED MEASUREMENTS:

Sizes:	Small	Medium	Large
Chest:	43½"	46½"	49½"
Back width at underarm:			
	21¾"	23¼"	24¾"
Sleeve width at upperarm:			
	18¾"	19¾"	20¾"

Note: Always twist yarns when changing colors to prevent holes. Carry colors not in use loosely at back of work, being careful to maintain gauge.

DIRECTIONS:

1. BACK: With smaller needles and MC cast on 80 (86-92) sts. Work in k 1, p 1 ribbing. Work 2 rows MC, 2 rows B, 2 rows A, 4 rows MC, 2 rows B, 4 rows A, 2 rows B, 2 rows MC. With MC p 1 row, inc 9 sts evenly across, - 89 (95-101) sts. Change to larger needles and St st. Beg pat following FIG. 6. Rep 20 rows of chart for pat throughout. Work to 24½ (25-25½)" from beg, or desired length, end with a p row.

2. Shape Shoulders: Keeping to pat, bind off 9 (11-11) sts at beg of next 2 rows, then bind off 10 (10-11) sts at beg of next 4 rows. Bind off remaining 31 (33-35) sts for back neck edge.

3. FRONT: As back until piece measures 21½ (22-22½)" from beg, end with a p row.

4. Shape Neck: Keeping to pat, work 39 (41-43) sts, sl to a holder. Bind off center 11 (13-15) sts, work 39 (41-43) sts. Working one side only, at neck edge bind off 2 sts every other row 5 times, - 29 (31-33) sts. Work to same length as back to shoulder, end at side edge.

5. Shape Shoulder: Keeping to pat bind off 9 (11-11) sts once. Work 1 row. Bind off 10 (10-11) sts every other row twice. Sl sts from holder to a larger needle. Work as other side, reversing shaping.

6. SLEEVES: With smaller needles and MC cast on 41 (45-49) sts. Work in rib and stripe pat as on lower back.

With MC p 1 row, inc 8 (6-6) sts evenly across, - 49 (51-55) sts. Change to larger needles and St st. Beg pat as indicated for sleeves. Inc 1 st each end every 4th row 14 (15-15) times, working new sts into pat, - 77 (81-85) sts. Work to 21" from beg, or desired length. Bind off.

7. FINISHING: Sew left shoulder seam. **Neckband:** From right side, with smaller needles and MC, beg at right back neck edge, pick up and k 87 (91-95) sts around neck. Work in k 1, p 1 ribbing. Work 1 row MC, 2 rows B, 2 rows A, 1 row MC. Bind off with MC. Sew right shoulder and neckband tog. Match center top of sleeves to shoulder seams. Sew top of sleeves to front and back. Sew side and sleeve seams. Block lightly to measurements.

MAN'S "CREST" MOT
CREWNECK

CHALLENGING: Requires more perience in knitting.
Directions are for Small (36-
Changes for Medium (40-42)
Large (44-46) are in parentheses.
MATERIALS: Worsted wei
100% wool (3.5 oz. skeins): 5 (
Oyster White (MC) 1 oz. each M
um Green (A), Soft Green (B),
(C), Purple (D), Yellow (E) and B
(F), 1 ball Gold Lurex (G). Size 6
8 knitting needles, OR ANY SIZE
DLES TO OBTAIN STITCH GAUGE BEL
2 Stitch holders; 8 Bobbins.
GAUGE: St st on larger needles:
= 1"; 6 rows = 1". TO SAVE T
TAKE TIME TO CHECK GAUGE.

FINISHED MEASUREMENTS:

Sizes:	Small	Medium	Lar
Chest:	41"	44"	4
Back width at underarm:			
	20½"	22"	23
Sleeve width at upperarm:			
	19¾"	20½"	21

Note: Wind 2 bobbins with MC ar
each with A, B, C, D, E and F. Al
twist yarns when changing color
prevent holes. When working
more than 1 color (as on diag
stripes) carry color not in use loose
back of work, being careful to mair
gauge.

DIRECTIONS:

1. FRONT: With smaller needles
MC cast on 104 (112-120) sts. W
in k 1, p 1 ribbing for 2". Chang
larger needles and St st. Work t
from beg end with a p row. Beg C
(FIG. 7) pat. **Row 1:** With MC
(30-34), work Chart over next 52
with MC k 26 (30-34). Keepin
Chart over center 52 sts work until
74 is completed. Work with MC c

FIG, 6 FAIR ISLE PULLOVER

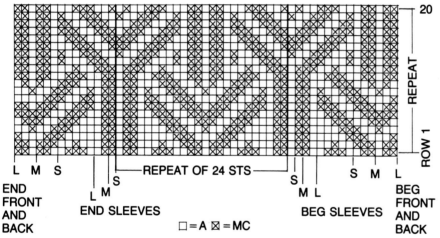

□ = A ⊠ = MC

rk to 22" from beg end with a p row.
hape Neck: K 45 (48-51) sts, sl
ter 14 (16-18) sts to a holder, join a
ball MC, k 45 (48-51) sts. Work
sides at once. P 1 row. **Dec Row:**
4 sts before neck edge, k 2 tog, k 2,
2nd ball k 2, sl 1-k 1-psso, k to
. Rep Dec row every k row 9 times
e - 35 (38-41) each side of neck.
rk 3 rows even. Bind off.

BACK: As front, eliminating
rt and neck shaping to top. **Shape**
: Bind off 35 (38-41) sts, k next 34
-38) sts, sl to a holder for neck
e, bind off remaining 35 (38-41)

SLEEVES: With smaller needles
MC cast on 47 (51-55). Work in k
1 ribbing for 2". Inc 1 st each end
ry 4th row 27 times - 101 (105-109)
Work to 20" from beg end with a p
. Bind off.

FINISHING: Sew left shoulder
m. **Neckband:** From right side with
ller needle and MC, beg at right
k neck edge, pick up and k 85 (89-
sts around neck, including sts on
ders. Work in k 1, p 1 ribbing for 5
s. Bind off in ribbing. Sew right
ulder and neckband tog. Duplicate
for crest following Chart. Match
ter top of sleeve to shoulder seam.
in sleeve. Sew side and sleeve
ms. Block lightly to measurements.

FIG. 7 "CREST" MOTIF CREWNECK

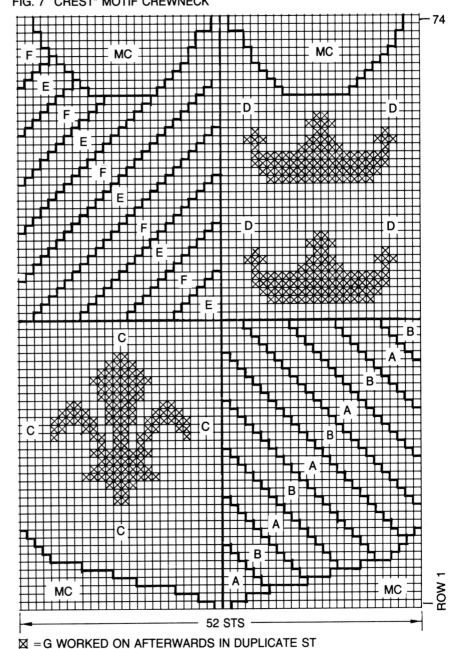

⊠ = G WORKED ON AFTERWARDS IN DUPLICATE ST

MAN'S LOG CABIN PULLOVER

CHALLENGING: Requires more experience in knitting.
Directions are for Small (36). Changes for medium (38-40) and Large (42-44) are in parentheses by changing needle sizes.
MATERIALS: 100% worsted weight wool yarn (3½ oz. skeins) 2 each of Lt. Gray Heather (MC), Rose (A), Mahogany (B), Moss (C) Cinnamon (D) and Blue Heather (E). Size 4 (5-6) and 7 (8-9) knitting needles, OR ANY SIZE NEEDLES TO OBTAIN STITCH GAUGE BELOW; Bobbins.
GAUGE: Pat on size 7 needles: 5 sts = 1"; 19 rows = 3". **Pat on size 8 needles:** 9 sts = 2"; 6 rows = 1". **Pat on size 9 needles:** 4 sts = 1"; 17 rows = 3". TO SAVE TIME, TAKE TIME TO CHECK GAUGE.

FINISHED MEASUREMENTS:
Sizes: Small   Medium   Large
Chest: 36"   40"   45"
Back width at underarm:
                 18"   20"   22½"
Sleeve width at upperarm:
                 14"   15¾"   17½"

Note: Wind a bobbin for each color section. Always twist yarns when changing colors to prevent holes.

DIRECTIONS:
1. BACK: With smaller needles [4 (5-6)] and MC cast on 80 sts. Work in k 1, p 1 ribbing for 3", inc 10 sts evenly across last row - 90 sts. Change to larger needles [7 (8-9)] and St st. Beg pat following Chart. Work to 15" from beg or desired length to underarms, end with a p row. *Note:* If Row 82 of FIG. 8 has been completed, rep Chart starting with row 35. Rep Rows 35 thru 82 for pat.
2. Shape Armholes: Keeping to pat, bind off 4 sts at beg of next 2 rows. Dec

1 st each end every other row 4 times - 74 sts. Work even until armholes measure 9 (9½-10)", end with a p row.
3. Shape Shoulders: Keeping to pat, bind off 7 sts at beg of next 6 rows. Bind off remaining 32 sts for back neck edge.
4. FRONT: As back until armholes measure 6 (6½-7)", end with a p row.
Shape Neck: Keeping to pat, work 27 sts, bind off center 20 sts, work 27 sts. Working both sides at once, dec 1 st at each neck edge every row 6 times. Work to same length as back to shoulders. Shape shoulders as on back.
5. SLEEVES: With smaller needles [4 (5-6)] cast on 40 sts. Work in k 1, p 1 ribbing for 3", inc 8 sts evenly across last row - 48 sts. Change to larger needles [7 (8-9)] and St st. Beg pat as indicated for sleeves and starting with row 38, inc 1 st each end every 6th row 12 times - 72 sts. Work new sts into pat. Work to 19" from beg, or desired sleeve length, end with a p row. **Shape cap:** Keeping to pat bind off 4 sts at beg of next 2 rows. Dec 1 st each end every other row 10 times. Bind off 3 sts at beg of next 8 rows. Bind off.
6. FINISHING: Sew left shoulder seam. **Neckband:** From right side, with smaller needles and MC, beg at right back neck edge, pick up and k 85 sts around neck. Work in k 1, p 1 ribbing for 1". Bind off in ribbing. Sew right shoulder and neck band tog. Sew side and sleeve seams. Sew in sleeves. Block to measurements.

MAN'S CABLE V-NECK SWEATER

CHALLENGING: Requires more experience in knitting.
Note: This is a loose-fitting sweater that may be worked with a V-neck, crew neck or turtleneck.
Directions are for Small (38-40). Changes for Medium (42) and Large (44-46) are in parentheses.

MATERIALS: 100% worsted-we wool (100-gr. balls): **V-Neck:** 8 (9- Blue. **Crew and Turtleneck:** 9 (10- Blue. Size 5 and 8 knitting needles, ANY SIZE NEEDLES TO OBTAIN STI GAUGE BELOW; 16" circular needle 5. One double point needle (dpn Stitch holders.

GAUGE: St st on larger needles: 9 = 2"; 6 rows = 1". Cable Pat on la needles: 6 sts = 1"; TO SAVE T TAKE TIME TO CHECK GAUGE.

FINISHED MEASUREMENTS:
Sizes: Small   Medium   Lar
Chest: 44"   47"   50
Back width at underarm:
                 22"   23½"   25
Sleeve width at upperarm:
                 18"   19"   19¾

STITCH ABBREVIATIONS: 4
Front Cable (4FC): Sl 2 sts to a d hold in front of work, k 2, k 2 off d
4 St Back Cable (4BC): Sl 2 sts dpn, hold in back of work, k 2, k 2 dpn.

DIRECTIONS:
1. BACK: With smaller needles, on 104 (110-116) sts. Work in k 1, ribbing for 2½", inc 9 sts evenly ac last row, - 113 (119-125) sts. Cha to larger needles and pat. **Row 1 (r side):** K 35 (38-41) [p 1, k 1] twice 1, k 4, p 1, k 4, p 1, k 1] 3 times, p 1, p 1, k 35 (38-41). **Rows 2 and 4** the purl sts and k the knit sts. **Row** K 35 (38-41), [p 1, k 1] twice, [p 4FC, p 1, 4 BC, p 1, k 1] 3 times, p 1, p 1, k 35 (38-41). Rep these 4 r for pat. Work to 17" from beg or sired length to underarms, end w Row 2 or 4.
2. Shape Raglan Armholes: Bind o (4-5) sts at beg of next 2 rows- (111-115) sts. **Row 3:** K 1, sl 1 - k psso, in pat work to last 3 sts, k 2 tog 1. **Row 4:** Keeping to pat, w across. Rep Rows 3 and 4 for 35 (37) times more, - 35 (37-39) sts left. to a holder.

8 LOG CABIN PULLOVER

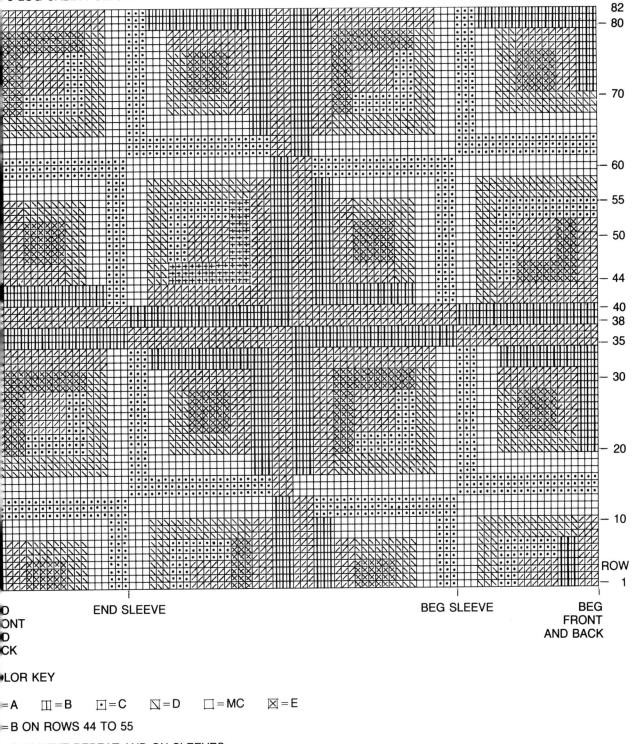

82
— 80

— 70

— 60

— 55

— 50

— 44

— 40
— 38
— 35

— 30

— 20

— 10

ROW
— 1

END SLEEVE   BEG SLEEVE   BEG
                                                           FRONT
                                                           AND BACK

D
ONT
D
CK

●LOR KEY

=A   ▥=B   ·=C   ◩=D   ☐=MC   ⊠=E

=B ON ROWS 44 TO 55

=E IN NEXT REPEAT AND ON SLEEVES

3. CREW AND TURTLENECK FRONT: Work same as back until there are 59 (61-63) sts left after start of raglan armholes, end with a right side row. **Shape Neck:** Keeping to pat work 19 sts, slip center 21 (23-25) sts to a holder, join a 2nd ball of yarn, work 19 sts. Working both sides at same time, dec 1 st at each neck edge every other row 6 times, AT SAME TIME, work raglan armhole shaping as on back until 2 sts remain each side of neck, end ready for a right side row. **Last Row:** Sl 1 - k 1 - psso, with 2nd ball k 2 tog. Fasten off.

4. V-NECK: Work as back to 1 row less than back to underarms. **Shape V-neck and Raglan Armholes:** Keeping to pat work 56 (59-62) sts, sl next st to a safety pin (point of V), join a 2nd ball of yarn, work 56 (59-62) sts. Working both sides at same time, shape raglan armholes as on back. AT SAME TIME, dec 1 st at each neck edge every 3rd row 17 (18-19) times.

5. SLEEVES: With smaller needles, cast on 48 (52-56) sts. Work in k 1, p 1 ribbing for 2½", inc 5 sts evenly across last row, - 53 (57-61) sts. Change to larger needles and pat. **Row 1 (right side):** K 17 (19-21) [p 1, k 1] twice, p 1, k 4, p 1, k 4, p 1 [k 1, p 1] twice k 17 (19-21). **Rows 2 and 4:** As Rows 2 and 4 of back. **Row 3:** K 17 (19-21), [p 1, k 1] twice, p 1, 4FC, p 1, 4BC, p 1 [k 1, p 1] twice, k 17 (19-21). Keeping to pat, inc 1 st each end every 5th row 18 times. Work new sts in St st, - 89 (93-97) sts. Work to 19" from beg, or desired length to cap, end with Row 2 or 4.

6. SHAPE RAGLAN CAP: Work same as back raglan armhole. Sl remaining 11 sts to a holder.

7. FINISHING: Sew raglan caps to front and back. Sew side and sleeve seams. **Crew Neck:** From right side, beg at right back neck edge, with circular needle pick up and k 104 (108-112) sts around neck, including sts on holders. Work round in k 1, p 1 ribbing for 1¼". Bind off in ribbing. **Turtleneck:** As crew neck but work to 7½". **V-Neck:** From right side beg at right back

neck edge, k 35 (37-39) sts off back holder, k 11 sts off sleeve holder, pick up and k 55 (59-63) sts down left front to point of V, k st off safety pin and mark this st, pick up and k 55 (59-63) sts up right front, k 11 off sleeve holder. Work round. Being sure to work marked st in k on every rnd, work in k 1, p 1, ribbing, dec 1 st each side of marked st every rnd. Work 8 rnds. Bind off in ribbing. Block lightly to measurements.

STENCILED GIFTS

EASY: Achievable by anyone.
MATERIALS: Self-adhesive ster and fabric-painting dyes (see Mate Shopping Guide, page 272); paper tow and cardboard; stencil brushes; chased slip and camisole, sheets, lowcases and towels, all of poly/cot blend; 2"-wide lace edging to t sheets and cases; **for pillow,** ½ white 50% poly/50% cotton fabri yds. lace and/or ribbon trim and pi form or stuffing.

DIRECTIONS:
HALF SLIP AND CAMISOLE
1. Place cardboard, well covered w paper towels, between the front back of the garment.
2. Rose Border: Remove from ste those areas which will be painted, off the paper backing and smooth s cil onto garment (see photo). Mix equal part of white tint-medium w each color you plan to use.
3. With a ¾" stencil brush for and leaves and a #6 scrubber brush roses, use a dry brush technique as lows: Dip brush in paint, blot, t dab or use a circular motion to br the paint through the stencil. W you peel off the stencil to reposit and continue the border, change paper towel padding. Clean the br with water and dry it with paper tow each time you change colors.
4. Let dry overnight. Cover fabric w a paper towel. Set iron one step ab setting for fabric and apply heat w circular motion for one minute. C iron to one step below setting for fat and iron for one minute.
5. To launder: Machine-wash at d cate; machine-dry at cool.
SHEETS AND PILLOWCASES
1. Following directions above (see and Camisole), stencil a basket at c ter of pillowcase border, then stenc rose at each side. Stencil a basket center of sheet border, then a r

nciled Gifts

der at each side; repeat to edge of
et.
Edgestitch 2″-wide lace edging to
sheet and the cases, above the
nciled border (*see photo*), turning
der the raw ends.

OWELS (*with at least 40% polyester
tent***)**
Pre-wash the towels, using fabric
tener on rinse cycle; machine-dry.
Follow direction for Slip and Cami-
e (*see* Steps 1-4), using colors full
ength and a #4 fabric brush. **For
h towel,** stencil a basket at center of
ge, between two rose borders. **For**

finger towel, stencil a basket at center
of edge. **For hand towel,** stencil a rose
border along edge. Let them dry overnight.
3. Machine-wash in cold water with a
mild detergent. Machine-dry at permanent press for forty-five minutes. Additional washings may be done in warm
water, warm rinse. Machine-dry.
PILLOW
1. Cut two 18″ squares of white fabric.
Place one (top) square on a well padded work surface.
2. Following directions for Slip and
Camisole (*see* Steps 2-4), stencil a rose

border across the center of the pillow-
top. Leaving ¾″ empty between, stencil a row of three baskets above and
below the rose border, then (after another ¾″) a rose border above and below the baskets.
3. Topstitch the trim between the
stenciled rows. Seam (½″) pillow front
to pillow back, right sides together,
around three sides and four corners.
Turn, stuff and slipstitch open edges
closed.
Basket—Use acrylic paint with stencil; no ironing necessary.

TEA TOWEL TOTE

AVERAGE: For those with some experience in sewing.

MATERIALS: Three tea towels; 2 yds. 45"-wide green chintz for lining and binding, 1¼ yds. 22"-wide nonwoven interfacing.

DIRECTIONS: (½" seams allowed)

1. Cutting: *From tea towels, chintz and interfacing,* cut Bag Front and Back, each 15½ x 12½", two Bag Sides each 15½ x 6½", Bag Bottom 12½ x 6½" and two Handles each 2½ x 15". Baste interfacing to wrong side of tea towel pieces. *From green chintz,* also cut enough 2"-wide bias strips to make, when pieced, 80" of binding.

2. Handles: With right sides together, stitch green lining to handles at the long edges. Turn right side out and edgestitch. Stitch a handle to the top (shorter) edge of Bag Front, right sides together and raw edges even, placing each end 2½" from center. Repeat on Bag Back.

3. Lining: With right sides together, stitch Bag Bottom between Bag Front and Back. Stitch lining the same. Pin lining pieces, right sides together, over tea towel pieces and seam the top edges; turn, press and baste raw edges together.

4. Assembly: Seam a Bag Side to each edge of the big piece with wrong sides together and top edges even (clipping bag to seam at lower corners). Turning in raw ends, stitch green binding over raw edges, mitering lower corners.

BOW TOTE

AVERAGE: For those with some experience in sewing.

MATERIALS: ¾ yd. each of sailcloth and lining fabric; 5 yds. 1½"-wide ribbon, 1¼ yds. 22"-nonwoven interfacing.

DIRECTIONS: (½" seams allowed)

1. Cutting: *See* Tea Towel Tote, Step 1, omitting the binding and handle linings.

2. Handles: Turn under ½" at l[o]ng edges of handles and press. Pin rib[bon] to wrong side and edgestitch. Sti[tch] handles to bags (see Tea Towel T[ote] Step 2).

3. Ribbons: With right sides togeth[er] seam Bag Bottom between Bag Fr[ont] and Back. Pin ribbon through the l[ength] center. Pin horizontal ribbons (str[ipes] matching) 6" below all top ed[ges]. Where ribbons intersect at the fr[ont,] pinch a pleat (to underline the bo[w].

4. Assembly: With right sides toge[th-]er, stitch Bag Bottom between [Bag] Front and Back. At each long edg[e of] this piece, seam three edges of a [Bag] Side, clipping bag at corners. Se[am] lining the same as bag, leaving [an] opening for turning. With right si[des] together, seam lining to bag at [top] edge. Turn right side out, turn in o[pen] edges and slipstitch.

5. Bow: Overlap remaining ribb[on] and topstitch, to double the width. [Tie] it in a bow and sew the knot to the [bag] over the pleats. Slant the raw ends [(see] *photo),* turn under ¼" and glue.

Tote Bag Duo: Teatowel Tote; Bow Tote

HOME, SWEET HOME

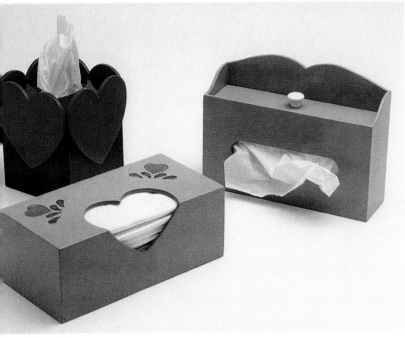

TISSUE-BOX COVERS

AVERAGE: For those with some experience in woodworking.

FIG. 9c

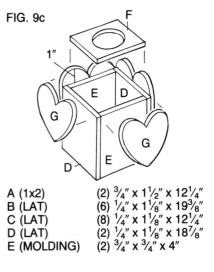

A (1x2)	(2) $\frac{3}{4}$" x 1$\frac{1}{2}$" x 12$\frac{1}{4}$"
B (LAT)	(6) $\frac{1}{4}$" x 1$\frac{1}{8}$" x 19$\frac{3}{8}$"
C (LAT)	(8) $\frac{1}{4}$" x 1$\frac{1}{8}$" x 12$\frac{1}{4}$"
D (LAT)	(2) $\frac{1}{4}$" x 1$\frac{1}{8}$" x 18$\frac{7}{8}$"
E (MOLDING)	(2) $\frac{3}{4}$" x $\frac{3}{4}$" x 4"

Tissue-Box Covers

G. 9a

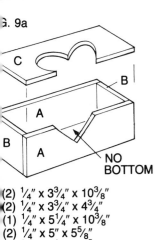

ALL BOXES
$\frac{1}{4}$" BIRCH
PLYWOOD

GLUE/CLAMP

(2) $\frac{1}{4}$" x 3$\frac{3}{4}$" x 10$\frac{3}{8}$"
(2) $\frac{1}{4}$" x 3$\frac{3}{4}$" x 4$\frac{3}{4}$"
(1) $\frac{1}{4}$" x 5$\frac{1}{4}$" x 10$\frac{3}{8}$"
(2) $\frac{1}{4}$" x 5" x 5$\frac{5}{8}$"
(2) $\frac{1}{4}$" x 4$\frac{1}{2}$" x 5$\frac{5}{8}$"
(1) $\frac{1}{4}$" x 4$\frac{1}{2}$" x 4$\frac{1}{2}$"
(4) $\frac{1}{4}$" x 5" x 4$\frac{3}{4}$"

FIG. 9b

DROP-IN
TOP

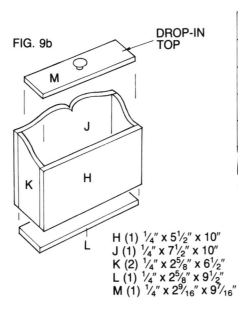

H (1) $\frac{1}{4}$" x 5$\frac{1}{2}$" x 10"
J (1) $\frac{1}{4}$" x 7$\frac{1}{2}$" x 10"
K (2) $\frac{1}{4}$" x 2$\frac{5}{8}$" x 6$\frac{1}{2}$"
L (1) $\frac{1}{4}$" x 2$\frac{5}{8}$" x 9$\frac{1}{2}$"
M (1) $\frac{1}{4}$" x 2$\frac{9}{16}$" x 9$\frac{7}{16}$"

TISSUE BOX PATTERNS   1 SQ. = 1"

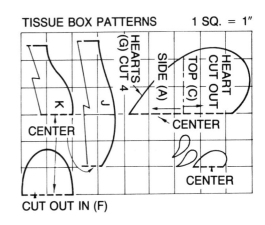

CUT OUT IN (F)

Spiderweb Tablecloth

IDERWEB TABLE-
LOTH

proximately 81 x 109")
d to fit 60 **x** 90" table or single bed.
Notes below to calculate additional
changes.

ERAGE: For those with some ex-
ence in crocheting.

TERIALS: Medium-weight cot-
thread, (325 yds.): 38 balls Ecru.
. 7, 4 and 3 steel crochet hooks OR
SIZE HOOKS TO OBTAIN STITCH
GE BELOW.

UGE: Motif = 4¾" square. TO
E TIME, TAKE TIME TO CHECK
GE.

es: This simple motif translates
ly into other sizes. One 325 yd.
make 14 motifs (each motif = 23
.). A 57"-square tablecloth requires
2x12 motif (57") square, using 11
s for motifs, plus an additional 6
s for sewing motifs together and
king fringe.

RECTIONS:

MOTIF (Make 391): Make a slip
t 6" from end of crochet thread.
h No. 7 hook ch 14, join with sl st
orm a ring. **Rnd 1:** Working over
h ch and 6" end, ch 3 for first dc,
k 31 dc in ring—32 dc counting

starting ch. Join with sl st to top of ch-
3 starting ch. Pick up 5" end and pull
snugly to draw center ring tog; secure
end at back of work. **Rnd 2:** Ch 3 for
first dc, dc in each dc around. Join with
sl st to top of starting ch-3. **Rnd 3:**
Change to No. 4 hook. From this point
on, work all dc between dc and work
over all loops at top of each st. Ch 6 for
first dc and ch 3, * dc in each of next 8
dc, ch 3 for corner. Repeat from * 2
times more, end dc in each of last 7 dc,
join with sl st to 3rd ch of ch-6 starting
ch. **Rnd 4:** Sl st in ch-3 space, ch 7 for
first dc and ch 4, dc in same space, * dc
between each dc to next corner, in corner work dc, ch 4, and dc. Repeat from
* 2 times more, end dc between each
dc along last edge—9 dc between ch-3
at each corner; 36 dc around. Join with
sl st to 3rd ch of starting ch. **Rnd 5:** Sl
st in ch-4 corner, ch 8 for first dc and
ch 5, dc in same corner, * dc between
each dc to next corner, in corner work
dc, ch 5, and dc. Repeat from * 2 times
more, end dc across last edge—10 dc
between corners. Join with sl st to 3rd
ch of starting ch. **Rnd 6:** Change to
No. 3 hook, sl st in ch-5 corner, ch 9
for first dc and ch 6, dc in same corner,
* dc between each dc to next corner, in
corner work dc, ch 6, and dc. Repeat
from * around as established—11 dc
between corners. Join with sl st to 3rd

ch of starting ch. **Rnd 7:** Sl st in ch-6
corner, ch 10 for first dc and ch 7, dc in
same corner, * dc between each dc to
next corner, in corner work dc, ch 7,
and dc. Repeat from * around as established—12 dc between corners. Join
with sl st to 3rd ch of starting ch. **Rnd
8:** Sl st in ch-7 corner, ch 11 for first dc
and ch 8, dc in same corner, dc between each dc to next corner, in corner work dc, ch 8, and dc. Repeat from
* around as established—13 dc between corners. Join with sl st to 3rd ch
of starting ch. Fasten off.

2. FINISHING: Sew motifs into a
17x23 motif rectangle as follows: Leaving 2 chs at center of each corner unstitched, whip stitch pieces together
along straight edges.
Note: The unstitched chs at the center
of all corners form a small diamond
shape.

Fringe: Cut a piece of crochet thread 7
yds. long. Fold piece in half (for a 3½
yd. length), fold again, and continue
folding in half until piece measures
about 22" in length. Draw folded piece
evenly through a st and knot; do not
cut ends. Working in this manner, on
each edge motif work a fringe in each
ch-space at corners; 3 fringes evenly
spaced between corners. Continue
working fringe until all 4 sides of rectangle are completed.

Log Carrier; Add-A-Layer Wine Rack; Wine Sacks

ADD-A-LAYER WINE RACK

AVERAGE: For those with some experience in woodworking.
MATERIALS: (per layer): Two 1 x 3 x 26¼" cross pieces; four 1 x 3 x 8" legs; seven ½ x 1½ x 8" lattice bottle supports; two ½ x 1 x 8" lattice handle bars; 26 No. 7x ¾" f.h. wood screws.

DIRECTIONS:
All outside edges flush, screw two bottle supports into ends of cross pieces; add five remaining supports between them, equally spaced. Screw handle bars into ends of pair of legs, edges flush, then screw the legs into each end of cross pieces, 3" down from top of handle bars.

WINE SACKS

EASY: Achievable by anyone.
MATERIALS (For one): T 6 x 13½" pieces firm cotton fabri yd. ⅞"-wide ribbon; purchased c screw with hole for hanging; pin shears.

DIRECTIONS:
1. Pink all edges of fabric pieces. S two pieces together (¼") around s and one end. Turn right side out. 2. Slip wine bottle into sack. T ends of ribbon diagonally. Slip rib through hole in corkscrew and around neck of bottle.

OG CARRIER

VERAGE: For those with some experience in woodworking.

FIG. 10 LOG/KINDLING CARRIER

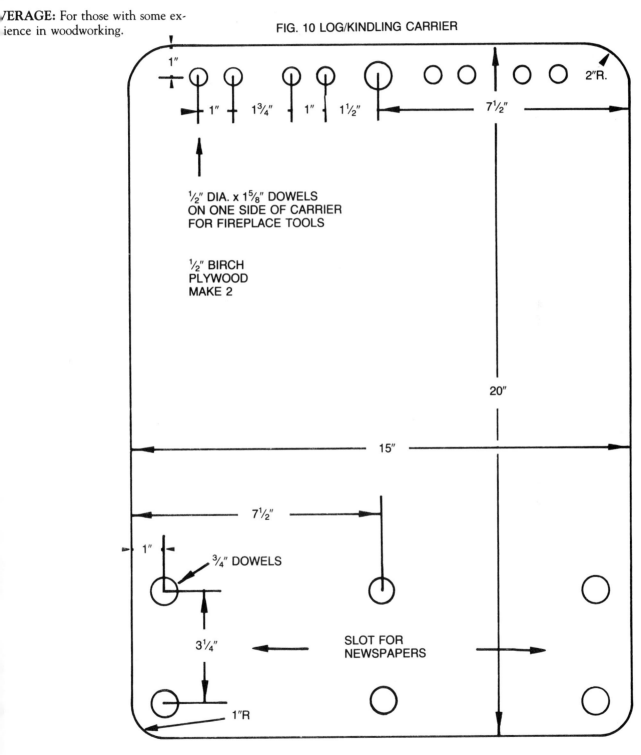

1"

2"R.

1"   1¾"   1"   1½"   7½"

½" DIA. x 1⅝" DOWELS
ON ONE SIDE OF CARRIER
FOR FIREPLACE TOOLS

½" BIRCH
PLYWOOD
MAKE 2

20"

15"

7½"

1"

¾" DOWELS

3¼"

SLOT FOR
NEWSPAPERS

1"R

KISS THE COOK!

Potholder Hanger; Lazy Cat Planter; Cow Shelf; Rooster Planter Cart

OTHOLDER HANGER

ERAGE: For those with some ex-ience in woodworking.

. 11 POTHOLDER HANGER
"W. x 9½"H.)

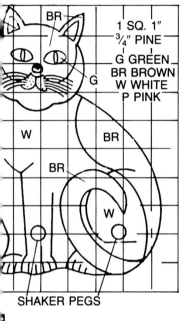

1 SQ. 1"
¾" PINE
G GREEN
BR BROWN
W WHITE
P PINK

SHAKER PEGS

AZY CAT PLANTER

VERAGE: For those with some ex-rience in woodworking.

. 12 LAZY CAT PLANTER
W. x 7½"H. x 9½"L.)

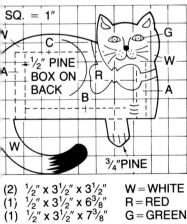

1 SQ. = 1"

½" PINE
BOX ON
BACK

¾"PINE

(2) ½" x 3½" x 3½"	W = WHITE	
(1) ½" x 3½" x 6⅜"	R = RED	
(1) ½" x 3½" x 7⅜"	G = GREEN	

COW SHELF

AVERAGE: For those with some ex-perience in woodworking.

FIG. 13 COW SHELF
(6" W. x 21" L. x 12" H.)

1 = BROWN   A (PINE) (1) ¾" x 11¼" x 20"
2 = BLACK   B (PINE) (1) ½" x 5½" x 20"
3 = WHITE   C (LAT) (6) ½" x ½" x 4"
4 = GREEN   D (LAT) (6) ⅜" x ⅞" x 5½"
5 = PINK   D1 (LAT) (3) ⅜" x ⅞" x 20¾"

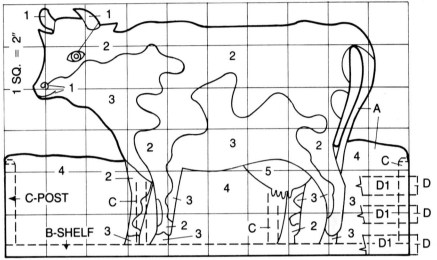

1 SQ. = 2"

C-POST
B-SHELF

ROOSTER PLANTER CART

AVERAGE: For those with some ex-perience in woodworking.

A circus type motif incorporating ini-tials is painted on the sides of the wagon.

FIG. 14. ROOSTER PLANTER CART

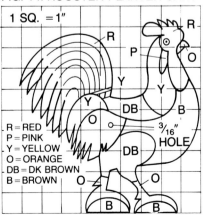

1 SQ. = 1"

R = RED
P = PINK
Y = YELLOW
O = ORANGE
DB = DK BROWN
B = BROWN

³⁄₁₆"
HOLE

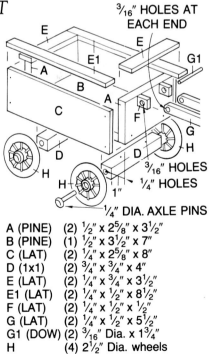

FIG. 14A

³⁄₁₆" HOLES AT
EACH END

³⁄₁₆" HOLES
¼" HOLES
¼" DIA. AXLE PINS

A (PINE)   (2) ½" x 2⅝" x 3½"
B (PINE)   (1) ½" x 3½" x 7"
C (LAT)   (2) ¼" x 2⅝" x 8"
D (1x1)   (2) ¾" x ¾" x 4"
E (LAT)   (2) ¼" x ¾" x 3½"
E1 (LAT)   (2) ¼" x ½" x 8½"
F (LAT)   (2) ¼" x ½" x ½"
G (LAT)   (2) ¼" x ½" x 5½"
G1 (DOW) (2) ³⁄₁₆" Dia. x 1¾"
H   (4) 2½" Dia. wheels

Christmas Potholders

CHRISTMAS HEART POTHOLDER

AVERAGE: For those with some experience in sewing.

MATERIALS: Two 12″ squares red with-white-dot cotton fabric; one 9″ square Christmas green heart print cotton; one 3½″ tall heart cut from Christmas red heart print cotton; **OR:** assorted fabrics of the previous 3 counts; one 12″ square batting; 1½ yd. white ½″ lace; ¼ yd. ½″-wide red satin ribbon.

DIRECTIONS:

Potholder Front: Cut lace into four pieces and arrange on potholder to form a 6½″ square. Stitch in place. Press under edges of green heart square down all sides. Place in center of square formed by lace. Top stitch in place.

Place front to back, right sides together. Place batting on wrong side. Stitch ⅝″ seam around edges, leaving open. Turn. Press. Top stitch ¼″ around all edges.

Place heart in center of green square and stitch in place, using blanket stitch (*see Embroidery Stitch Guide, page 269*) or appliqué by machine. Stitch 1″ in from green edge all around, forming quilted square around heart.

Make red satin bow and stitch in upper left hand corner.

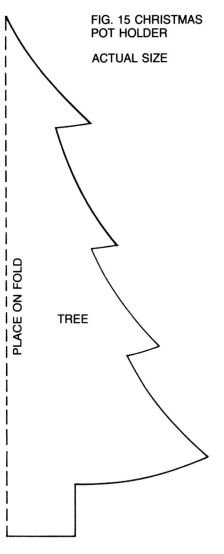

FIG. 15 CHRISTMAS POT HOLDER

ACTUAL SIZE

PLACE ON FOLD

TREE

CHRISTMAS TREE POTHOLDER

AVERAGE: For those with some experience in sewing.

MATERIALS: Two 12″ square white-with-green-dot cotton; one 12″ square batting; one 5″ square dark green print cotton; 1 small green ball fringe for tree top; ¼ yd. ¼″-wide red satin ribbon for bow; ⅔ yd. ½″-wide lace in white.

DIRECTIONS:

1. On right side of potholder front, place two 12″ strips of white lace on outside edges, right sides together (FIG. 15a) and baste in place.

2. Place front to back, right sides together. Place batting on wrong side of potholder back. Stitch ⅝″ seams through all 3 layers leaving 3″ open. Clip corners. Turn. Press. Top stitch ¼″ around all outside edges. Top stitch again 1″ in from edges.

3. Cut tree using pattern in FIG. 15 from dark green fabric. Place tree in center of potholder with ball on top. Using blanket stitch (*see Embroidery Stitch Guide, page 269*) or appliqué by machine, stitch tree to potholder.

4. Make bow front ribbon and stitch to upper left corner.

FIG. 15a

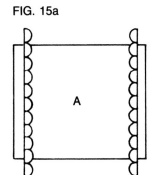

A

Patchwork Clock And Tray; Cheeseboard

PATCHWORK CLOCK

AVERAGE: For those with some experience in woodworking.
MATERIALS: $\frac{1}{2}$ x 2 x 48" lattice; $10\frac{1}{2}$" square of $\frac{1}{4}$" hardboard; 4 feet of $\frac{3}{4}$" Qtr-rnd; matte-white spray paint; sandpaper; matte finish/glue medium (*see Materials Shopping Guide, page 272*); 2" sponge brush; 5 fabric patterns of $\frac{7}{8}$"-wide craft ribbon (*see Step 4*).

DIRECTIONS:
1. Make a frame of $\frac{1}{4}$ x 2 x 11" l[...]tice. Miter corners, glue and cla[...] square. When dry, stain.
2. Cut four $\frac{3}{4}$" Qtr-rnd x $10\frac{1}{2}$". Mi[...] corners and glue to inside of latt[...] frame $\frac{3}{4}$" from top edge.
3. Cut a $\frac{1}{4}$ x $10\frac{1}{2}$ x $10\frac{1}{2}$" piece [...] hardboard. Spray paint matte whi[...] Sand lightly.
4. Select the 5 fabric patterns in t[...] following mounts: Color A: $1\frac{1}{4}$ yds[...] and C: 1 yd each; D: $\frac{3}{4}$ yd; E: $\frac{1}{2}$ y[...]

Paint the hardboard with a thin [c]at of glue medium using the dam-[n]ed sponge brush. Allow to dry. Cut fabric (see FIG. 16). To glue in [pla]ce, paint back of each piece with [glu]e medium. After strips are in place, [ch]eck for bubbles before they dry. [W]hen thoroughly dry, paint with sev-[er]al coats of glue medium; dry com-[ple]tely between coats. Drill hole in [ce]nter for clock.

[FIG]. 16 PATCHWORK CLOCK [(9]" x 11") QUARTER PATTERN

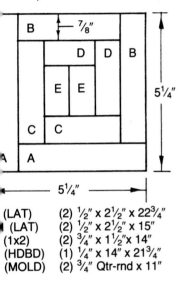

(LAT)	(2) $\frac{1}{2}$" x $2\frac{1}{2}$" x $22\frac{3}{4}$"
(LAT)	(2) $\frac{1}{2}$" x $2\frac{1}{2}$" x 15"
(1x2)	(2) $\frac{3}{4}$" x $1\frac{1}{2}$" x 14"
(HDBD)	(1) $\frac{1}{4}$" x 14" x $21\frac{3}{4}$"
(MOLD)	(2) $\frac{3}{4}$" Qtr-rnd x 11"

[C]HEESE BOARD
[(1" x] $12\frac{1}{2}$" x $14\frac{1}{2}$")

[A]VERAGE: For those with some ex-[pe]rience in woodworking.

[DI]RECTIONS:
[Th]e cutting board is made of an oak [bo]ard 1" thick, x $12\frac{1}{2}$" x $14\frac{1}{2}$". Rout [$\frac{3}{8}$]" deep x $\frac{7}{8}$" wide groove in the top [1"] from all four edges. The outside cor-[ne]rs of the routed groove are round, [th]e inside corners are square (90°).

PATCHWORK TRAY

AVERAGE: For those with some ex-perience in woodworking.
See FIG. 17 for assembly, FIG. 17A for patchwork design. *See text in* FIG. 16 Patchwork Clock for fabric applica-tion.

FIG. 17 TRAY ($2\frac{1}{2}$" H. x 15" W. x $22\frac{3}{4}$" L.)

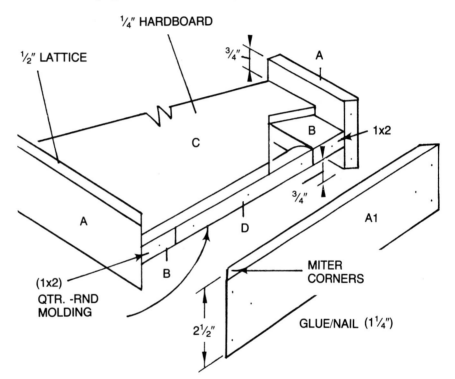

FIG. 17A FABRIC CUTTING DIAGRAM

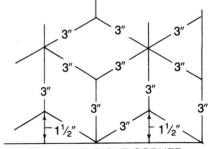

START LOWER RIGHT CORNER
GLUE FABRIC TO HARDBOARD

WOODEN RING TRIVET

EASY: Achievable by anyone.
MATERIALS: Wooden drapery rings (amounts and size of rings will depend on size desired; we used seven $2\frac{3}{4}$" rings); 4 yds. rope; glue.

DIRECTIONS:

1. Arrange rings on a flat surface according to desired size.
2. Cut a piece of rope approximately 6" long. Wrap the rope around 2 rings to join them. Tie; glue the tie and tie again. Repeat this until all rings are joined.
3. Wrap each ring again, adjacent to the first piece of rope.

Wooden Ring Trivet

BABES 'N TOYLAND

og Cabin Playbox; Teddy Bear Clock; Stenciltop Foot Stool

OG CABIN PLAYBOX

HALLENGING: Requires more ex-
rience in woodworking.
ATERIALS: See FIGS. 18 and 18a
r specifics.

DIRECTIONS:
1. First, paint the luan mahogany with a walnut stain. The front, back and sides are notched $\frac{1}{2}$ x $\frac{3}{4}$" to simulate log cabin construction.
2. A "V" shaped gouge is used to cut the "log" grooves. The cuts are about $\frac{1}{8}$" deep, $\frac{3}{4}$" apart and aligned with the notches. The groove spacing varies where the roof gable begins at the sides, (see FIG. 18).

3. Roof half (E) is notched for the chimney, (see detail), and is glue/nailed ($1\frac{1}{4}$") to the sides (B). Roof (E1) is removable, do not nail. [See detail for stop (F) on roof (E1)].
4. The plywood base beneath the veneer is exposed in the "V" grooves to define the logs. The window frames are natural. The inside walls are painted light green, roof is orange, chimney is white.

FIG. 18 LOG CABIN
(10"W. x 16"L. x 16"H.)

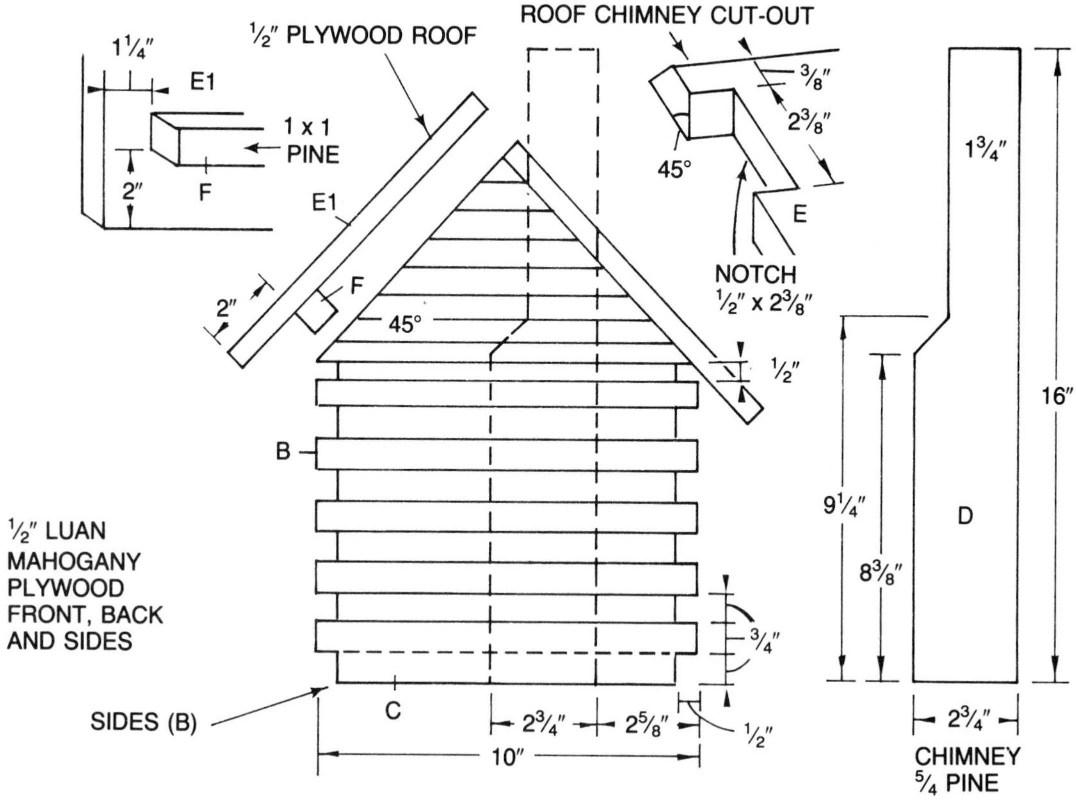

1/2" PLYWOOD ROOF
ROOF CHIMNEY CUT-OUT
1 1/4"
E1
1 x 1
PINE
2"
F
E1
2"
F
45°
3/8"
2 3/8"
45°
E
NOTCH
1/2" x 2 3/8"
1/2"
1 3/4"
16"
B
1/2" LUAN
MAHOGANY
PLYWOOD
FRONT, BACK
AND SIDES
9 1/4"
8 3/8"
D
3/4"
SIDES (B)
C
2 3/4"
2 5/8"
1/2"
10"
2 3/4"
CHIMNEY
5/4 PINE

FIG. 18A

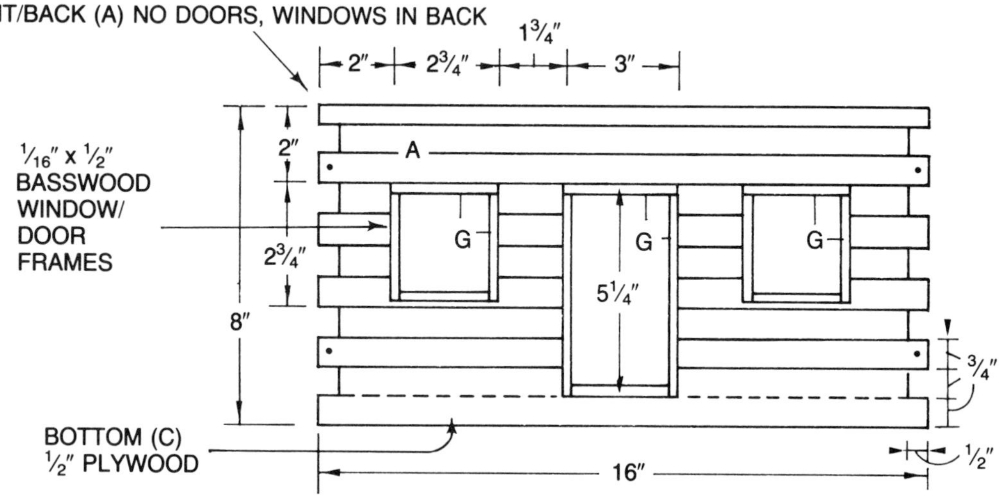

FRONT/BACK (A) NO DOORS, WINDOWS IN BACK
1 3/4"
2"
2 3/4"
3"
2"
A
1/16" x 1/2"
BASSWOOD
WINDOW/
DOOR
FRAMES
G
G
G
2 3/4"
5 1/4"
8"
3/4"
BOTTOM (C)
1/2" PLYWOOD
1/2"
16"

A (PLY)	(2) 1/2" x 8" x 16"	E (PLY)	(1) 1/2" x 8 7/8" x 17 1/2"
B (PLY)	(2) 1/2" x 13" x 10"	E1 (PLY)	(1) 1/2" x 9 1/4" x 17 1/2"
C (PLY)	(1) 1/2" x 9" x 15"	F (1x1)	(1) 3/4" x 3/4" x 15"
D 5/4 (PINE)	(1) 1 1/8" x 2 3/4" x 16"	G (BASS)	1/16" x 1/2" As req'd.

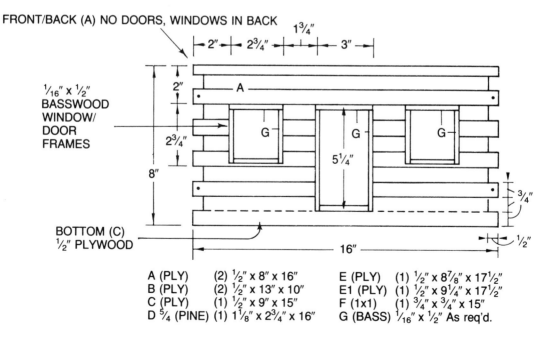

ΞDDY BEAR CLOCK
L x 8"W x 13"H)

VERAGE: For those with some ex-
ience in woodworking.

RECTIONS:
ill the clock hole in 2 x 10 pine to
your clock. The clock shown in
oto has a tapered case. To make this
ck fit, 3 holes were drilled; the first
4" dia. through the bear; next a 3"
le ⅞" deep centered over the first
le; third hole 3¼" dia. x 1½" deep
itered over the previous 2 holes.
le inside hole edges were filed with a
p to create a tapered hole.

G. 19 TEDDY BEAR CLOCK
W x 8"L x 13"H)   1 SQ. = 1"

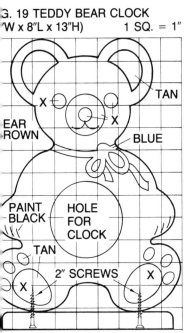

TAN

EAR
ROWN

BLUE

PAINT
BLACK

HOLE
FOR
CLOCK

TAN

2" SCREWS

X

4 x 8" BASE, PAINT BLUE
= ⅛" THICK PINE OR PLYWOOD

🔒 STENCILTOP FOOTSTOOL

AVERAGE: For those with some experience in woodworking.

DIRECTIONS:
The rabbits and name are stencilled on
the top (D) (*see* FIG. 20). Stencil letters are available at art stores.

FIG. 20 BENCH
(11¼"W x 14"H x 17¼"L)   7°

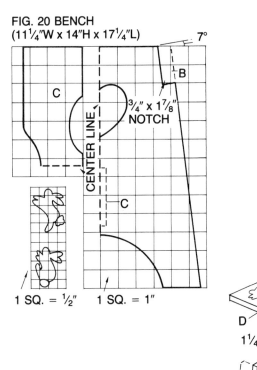

C

B

¾" x 1⅞"
NOTCH

CENTER LINE

C

1 SQ. = ½"   1 SQ. = 1"

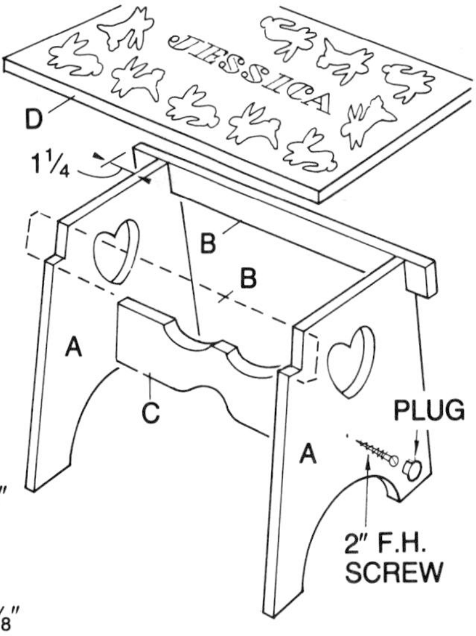

D

1¼

B

B

A

C

A

PLUG

2" F.H.
SCREW

A (1 x 12)	(2)	¾" x 11¼" x 13"
B (1 x 3)	(2)	¾" x 1⅞" x 17"
C (1 x 4)	(1)	¾" x 3½" x 13"
D (1 x 10)	(1)	¾" x 9¼" x 17⅜"

Child's Norwegian Cardigan And Hat

HILD'S NORWEGIAN ARDIGAN

HALLENGING: Requires more ex-
rience in knitting.

rections are given for Size 2.
anges for Sizes 4 and 6 are in paren-
ses.

ATERIALS: 100% Wool (100 gr.
in) fingering yarn: 3 (3-4) skeins
f-White (A), 1 (2-2) skeins of Blue
and 1 (1-1) skein Red (C); knitting
dles, one pair each #2 and #5, OR
Y SIZE NEEDLES TO OBTAIN STITCH
UGE BELOW; 5 (6-6) ³⁄₈"-dia. silver
tons.

AUGE: In Stockinette Stitch (k 1
w, p 1 row) using larger needles: 6 sts
1"; 8 rows = 1". TO SAVE TIME,
KE TIME TO CHECK GAUGE.

ES:	(2)	(4)	(6)
dy Chest:	21"	23"	25"

NISHED MEASUREMENTS:

est:	22"	24"	26"
idth across back at underarms:			
	11"	12"	13"
idth across each front at underarms cluding front band):			
	6"	6½"	7"
idth across sleeve at upper arm:			
	10"	11"	12"

te: When changing colors always
ist yarns on wrong side to prevent
les. Carry color not in use loosely in
ck of work, being careful to maintain
ige.

RECTIONS:

BACK: Starting at lower edge with
aller needles and B, cast on 66 (72-
) sts. work in k 1, p 1 ribbing for 1¼
½-1½)", decreasing one st on last
w (worked — 65) (71-77) sts.
ange to larger needles and stockin-
e stitch (st st). Now beg FIG. 21a
til completion of Row 10. Change
dot pattern as follows working in st
throughout: **Row 1 (right side):**
ith * A k 3, join B and with B k 1;
 from * 15 (16-18) times more, end-
g with A k 1 (3-1). **Rows 2-5:** With
only work 4 rows. **Row 6:** With A p

1, with * B p 1, with A p 3; rep from *
15 (16-18) times more, ending Size 4
only with B p 1, with A p 1. **Rows 7-
10:** With A only work 4 rows. Rep
Rows 1-10 for dot pattern until total
length is 8 (9-11)" from beg, ending
with a wrong-side row. **Armhole Shaping:** Continuing in dot pattern, bind
off 3 sts at beg of next 2 rows — 59
(65-71) sts. Work even in dot pattern
until armhole measures 2 (2½-3)",
ending with 4 A rows. Now beg FIG.
21b until completion of Row 22. **Neck
Shaping: Next Row:** Continuing to
follow FIG. 21b, work across first 15
(18-21) sts, place center 29 sts on a st
holder; join a 2nd ball of yarn and complete row. Work both sides at once
with a separate ball, until completion
of Row 24. Bind off 15 (18-21) sts on
each side for shoulders.

2. RIGHT FRONT: Starting at lower
edge with smaller needles and B, cast
on 38 (42-44) sts. Work in k 1, p 1
ribbing for 1¼ (1½-1½)", decreasing
1 (2-1) st on last row worked — 37
(40-43) sts. Place first 7 sts on a st
holder to be worked for front band.
Change to larger needles and st st.
Now beg FIG. 21a until completion of
row 10. Change to dot pattern as follows, working in st st throughout: **Row
1 (right side):** With * A k 3, join B
and with B k 1; rep from * 6 (7-8) times
more, ending with A k 2 (1-0). **Rows
2-5:** With A only work 4 rows. **Row 6:**
With A p l, with * B p 1, with A p 3;
rep from * 6 (7-8) times more, ending
with B p 1 (0-1), and A p 0 (0-2).
Rows 7-10: With A only work 4 rows.
Rep Rows 1-10 for dot pattern until
total length is 8 (9-11)" from beg, ending with a right-side row. **Armhole
Shaping:** Continuing in dot pattern,
bind off 3 sts at beg of next row. Work
even in dot pattern until armhole measures 2 (2½-3)", ending with 4 A rows.
Now beg FIG. 21c at size indicated until
completion of Row 14. **Neck shaping:
Row 15:** Continuing to follow FIG.
21c, bind off 5 sts at beg of row for front
neck edge. Dec one st at neck edge
every row 7 times - 15 (18-21) sts.
Work even on rem sts until completion

of Row 23. Bind off all sts. **Right Front
Band:** Slip 7 sts from st holder onto
smaller needles and work in k 1, p 1
ribbing same as Back until front band is
long enough to meet the bound-off sts
of neck shaping. Slip sts onto st holder.
Mark the position of 5 (6-6) buttons
with the first buttonhole ½" from the
bottom edge and the last buttonhole
½" from the top of band, evenly spacing the remaining buttonholes on the
front band.

3. LEFT FRONT: Work to correspond to Right Front, reversing shaping. **Left Front Band:** Slip 7 sts from st
holder onto smaller needles and work
in k 1, p 1 ribbing to first marker. **Buttonhole row:** Rib 2, bind off 3 sts, rib
2. On next row rib across, casting on 3
sts over bound-off sts. Continue to
work in ribbing making 5 (6-6) buttonholes in all opposite markers.

4. SLEEVES: Starting at lower edge
with smaller needles and B, cast on 44
(46-48) sts. Work in k 1, p 1 ribbing
for 1½". **Next Row:** P across, increasing 5 sts evenly spaced — 49 (51-53)
sts. Change to larger needles and st st.
Now beg FIG. 21a until completion of
Row 10. Change to dot pattern as for
Back, increasing one st each end every
6th row 6 (8-10) times — 61 (67-73)
sts. Work even in dot pattern until total length is 7 (9¼-10¼)" from beg,
ending with Row 1 or 6 of dot pattern.
Now beg FIG. 21d until completion of
Row 9. Bind off all sts.

5. FINISHING: Sew shoulder seams.
Sew front bands in place. **Neckband:**
With right side facing you, using smaller needles and B, k 7 sts from Right
Front Band st holder, pick up 19 sts
along right neck edge, k 29 sts from
back st holder, pick up 19 sts along left
neck edge and k 7 sts from Left Front
Band st holder — 81 sts. Work in k 1, p
1 ribbing for 1". Bind off loosely in
ribbing. Sew side and sleeve seams.
Sew in sleeves. Sew on buttons.

CHILD'S NORWEGIAN HAT

DIRECTIONS:

1. With smaller needles and B, cast on 99 (103-107) sts. Work in k 1, p 1 ribbing for 1¼". Break off B, join A. Change to larger needles and St st. Work 2 rows. Beg dot pat.
2. Row 1 (wrong side): K 3 A, * k 1, B, k 3 A, rep from * across. **Rows 2 thru 5:** With A only work 4 rows. **Row 6:** P 1 A, p 1 B, * p 3 A, p 1 B, rep from * end p 1 A. **Rows 7 thru 10:** With A only work 4 rows. Rep Rows 1-10 for pat. Work to approx. 4" above ribband, end with Row 3, 5, or 9. With A p 1 row, dec 2 (0-4) sts evenly spaced, 97 (103-103) sts. Beg FIG. 21d as indicated for sleeve. Work to top of chart. Break off A and B. With C only work 7 rows more. **Dec Row:** K 1, * k 2 tog, rep from * across. Break off C leaving a long strand. With a tapestry needle draw strand thru stitches on needle. Pull tight and sew top tog. Sew back seam.
3. Pom Pom: Wind B around a 4" piece of cardboard approx. 50 times. Cut 4 B strands approx. 27" long. Fold in half and tie around middle of pompom. Cut ends and trim neatly. Sew to top of hat.

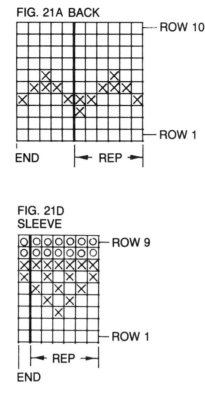

FIG. 21A BACK — ROW 10 / ROW 1 / END / REP

FIG. 21D SLEEVE — ROW 9 / ROW 1 / REP / END

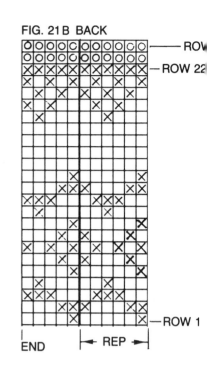

FIG. 21 B BACK — ROW / ROW 22 / ROW 1 / END / REP

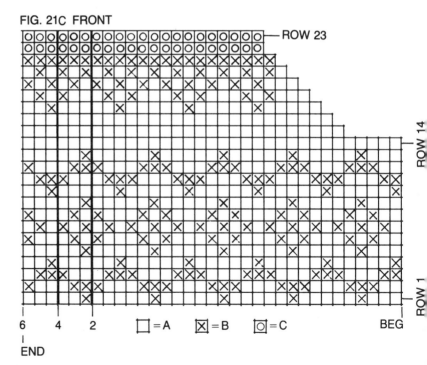

FIG. 21C FRONT — ROW 23 / ROW 14 / ROW 1 / 6 4 2 / END / BEG

□ = A   ⊠ = B   ⊙ = C

Christmas Puppets

CHRISTMAS PUPPETS

EASY: Achievable by anyone.
MATERIALS: $\frac{3}{8}$ yd. desired base color; assorted scraps of felt for details; fusible webbing; $\frac{1}{4}''$ wiggle eyes; jingle bells; red ribbon; glue; string.

DIRECTIONS:

1. Enlarge pattern from FIG. 22 following the directions on page 271. Cut two puppet pieces from the base color. Cut out details from the scraps of felt, following pattern. Appliqué or glue the pieces to the puppet front.

2. Antlers: Top stitch two pieces of felt together along the design lines. Trim close to stitching. Baste antlers in place to wrong side of puppet front. Top stitch puppet front to back, stitching close to edge.

3. Collar: Fold collar pieces over a length of string and stitch. Gather up and tie around neck. Tack one bell to each point.

4. Hat: Top stitch 4 hat pieces together. Tack bell at point. Baste to back of puppet head.

5. FINISHING: Glue wiggle eyes in place. Tack bells to reindeer's belt. Tie bow at neck with red ribbon.

FIG. 22 CHRISTMAS PUPPETS

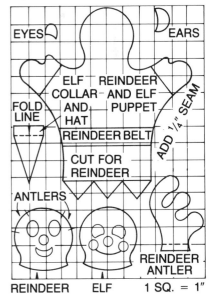

Here are some smart choices for those special children on your gift list.

WHAT BABIES LOVE (BIRTH TO AGE 1)

Babies learn about colors, shapes and sizes from their toys, but it's best not to overload them with too much stimulation at once. Always allow your baby sufficient time to get used to one toy, before you introduce another. If you've got a baby to shop for, consider the following.

Mobiles provide color, movement, even sound (if they have music box attachments) and relaxation. A baby loves to watch a mobile turn, especially just before going to sleep and when waking up. **Stuffed toys,** designed especially for baby in a washable fabric with secured eyes and nose and tight seams, are touchable, huggable friends that help little ones calm themselves. **Bath toys,** from the famous rubber ducky to the newer washable toys that sometimes double as washcloths and soft puppets, will help make bathtime fun. **Crib and playpen toys,** such as activity centers and crib gyms, offer exercise and self-amusement that baby will return to time and again. Choose those that have a variety of textures—hard (wood and plastic) and soft (fabric or rubber). **Music boxes** stimulate your baby's ear for music and are soothing.

TOPS IN TOYS FOR TODDLERS (AGES 1 TO 2)

Any toy that challenges a toddler's developmental abilities is a good choice. **Puzzles** teach toddlers to solve problems and improve their dexterity; **shape-sorting boxes** and **ring stacks** encourage logic, eye-hand coordination, shape and color recognition; **activity centers** offer exercise and stimulation. Push-pull toys, pounding sets, building blocks, telephones, puppets, wagons and ride-on toys are all guaranteed to delight the toddler while improving such skills as communication, coordination and creativity.

Picture books, audiocassettes and videotapes, dolls and stuffed animals improve language skills, and dolls also encourage the development of emotional attachments.

BEST THINGS FOR PRE-SCHOOLERS (AGES 3 TO 5)

The 3- to 5-year-old is curious about everything. This is the time for imaginative play, when children love to dress up. They enjoy playing with miniature towns, firehouses, garages; and doing art projects such as finger-painting and coloring with crayons. Since outdoor play is also gaining in importance, swing sets, tricycles, sand pails and shovels are all good picks for preschoolers. Blocks continue to be popular. So are books, audiocassettes and videotapes, puzzles and puppets. And because pre-school children are actively learning social roles, they're interested in everyday items such as tables and chairs, and household objects they can pretend to "cook" or "clean" with. Choose typewriters, cash registers, play money and other props that can be used in a make-believe office or store.

Now is also the time for introducing simple musical instruments. Also choose board games, lacing cards, Viewmasters, blackboards, tool kits and ring-toss sets.

GOOD GIFTS FOR SCHOOL-AGE CHILDREN (AGES 6 TO 12)

As children grow, their playthings change to match their interests. Art supplies and hobby kits are enjoyable and give children a sense of accomplishment. Construction and transportation toys—trains, cars, trucks, boats, fire engines—provide them with things to build and to manipulate with their hands. Stuffed animals and dolls are still important; children use them in two ways—for reassurance when things get difficult and for acting out roles that help them understand the goings-on in their own families.

Board games are also excellent gifts; they help improve communication skills and social interaction.

Other good bets are bicycles, tools, kites, marbles and yo-yos.

FROM THE KIDS

rette Box; Barrettes

ARRETTE BOX

SY: Achievable by anyone. (Chil-
n will need help from an adult.)

TERIALS: 10 x 13″ plastic need-
oint canvas, 7-mesh-per-inch; 10
. each dark blue, medium blue,
it blue Persian or Persian-type
dlepoint yarn; tapestry needle.

RECTIONS:
Cut the following pieces measuring

by mesh count: 26 x 26″ for box top,
four 5 x 26″ for top side panels,
24 x 24″ for box bottom, four 8 x 24″
for bottom side panels. Leave the edges
unworked around all pieces for joining.
2. Using medium blue, work in scotch
stitch (repeat one-quarter of scotch
stitch design in *Embroidery Stitch
Guide, page 269*) around outside edge
of top.
3. Change to light blue and fill in center of top and four top side panels in
scotch stitch; using mosaic stitch (*see
Stitch Guide*), fill in box bottom.

4. Using dark blue and mosaic stitch,
work bottom side panels.
5. Using dark blue and whip stitch,
stitch panels to top and bottom, making 3 whip stitches in corner hole
wherever 3 canvas pieces come together—first stitch panels together end to
end, then stitch panels to top and
bottom.

BARRETTES

EASY: Achievable by anyone. (Children will need help from an adult.)
MATERIALS: Plain barrettes in desired shapes and sizes; ribbons and trims in narrow widths and desired colors and print; small buttons with prints; glue.

DIRECTIONS:

1. To make a woven barrette: Use 1 or 2 colors of narrow ribbon and a barrette with a slit in the middle. Glue the ends of 2 different ribbons or the center of one ribbon to the under side of one end of barrette. Bring each end alternately around from back and down through center slit until barrette is covered. Secure ends to back of barrette with glue, tie a bow or leave long strips hanging free at end of barrett.
2. To make barrettes with bows, simply fold a bow shape, tack bow to secure and glue to barrette. Glue or sew a button to center of bow for trim.
3. To make a barrette with bow and lace, make a circle from lace by gathering a piece of lace along one edge and tacking ends together. Glue on a bow and button.

NOVELTY SPONGES

EASY: Achievable by anyone.
MATERIALS: Supermarket sponges (buy a bagful); scissors; paper and pencil for patterns.

DIRECTIONS:

1. Enlarge patterns in FIG. 23, following the directions below.

FIG. 23 SPONGES   **1 SQ. = 1"**

BATH MITTS AND POUCH

EASY: Achievable by anyone. (Children will need help from an adult.)
MATERIALS: Washcloth and ¼ yd. narrow elastic for each mitt; ½ yd. lace trim and ¾ yd. grosgrain ribbon for drawstring bag; scrap of red fabric and 6-strand cotton (black and white) for eyes on creature mitt.

DIRECTIONS (½" seams allowed)
1. Striped Mitt: Cut 8" long ela[...] and sew it to wrong side of washclo[...] 3" from one (wrist) edge. Seam l[...] edge and short end. Turn right [...] out.
2. Creature Mitt: Cut 3" red square [...] tongue. Fold it in half, right sides [...] gether. Stitch a curved short edge [...] the long edges. Turn right side [...] Follow Step 1, inserting tongue (r[...] sides together and facing upward[...] bottom seam. Take 1" tuck about [...] inch above the tongue. Embro[...] round eyes—black satin stitch [...] rounded by white chain stitch, usin[...] strand floss.
3. Drawstring Bag: Fold washcloth [...] half, seam one short (bottom) end [...] the long edges, stopping 3" from [...] top. Turn right side out. At top [...] turn down a cuff 2½" to the out[...] and stitch lace trim to edge. Topst[...] ½" from fold to make a casing and [...] sert the ribbon.

Novelty Sponges and Bath Mitts

REETING CARDS AND TATIONERY

SY: Achievable by anyone.
ATERIALS: Assorted colored pa-
; ⅛″ and ¼″ hole punch tools; rib-
and yarn.

RECTIONS:

ng photo as a guide, punch out
orative designs from paper, folding
e sheets to make cards. Draw rib-
or yarn through holes before tying
bows.

Greeting Cards And Stationery

MORE GIFTS THE KIDS CAN MAKE

MARBLEIZED ROCK PAPERWEIGHT

EASY: Achievable by older children; younger children may need adult supervision.

MATERIALS: 3 cans spray paint, preferably petroleum-based (one white or very light color); 1 can clear acrylic spray; scrap of felt; glue; rock with a flat bottom; disposable containers.

DIRECTIONS:

1. Spray rock with light color. Dry thoroughly.
2. Fill disposable container with enough water to cover rock. Spray rows of two colors on surface of water.
3. Dip rock carefully in water. (We made a "cradle" from 2 wire coat hangers to hold the rock.) Allow to dry. Glue felt to bottom of rock. Spray top with clear acrylic.

EGGS-TRAORDINARY ORNAMENTS

EASY: Achievable by older children; younger children may need adult supervision.

MATERIALS: Whole empty eggshells; white glue; bits of ribbon, rickrack; real or paper lace; Christmas wrapping paper; holiday cards; glitter; different colored felt-tip pens; clear nail polish.

DIRECTIONS:

1. **To hollow out eggshells** (you may want to get some help with this part): With a small nail scissors, carefully make a small hole in both ends of an egg. This isn't as hard as it sounds: just tap firmly but gently on the eggshell. Push the point of the scissors in slightly to break the membrane of the egg.
2. Hold the egg over a bowl and blow into one hole: the egg will slowly come out of the other end. (You can scramble the egg for breakfast!) Don't worry if the shell cracks a little around the holes: you can hide that with decoration.
3. Rinse the eggshell and let it drain for awhile. An empty egg carton is a good place to store your hollow eggshells.

4. **Shell decorations:** ● Glue bits : pieces of ribbon, rickrack, figures from old wrapping paper or cards the shell surface. Let glue dry. ● **decorate with glitter:** Spread glue shell, sprinkle glitter on top and, a the glue has dried, tap loose glitter
● **To draw or write a message on shell:** Use a felt-tip pen. Let the dry a bit—it will smear if you to it—and then cover the design wit coat of clear nail polish.
5. **To hang shell ornaments:** Glue a ribbon or cord. A good way to do t is to poke the end of the ribbon i and around the hole. When the g dries, the ribbon will stay in place. you can glue a bow with long stream to the top and tie the streamers toge er to make a hanger.

CHRISTMAS PACKAGES FOR A LARGE FAMILY
To keep who-gets-what straight, color-coordinate packages by family. For instance, when buying lots of presents in advance, wrap one se of presents in blue paper; when wrapping them for mailing, use blue ink for the addresses. Another family group could get parcels with a green color scheme, and so on.

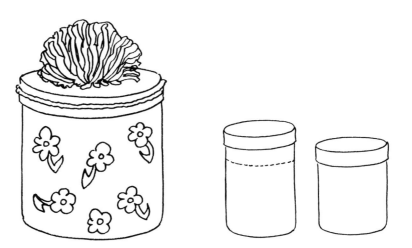

STRINGY GIFT

e a neat string holder with these easy
tions.

SY: Achievable by older children;
nger children may need adult su-
vision.

TERIALS: Small oatmeal box;
e darning needle; 2″ length of wire;
t or scraps of material; yarn; glue;
of string (which you can get in a
e store or hardware store).

RECTIONS:

ery **carefully** cut off about two
es from the top of the oatmeal
. **(A)** The lid will still fit.

Decorate the box and lid: You can
t it or glue material around it. Cut
flower or other shapes from materi-
Make yarn stems and flowers. Glue
around edge of lid.

o make "flower" for lid: (B)
d yarn around a 1½″ strip of card-
rd. How much yarn you use de-
ds on how full you want the flower
e. Tie a short piece of yarn tightly
nd one end, then cut through yarn
pposite end and remove cardboard.
h darning needle, poke two holes
e together in center of lid. Put one
of the tie through each hole and
e a knot on the other side.

o make hanger for string holder
Poke two holes about ¾″ apart in
k of box, about 1¼″ from the top
e. Push ends of wire through holes
twist together. Poke another hole
enter of the bottom of box, put ball
tring inside and push the end of
g through the hole. Replace lid.

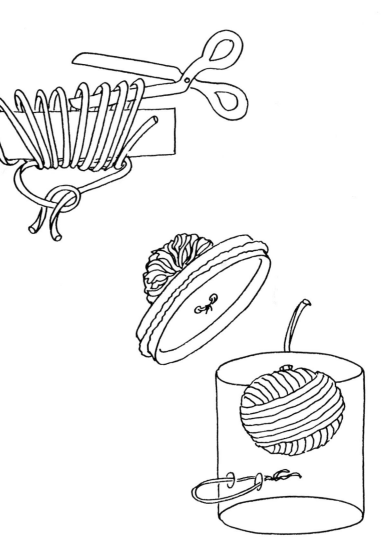

GIFTS FROM THE HEART

*Wonderful presents that require
more love than money.*

● Use the front of an old Christmas card to decorate a dime-store notebook; trim with ribbon scraps.

● Recycle art-quality greeting cards by slipping them into a pretty frame. Or, mat the card (or a favorite photo) with a border cut from a doily before placing it in the frame.

● Give a gift of service to a friend, be it several nights of baby sitting, gardening, or some ready-to-serve meals.

● Have a personalized ink stamp made for a friend; give it with several different colors of ink.

● Make a family photo montage for grandparents: Arrange different photos—some old, some new—and mount them with double-stick tape in an inexpensive frame.

● Take cuttings of your own plants and repot them in small decorative pots or pretty coffee mugs (for coffee mugs, use a layer of gravel on the bottom to make sure there is adequate drainage).

● If you have a special recipe for a baked treat, jam or sauce, copy it onto an attractive piece of durable paper, mount it onto a small cutting board and varnish over it (or use polyurethane). Accompany the recipe with the real thing for a sure-to-delight gift.

● Decorate T-shirts with acrylic fabric paints to suit someone's special tastes.

● Make your own dried flower arrangements, using flowers and anchoring bases available at florist supply shops. (Baskets, vases, even attractive bottles, make lovely containers!)

● Sew novelty buttons or embroidered appliques (available at five-and-dime stores and notion shops) onto the cuffs of a pair of socks.

● Give a plant in a candy cane plant holder: Use an empty plastic container that is big enough to hold a small plant. With white glue, affix candy cane sticks around the container. Place a rubber band around the candy canes until they dry. Attach a felt or cardboard base, if you wish, and store the holder (without the plant) in a cool place or the refrigerator until gift-giving time. Decorate with a red bow.

● Make a fragrant eucalyptus wreath: Bend heavy wire or a clothes hanger into a heart shape, bending the ends together at the lower tip. With florist wire, affix sprays of eucalyptus to the wire. Decorate with baby's breath in the spaces and a big ribbon bow.

● Make potpourri sachets by purchasing potpourri in bulk and placing it in squares of fabric remnants cut with pinking shears; tie with satin ribbon and decorate with bits of lace, if desired.

● Another "potpourri": Fill fabric squares with shavings of perfumed soap.

● Make a message center by decorating the frame of a small blackboard with precut wooden shapes, buttons, etc., affixed with white glue. Attach a small basket to a lower corner of the blackboard, using glue. Tie a pencil with a long piece of sturdy ribbon and attach

to the message center.

● Make your own tin-punch desi[?]
1. Buy a 9-inch tin pie pan. Enlar[?] simple pattern on folded pa[?]
2. Cover an old table with at lea[?] 1/2" thickness of cardboard. Tape c[?] board to table so it won't slip. T[?] pattern to tin. Punch holes wit[?] hammer and awl. 3. Add wire or st[?] for hanging, if desired.

● Make a Map Case for the seaso[?] traveler: Unglue the side seams of a[?] Manila file envelope, so you have a[?] piece. Carefully remove the ela[?] With rubber cement, glue a map [?] the outside surface, and fold abou[?] over to what will be the inside of [?] flap. Cut the map flush with the c[?] board edges. Let dry, then reglue [?] side seams and replace the elastic. [?] with a notepad that has also been d[?] rated with the map, pencils and—[?] course!!—maps.

● If your friend has recently put [?] some wallpaper, get a piece for a de[?] sample. Trace the design onto a p[?] of needlepoint canvas, and use to m[?] a pillow or frameable piece.

● For holding potpourri, your t[?] sured sauces and preserves or a bu[?] of pretty flowers, buy antique ma[?] jars at flea markets, or go to a labor[?] ry supply store for flasks and cov[?] glass dishes.

● Great for children: Record a se[?] tion of stories on a cassette tape. [?] you turn each page, ring a bell. G[?] the cassette and the book as the [?]

LAST-MINUTE GIFTS THAT DON'T LOOK IT

ll a gold lamé sock with an assort-
t of small cosmetics, such as lip-
, eyeshadow and nailpolish. (At-
the other sock, too!) Tie with
cord.

ake a breakfast-in-bed tray: Fill a
er tray with supermarket goodies:
a, coffee, muffins or croissants,
s and napkins. Cover with plastic
p and tie with a jumbo bow.

ine a tray basket with tissue paper;
with custard cups that hold a vari-
of special spices.

ine a clear acrylic shoe box with
active seed packets; add a variety of
ener's delights, from peat pots to
t hooks.

or the seamstress, fill a thread box
h threads and needles (don't forget
needle threader!). Tie with tape
sures and top with a pincushion.

or the knitter, buy a canvas bag
h lots of pockets. Fill the bag with
tting books, yarn and needles.

● Fill a magazine rack with an assortment of magazines and catalogs you
know the recipient will enjoy. And
perhaps a note about a magazine sub-
scription, too.

● Fill a satin-covered, ceramic, velvet
or wooden box with costume jewelry.

● For the person who never has
enough storage containers, buy a set of
nesting canisters; place one inside the
other, with a special surprise in the
smallest one!

● Know a wine lover? Place a bottle of
wine in a clay or other type of wine
cooler; wrap with a bow and attach a
corkscrew or a wine thermometer to
the bow.

● Fill glass storage jars (they can be
dime store or cut crystal, depending on
your budget) with sweets; top with
bows made from button candy.

● Pamper someone with a basket of
bath delights: a loofa mit, an assortment of soaps, sponges, brushes and
bubble bath. Add a good paperback
novel, too.

● For the inveterate reader, buy a special bookmark and attach it to a page of
your favorite book; or attach it to a log
for recording books read.

● For the teenager, buy a diary and a
fountain pen.

● Give a set of mixing bowls to a favorite chef. Decorate with a set of wooden
spoons (every cook needs more of
these) tied with ribbon.

● For the child beginning to explore
nature, buy a magnifying glass and attach it to a book for drawings and sam-
ples of leaves and flowers.

● For the hostess on New Year's Eve:
Accompany a bottle of champagne
with a set of champagne glasses
wrapped in tissue paper that also holds
confetti. Affix streamers and masks to
the outside.

WRAPPING IT UP

Follow these step-by-step directions for wrapping with professional-looking results!

LINING THE BOX

Materials: Tissue paper; adhesive seal; gift box.

Directions:
1. Pleat two or three thicknesses of the tissue as wide as the width of the box.
2. Do the same for the length.
3. Cross the tissues to line the box.
4. Place the gift in the tissue and fold the lining over the gift. Use an adhesive seal to close the layers of tissue and "dress up" your package.

WRAPPING THE PACKAGE

Materials: Gift wrap; cellophane tape; ribbon and bow.

Directions:
1. Center the wrapping paper beneath the box.
2. Cut the paper to allow sufficient overlap. Secure with tape.
3. The paper should extend over both ends of the box a little more than half the depth of the box. Fasten the ends by folding the sides in, the top flap down and then the bottom flap. Secure with tape.
4. Turn the package over and decorate with ribbon and bow.

ARATE LID

erials: Gift wrap; cellophane tape.

ections:

Cut the paper to a size that will fold
r the sides and inside the lid.
At the four corners of the lid, snip
paper even with the edge of the lid.
Fold two edges up and tape them
de. Fold the end flaps up and tape
n inside.
Wrap the bottom in the same way.

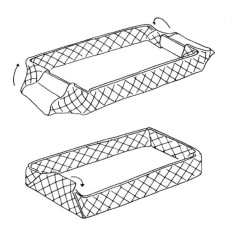

UND BOXES

terials: Gift wrap; pencil; ribbon,
or yarn pompon.

ections:

Trace the top and bottom of the box
. cut out two circles.
Wrap the box, allowing enough pa-
for sufficient overlap to extend
r the top and bottom. Tape to
ure.
Fold the edges of the wrapping pa-
at each end of the box and tape to
ure.
Attach the pre-cut circles to the top
bottom with paste or tape.
Adorn with ribbon or yarn and top
h a yarn pompon, pre-made bow or
wball bow.

**KEEPING GIFTS UNDER
WRAPS**
● *For an oversized or unusually
shaped gift—like a cuddly bear—use
a designed gift bag. All you need to
do is add the tag and draw the top
closed with a bow of yarn.*
● *For crazy shapes—bottles, base-
ball bats, soccer balls—avoid the
haphazard look by using reversible
wrapping paper.*
● *Package small children's toys that
come without containers in tin
banks...a nice gift in their own
right.*
● *Select foil papers to add sparkle to
the gifts under your tree. Several
foil papers, strategically placed beneath the tree, will reflect the lights
and colors of your holiday decorations.*

*To estimate how much wrapping
paper you will need to cover a boxed
gift, use enough to go around three
of the box's sides one time and one
of the narrow sides two times.*

BOTTLES

Materials: Gift wrap; gift wrap cord or yarn tie.

Directions:
1. Measure height of the bottle.
2. Cut gift wrap into a square, with edges a few inches longer than the height of the bottle. Fold into triangular shape at least three times. Round off the edge of the triangle. When the paper is unfolded, it should be in a circular shape.
3. Place the bottle in the center of the circle. Draw up sides and tie with gift wrap cord or yarn tie. Flare the top for a ruffled look.

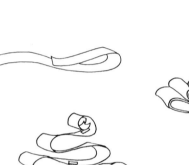

TAILORED BOW

Materials: Shiny ribbon; cellophane tape.

Directions:
For a six-inch bow, cut a piece of ribbon 2 feet long. Form a loop three inches long and secure with tape. Add a matching loop to the other side (do not cut ribbon), building slightly smaller loops each time and securing each with tape. End with a small loop in the center.

SNOWBALL BOW

Materials: Curling ribbon; scissors.

Directions:
1. For a three-inch snowball, cut an eight-yard piece of ribbon. Draw the entire length over a dull blade of the scissors to curl it.
2. Gather the curls into a ball and tie them with a separate piece of ribbon, catching stray curls into the ball.

For variety, wrap packages in differently shaped containers.

RN BOW

TERIALS: Yarn tie.

ections:

oop the yarn back and forth until
desired number of loops is reached.
ie very tightly in the center with a
arate piece of yarn and flare the
ps out to form the bow. You may tie
ts in the loose ends of the yarn.

WRAPPING: THE FINAL TOUCH

Try placing ribbons slightly off
center. Split the ribbon to varying
widths for a decreasing stripe effect.
Two colors or shades of ribbon can
easily be woven into a nostalgic bas-
ket-weave pattern.

● Use paper for wrapping and
trimming. Make a bow by stapling
strips of paper together like the
spokes of a wheel. Draw the paper
over a dull edge to create curls.

● Ordinary items such as small
toys, candy and old greeting cards
make eye-catching trims and may
be used to hint at the contents of the
package. If you run low on a fa-
vored gift-wrapping paper, wrap the
gift in a matching solid and use the
scraps as trim.

● Dress up the obvious. If the gift is
a tie, or a giveaway shape, use trims
and bows to give the package a little
extra pizzazz. You may even be able
to hide the shape. Coordinate the
wrappings of different gifts for a
dazzling foot-of-the-tree array.

To add a touch of surprise, wrap
your gift to disguise it. A large box,
for example, can hold a small piece
of jewelry. Use tissue to further
camouflage the shape of the gift.

Be sure to see page 253 for informa-
tion on packing food gifts.

TO SEND A GIFT BY MAIL

Select the proper container

Fiberboard containers (commonly found in supermarkets or hardware stores) are generally strong enough for mailing things of average weight and size—up to 10 lbs. Paperboard cartons (similar to suit boxes) can also be used for items of up to 10 lbs. Some boxes have what is known as a "test board" rating, which indicates how strong they are. For example, a corrugated fiberboard box (125-lb. test board) is good for mailing weights up to 20 lbs. High-density items, such as tools, require a stronger container (strength is indicated by a round imprint on a bottom corner of the box).

How to package your gifts

● *Soft goods,* like clothing, pillows and blankets, should be placed in a self-supporting box or tear-resistant bag—the box closed with reinforced tape, the bag sealed properly.

● *Perishables,* such as cheese, fruit, vegetables, meat or anything with an odor, must be placed in an impermeable container, filled with absorbent cushioning and sealed with filament tape.

● *Fragile items,* such as glasses, dishes or photography equipment, are safest packaged in fiberboard containers (minimum 175-lb. test board) and cushioned with foamed plastic or padding. Seal the package and reinforce with filament tape.

● *Shifting contents,* including books, tools or nails, should be packaged in fiberboard containers (minimum 175-lb. test board). Make sure that you use interior fiberboard separators or tape to prevent the contents of the parcel from shifting in transit. Seal the package and reinforce it with filament tape.

● *Awkward loads,* such as gloves, pipes or odd-shaped tools or instruments, re-quire special packaging. Use fiberboard tubes or boxes with length not more than 10 times their girth. Cushioning must be of preformed fiberboard or foamed plastic shapes, and the closure should be as strong as the tube itself.

Use adequate cushioning

If you are mailing several gift items in one package, wrap them individually and protect each one from the other with padding or foamed plastic. To prevent one item from damaging another, make sure you fill the box completely with cushioning material, leaving no empty space. Polystyrene, shredded, rolled or crumpled newspaper, "bubble" plastic and fiberboard are all good cushioning materials. So are plastic foam chips or egg cartons, cut into pieces and packing straw. Commercially available foam shells or air-pocket padding can also be used, as well as padded mailing bags (good for small items).

Seal your carton properly

Use one of three recommended types of tape to secure your parcel: pressure-sensitive filament tape, nylon-reinforced Kraft paper tape or plain Kraft paper tape. All three types are available in stationery stores or dime stores. There's no need to wrap your container with brown paper or tie it with twine. Paper sometimes rips in handling, and twine often gets entangled in mail-processing equipment.

Request special markings

Certain phrases printed on the outside of your parcel will alert Postal Service employees to the nature of its contents. Mark breakable objects FRAG-ILE in three places; above the address, below the postage and on the reve side. Packages of food or other ite which can decay should be mar PERISHABLE in the same locatio The words DO NOT BEND on y package will signal a fragile item, the sender must have first protec these and similar articles with stiff ing material. When you take y packages to the post office for maili ask the clerk to stamp them appro ately.

Insure your packages

Any gift sent by mail should be sured. You can insure your package varying amounts for up to $400. T cost is minimal, and you have the a ed security of knowing that in case a thing does happen to the package, y will be reimbursed. If you are maili something that is worth more th $400 or if you are sending cash or irreplaceable item through the ma send it by registered mail.

Use ZIP codes

The easiest way to delay delivery mail is to forget the ZIP Code, or to

wrong one. So, when addressing
r package, be sure to include the
code in both the recipient's and
r return address.

he it right
e Postal Service offers a wide range
delivery options for mailing pack-
s, depending on the amount of
ney you want to spend and the time
've allowed for delivery. A good
eral rule to follow is to mail early in
day and early in the month. As for
t-class letters and cards, those sent
st-to-coast should arrive within 3 to
ays; those greetings sent within the
e should arrive within 2 to 3 days;
I those mailed to an address within a
should reach their destination in 2
s. However, as we all know, the
ristmas season is the busiest time of
year for mail carriers, so it's best to
ow at least two weeks for domestic
ivery of holiday cards and gifts just
be on the safe side.

DOMESTIC MAIL SERVICES

You can choose any one of three services to send packages up to 70 lbs. and 108 inches (length plus girth) by mail.

SERVICE	DESCRIPTION	COST	TIME
PRIORITY MAIL	Packages receive the same attention as first-class letters. Shipped by air these parcels can be send from any post office station or branch, to any address in the U.S.	Determined by weight and distance traveled. A 2-lb. package from New York to Chicago: $2.88; a 5-lb. package: $4.83. A 2-lb. package from New York to Los Angeles: $3.57; a 5-lb. package: $6.54.	3-4 days
PARCEL POST	Takes longer than priority mail, but costs less. Packages can be mailed from any post office station or branch, and are delivered directly to the addressee.	Determined by weight and distance traveled. A 2-lb. package from New York to Chicago: $1.83; a 5-lb. package: $2.52. A 2-lb. package from New York to Los Angeles: $2.48; a 5-lb. package: $4.07.	8 days
EXPRESS MAIL	Guaranteed to be delivered on time to the addressee by 3 P.M. the next business day. Packages are automatically insured for up to $500. If mail is late, you can obtain a full postage refund by applying to originating post office.	Determined by weight and distance traveled. A 2-lb. package from New York to Chicago: $9.35; a 5-lb. package: $12.10. A 2-lb. package from New York to Los Angeles: $9.35; a 5-lb. package: $14.50.	Overnight

Note: Prices are accurate at time of press.

Follow these other pointers on mailing gifts, so they arrive in perfect condition:

● **Use a heavy gift wrap.** Thicker, heavier paper has a better chance of arriving without being torn.
● **Consider a designed gift box.** Many boxes come decorated with holiday motifs.
● **Bows don't travel well.** Instead, decorate packages with flat trims, stickers, yarn or tinsel tie.
● **Always mail a wrapped present inside another box.** Many gift boxes just aren't meant for shipping, so be sure to choose a box that is sturdy enough to support its contents and withstand the wear and tear of delivery.

ternational Mail

Destination	Air Parcels	Airmail Letters/Card
orth and Northwest Africa	24 Nov	1 Dec
ustralia	24 Nov	24 Nov
aribbean/West Indies	12 Dec	12 Dec
ntral And South America	5 Dec	5 Dec
rope	1 Dec	5 Dec
r East	1 Dec	5 Dec
id-East	24 Nov	28 Nov
utheast Asia	24 Nov	24 Nov
utheast Africa	24 Nov	1 Dec
est Africa	24 Nov	1 Dec

ote: These dates are for mailing from the continental U.S. only.

Romance and Lace: A Victorian Christmas tree and all the trimmings.

Legend has it…Under the mistletoe wasn't always a place to be kissed. In Roman times, this plant was a symbol of peace. When people warring with each other met under a mistletoe-covered tree, they would stop fighting—at least temporarily. Later on, in England and Scandinavia, the plant was hung over entryways; anyone passing under it would receive a friendly greeting—such as a kiss. Today's custom of kissing under the mistletoe was probably derived from this. And part of the fun, according to tradition, is that you can't refuse a kiss from anyone who catches you there!

Chapter
VI

HOME FOR THE HOLIDAYS

Low-Cost

Make-Ahead

Quick and Easy

Low-Calorie

Bazaar

"Oh, there's no place like home for the holidays…" We couldn't agree more, so we've put together this special chapter to help you achieve the Christmas of your dreams. It's all here: ornaments and decorating projects, dinners and desserts—even afghans to complete the mood! There are five beautiful themes to choose from: Romance & Lace, for lovers of Victoriana; South of the Border, for Christmas on the sunny side; Homespun Holiday, to celebrate nature; American Country, for an old-fashioned Yule; and Nice and Easy, for those short on time, but not on spirit. Take a look— and may all your Christmas dreams come true!

Lace Wreath

Frothy and delicate decorations, lavish dinners, splendid presents. The charm of this turn-of-the-century style evokes a time long gone, but still fondly remembered. This year, you can make it happen in your home.

ROMANCE AND LACE

Nosegay Ornaments; Satin-Covered Balls

TO FURTHER THE VICTORIAN FEELING:

● Coordinate your gift wrappings with the other decorations: Choose shiny silver paper and lace or ribbon ties; trim with a rose or ruffled paper doilies.

● Or, wrap gifts in scraps of moire fabric and trim with lace.

● Scent the air with flowers, especially roses, for a romantic fragrance throughout the house.

● Display antique treasure on a sled or in an old hat box.

● Don't forget the mistletoe!

SATIN STOCKINGS

AVERAGE: For those with some experience in sewing.

MATERIALS: (for one) ½ yd. 45″-wide satin; lace and ribbons; green stamens; white floral tape; clear acrylic spray to size fabric (*see Materials Shopping Guide, page 272, for these items*); artificial leaves.

DIRECTIONS (*½″ seams allowed*):
1. Enlarge the pattern in FIG. 1, following the directions on page 271.
2. To size the fabric, spray with two coats of acrylic, allowing for enough time to dry between coats.
3. Cut stocking front and back. On stocking front, pin laces and ribbons (*see photos*). Stitch in place. With right sides together, seam back to front except top edge.

Satin Stockings

FIG. 1 RIGHT SIDE   1 SQ. = 1″

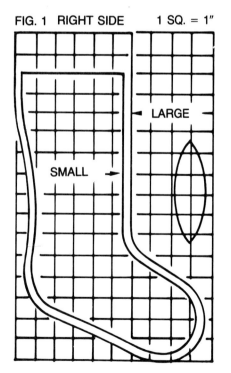

4. Cuffs: Cut a 5″-wide strip of satin 1″ longer than top edges of stocking. Stitch trims across cuff. Seam short ends together. Stitch cuff to stocking, along top edges, with wrong sides up.
5. Turn stocking right side out and turn cuff down. Fasten flowers or rosettes to cuffs.
6. Flowers: Cut 6″ pieces of 1¼″-wide lace or ribbon. Glue cut ends together.

Make running stitch at bottom ed[
pull up tightly, fasten ends and ins[
pearl stamens at center. Wrap gather[
edge of ribbon and stems with flo[
tape. Add leaves or ribbons.
7. For lace rosettes, gather up one e[
of 12″ strip of 2½″-wide lace, add b[
of colored ribbons and tack to cuff[
8. Tack ribbon loops to inside of ba[
seam, for hanging.

OSEGAY RNAMENTS

EASY: Achievable by anyone.
MATERIALS: 2½"-wide white lace; and 1½" picot taffeta ribbon; clustered pearl stamens; white floral tape; white glue (see *Materials Shopping Guide on page 272*); white plastic (disposable) plate.

DIRECTIONS:
Cut 26" of lace. Make running stitches along one edge and gather up, leaving center opening about 1" wide. Cut 3" scalloped circle from plate and cut two short crossed slits at center. Glue scalloped circle behind lace circle and allow enough time for drying. Make flowers as for stockings (see Satin Stockings how-to's, *page 132*), with 3½" long stems. Insert flower stems into center of lace and through slits. Tie ribbon around flowers (over stems) for streamers. Hang by stems.

SATIN-COVERED BALLS *(3"-dia.)*

EASY: Achievable by anyone.
MATERIALS: Satin (¾ yds. makes one dozen balls); ½"-wide white lace (24" per ball), 1¼"-wide white lace (12" per ball); ½"-wide picot ribbon (16" per ball); clear acrylic spray to size fabric (see Step 2, Satin Stockings, *page 132*); white glue (see *Materials Shopping Guide on page 272 for items above*); straight pins; cardboard.

DIRECTIONS:
1. Following the directions on page 271, enlarge ball section (see segment in Fig. 1) onto cardboard.
2. From satin, cut eight sections for each ball. Pin (at ends) each section to ball overlapping sides and ends. Covering all seams, wind and pin ½" lace around ball. Pin 3 lace flowers (see Step 6, Satin Stockings, *omitting stamens*) to top of ball. From 6" ribbon, make bow and pin to top.

LACE WREATH

EASY: Achievable by anyone.
MATERIALS: (*see* Materials for Nosegay Ornaments, *at left*, omitting plastic plate): Styrofoam® wreath form; 13 yds. of 2½"-wide lace for bows (20" each bow); 2¾ yds. of 1"-wide lace to bind wreath; green velour leaves (see *Materials Shopping Guide page 272*); pipe cleaners; white hair pins; dried baby's breath.

DIRECTIONS:
1. Glue 1"-wide lace around inner and outer flat edges of wreath form.
2. Cut 2½"-wide lace into 20" lengths and fold into quarters, to make bow. Wrap across center with 3" pipe cleaner, twist the ends and stick them into the wreath. Repeat until wreath is covered. (see Step 4 of Satin Stockings *to make flowers*).
3. Pin, with ribbons or leaves to wreath (see *photo*). Add dried baby's breath.

SPICY POMANDER BALLS TO MAKE IN MINUTES

You'll find everything you need for these old-fashioned pomander balls right in your kitchen.
● *With a light tack hammer, "nail" whole cloves into oranges or lemons, covering the entire surface of the rind.*
● *Using one clove "nail," attach a ribbon loop hanger.*
● *Pile pomander balls in a bowl or basket so that the air circulates around them; this "drying out" makes them fragrant.*
● *Keep some for yourself to use as delightful air fresheners or to decorate a door or tree. They're welcome gifts, too. But don't wrap until the last minute—wrapping will retard the drying process.*

Rose Garden Quilt

OSE GARDEN QUILT
(out 85"x93")

ERAGE: For those with some ex-
ience in quilting.

ATERIALS: 44/45"-wide cotton
adcloth, as follows: 12½ yds. white
patches and quilt back) and 1¼
. pink (for border patches); scraps of
ric for patches. We used about ¼
each of six solids (including yel-
), ⅜ yd. each of seven prints and ½
each of two prints; 90x108" quilt
t; 12 yds. of wide pink bias binding;
ap of thin cardboard.

RECTIONS *(¼" seams allowed):*
te: The patches will be sewn into
ettes and diamonds. Then these are
ned to make two alternating rows
e FIG. 2c). The rows are repeated
d sewn side by side. A border is add-
left and right to finish the quilt top.
en you quilt the layers (quilt top,
ting and quilt back) together and
d the edges.

FIG. 2B

FIG. 2C

FIG. 2D

G. 2A

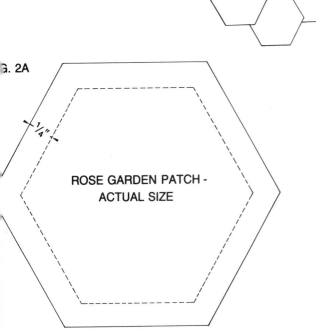

ROSE GARDEN PATCH -
ACTUAL SIZE

¼"

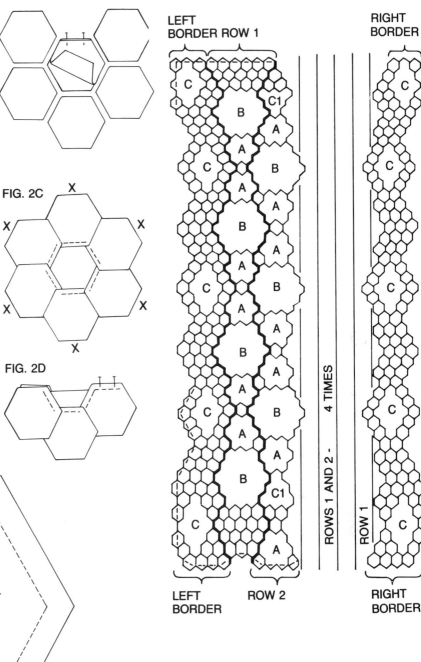

FIG. 2E JOINING DIAGRAM

LEFT
BORDER ROW 1

RIGHT
BORDER

ROWS 1 AND 2 - 4 TIMES

ROW 1

LEFT
BORDER

ROW 2

RIGHT
BORDER

1. Cutting Pattern: Carefully trace or cut out the hexagon (*see* FIG. 2a). With glue or transparent tape, fasten it smoothly to cardboard and cut on solid lines. The broken lines represent the seamlines. Whenever you sew patches together, sew only *on the broken lines;* don't sew all the way to the edges.

2. Cutting: From the white fabric, cut two 98″ lengths the full width of the fabric and seam them at long edges to make a quilt back 98″x87/89″. Then cut 1,041 white hexagons, trace carefully (with a sharp pencil) and lay them out with common edges in intersecting rows (like the quilt) to save fabric and time. From pink, cut 166 (for border) and from yellow cut 39 (for rosette centers). From plain pastels, cut 39 sets of six same-color patches and from prints, cut 39 sets of twelve same-color patches.

3. Block A (*White Rosettes*): With right side up, lay out a ring of six white patches around a central white patch. Turn one patch over the center (*see* FIG. 2b); pin on seamline (*see* Note) and stitch. Repeat with five other patches (*see* FIG. 2c). With right sides together, bring two outer patches together and stitch (*see* FIG. 2d). Repeat with other five to complete the ring. Press but don't open seams. Make 71 A Blocks.

4. Block B (*Colored Rosettes*): Using a yellow center patch and a ring of solid-color patches, make a Block A. Around it lay another ring, of twelve printed patches, and seam every other one to an ouside edge (*see* x's in FIG. 2c). Seam the intervening patches at two sides each. Seam their side edges to complete the ring. Make 39 B Blocks.

5. Block C (*White Diamond*): Make an A block. Add one white patch at an inside corner (seaming two edges). Add another opposite this to finish the diamond. Make 10 C Blocks.

6. Block C-1 (*White and Pink Diamond*): Make an A block using two adjoining pink patches in the ring (*see* FIG. 2E). Add one white patch be- tween them and another opposite, to make a diamond. Make 10 C-1 blocks.

7. Row 1: Join six A blocks, four B Blocks and fifteen white filler patches; add pink and white patches at each end (*see* FIG. 2E). Make 6 Rows 1.

8. Row 2: Join seven A blocks, three B Blocks, two C-1 Blocks and four white filler patches (*see* FIG. 2e). Make 5 Rows 2.

9. Quilt Top: Alternating six Rows 1 with five Row 2 (*see* FIG. 2e), seam them together. Add five white patches to ouside of each B Block. Add pink patches, C Blocks and white patches (*see* FIG. 2e) to complete the side borders.

10. Basting: Spread out the quilt back, wrong side up on the floor, and tape down the corners. Over it, center the batting and spread it out smoothly. On this, center the quilt top, right side up. With long stitches, baste through layers from the center outward to each corner and to middle of each edge. Add more basting rows (six or eight inches apart) so the layers are well bonded. Untape the corners.

11. Quilting: Thread needle with a single strand of sewing or quilting thread and knot one end. Begin near the quilt center and work outward, with the quilt in a hoop or frame if you have one. Bring needle from quilt back to quilt top on a seam, give it a small tug to pull the knot into the batting. Stitch with even running stitches, in the ditch of all the seams. Baste (through all layers) from corner to corner around outside edges (*see broken lines in* FIG. 2e) to make top edge straight, other edges scalloped. Trim off just outside the basting.

12. Finishing: With right sides together and raw edges even, stitch bias tape (along a fold) to quilt. Turn tape over the edge and slipstitch the fold to the quilt back. Remove basting.

VICTORIAN TABLE SETTING
(Shown on page 128)

AVERAGE: For those with some [ex]perience in sewing.

TABLECLOTH
(about 60″ x 80″)

MATERIALS : 4⅝ yds. 44″-wide [fab]ric; 8 yds. 1″-wide beaded lace.

DIRECTIONS:
1. Seams: Cut one full width of fa[bric] 82″ long. Cut two more strips [ ] long x 10″ wide, each with one selv[age] edge. Seam (½″) a narrow strip to e[ach] side of the wide (center) strip, w[ith] selvages matching; press seams op[en].
2. Edges: At each edge, turn ½″, th[en] ½″ again, to wrong side; pin a[nd] stitch. On right side, stitch lace al[ong] each edge, mitering corners.

LACE TABLECLOTH
(about 50″ x 70″)

MATERIALS: 4 yds. 44″-wide l[ace] fabric; 7 yds. 1½″ ruffled lace.

DIRECTIONS:
Cut two 26x70″ pieces of lace; se[am] them right sides together at a lo[ng] (center) edge. Trim seam; press to o[ne] side and stitch along raw edges. Tr[im] the 4 corners to round them. Seam la[ce] ruffle to tablecloth edges, right si[des] together. Turn lace outward and to[p] stitch along the seam.

...ABLE RUNNER
(...out 14" x 68")

...TERIALS: 2 yds. 45"-wide fabric; ...ds. 1"-wide beaded lace.

...RECTIONS:
...: 16 x 70" fabric. At each edge, ...n ½", then ½" again, to wrong side; ...and stitch. On right side, stitch ...e across lengthwise center of run-..., then against each long edge, and ...lly (turning under raw ends) ...inst each short edge.

...ARGE FAN HOLDER
(...out 2" wide x 24" long)

...ATERIALS: 4 x 24" mat board; 4 ... 1"-wide beaded lace; white glue; ...tal ruler.

...RECTIONS:
...ke score lines 1" inside each long ...ge of the mat board. With a ruler and ...ingle-edge razor blade or craft knife, ...re the two lines, without cutting all ...e way through. Fold up each side. ...ue lace around both long sides and ...ound both open ends, to make a nar-...w box. From the lace make a Bow ...e below), using three 17" lengths for ...ls and a 15", 11" and 4" length for ...e three loops. Glue to front of box.

...ARGE FAN
(...bout 12" high x 24" long)

...ATERIALS: 24 x 56" fabric; 4 yds. ...-wide beaded lace; fusible web; spray ...hesive; lightweight wire on a spool; ...hite glue.

...RECTIONS:
...ld fan in half (56 x 12"), right side ...t, and press. Open it and spray ...rong side lightly with spray adhesive; ...ld it again carefully and press lightly

with a warm iron. Fuse a strip of lace across each short end. Cut lace to fit across top edge of fan. Cut fusible web same size as lace and pin it across top edge of fan. Over the web, place a thin wire about ¼" from the edge, then the lace, then iron it to fuse. Repeat at top back edge. Fold the fan into 2"-wide accordion pleats, crimping the wire at the folds. Press the folds. At the bottom edge, staple each pair of ribs together. Unfold into a fan shape and glue the first and last ribs flat to inside bottom of fan holder.

FAN PLACEMARK

DIRECTIONS:
Holder: Cut 1¾ x 6½" posterboard. Follow directions for Large Fan Holder, scoring ½" from the edges and using ½" lace. **For bow:** Fold 18" and 2½" lace pieces into loops (*see directions for Bow, below*). Wrap them together and glue them to box front (*see photo*). **For card:** Cut 1½" high x 3" half moon from posterboard. Glue ruffled lace behind its curved edge. Print the name on the card and glue it behind the front of the box. **Fan:** Cut fabric 15 x 6½" and fold to 3¼". Follow directions for Large Fan, omitting wire and folding into ⅝"-wide pleats.

BOW *(under plate—about 7" wide x 20" long)*

MATERIALS: 3¼ yds. 1⅜"-wide flat ribbon.

DIRECTIONS:
1. Cut lengths of ribbon: 3 at 20", 1 at 11", 1 at 16", 1 at 4½", 1 at 8½", 1 at 2" and 1 at 8".
2. Overlap one 20" piece about ½" over another at top end, angled so the bottom ends splay out about 2" apart. Place the third 20" strip centered over them, top edges even. Staple top edges.

3. Fold ends of 16" piece to the back, overlapping them at the center; staple. Do the same with an 11" piece. Place small loop over large one; staple at centers. Fold 4¼" piece across the center and glue its ends to back.
4. Assembly: Glue bow to top of tails, centers matching. Glue 8" piece behind the bow and notch each end (*see photo*). Also notch tail ends. Place a heavy book on the bow to flatten it.

NAPKINS *(20" square)*

DIRECTIONS:
Trim the edges of a 21" square of fabric with pinking shears or zigag stitch. Pin ruffled lace to napkin edges, right sides together, and seam along the gathering stitches. Turn lace outward; press; topstitch along the seamline.

MOIRE FANS
(Shown in centerpiece on table)

EASY: Achievable by anyone.
MATERIALS: 12" of 8"-wide moire; 76" length of lace ribbon (⅝" wide—*see Materials Shopping Guide, page 272*); 1 length of covered wire 18" (#28 gauge) cut in half.
Note: Instructions are for two fans.

DIRECTIONS:
1. Cut moire into two pieces down the center so there are two 4" wide pieces of moire 12" in length.
2. Glue lace ribbon to three sides of moire (2 short ends, 1 long side).
3. Make small bow with 18" of lace ribbon and secure with covered wire.
4. Accordion-pleat moire ribbon and secure by attaching bow at bottom of fan.
5. Finishing: Bow should be placed on side of moire that does not have lace trim (on cut edge).

Christmas Eve Dinner: Goose provides the centerpiece for this Victorian-style feast.

VICTORIAN CHRISTMAS EVE DINNER

(FOR 8)

Fruit Cut Noël*
Oysters Supreme*
with Toast Points*
Royal Roast Goose*
with Vegetable Della Robia OR:
Royal Roast Turkey*
Royal Gravy*
Savory Red Cabbage*
Glazed Sweet Potatoes*
Minted Peas*
Buttered Brussels Sprouts*
Tangy Cranberry Conserve*
Individual Relish Trays
Seeded Rolls
Christmas Plum Pudding*
with Hard Sauce
Victorian Lace Cake*

*Recipe follows

WORK PLAN

Two Months to Two Weeks Before
● Make and bake CHRISTMAS PLUM PUDDING.
Three Days Before
● Buy goose.
Two Days Before
● Trim vegetables for VEGETABLE DELLA ROBIA and refrigerate in plastic bags.
● Make HARD SAUCE and bake TOAST POINTS. Make APPLE-CORNBREAD STUFFING if making turkey. Thaw CHRISTMAS PLUM PUDDING and make layers for VICTORIAN LACE CAKE. Make "lace" for cake.

Early in the day
● Prepare RICH FUDGE FROSTING for cake. Frost and decorate cake.
Three hours before
● Roast ROYAL ROAST GOOSE or TURKEY.
Two hours before
● Prepare FRUIT CUP NÖEL and refrigerate.
One Hour Before
● Prepare OYSTERS SUPREME, GLAZED SWEET PO-TATOES, MINTED PEAS, BUTTERED BRUSSELS SPROUTS and SAVORY RED CABBAGE.
30 minutes before
● Make VEGETABLE DELLA ROBIA and GRAVY.
15 minutes before
● Heat rolls, open wine and make coffee.

During dinner
● Reheat CHRISTMAS PLUM PUDDING.

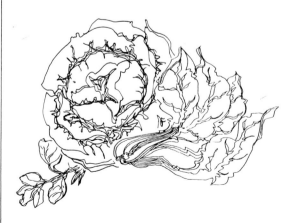

Fruit Cup Noël

An easy-to-prepare, yet smashing, appetizer.

Makes 8 servings.

½ cup cranberry liqueur or juice
8 navel oranges
8 large strawberries, hulled
   Fresh mint

1. Spoon 1 tablespoon of the cranberry liqueur or juice into each of 8 stemmed fruit compotes.
2. Pare the oranges; cut into thin cross-wise slices. Arrange, overlapping, in a circle over the cranberry liqueur or juice. Top each with a hulled strawberry, point side up. Garnish with fresh mint, if you wish.

Oysters Supreme

A superb choice for a party fish course.

Makes 8 generous servings.

2 pints (4 cups) fresh oysters
   OR: 4 cans (6 ounces each) whole oysters
2 cans condensed cream of onion soup
1 cup cream or milk
¼ cup lemon juice
   Toast Points (recipe follows)

1. Cook the fresh oysters in their liquid in a large saucepan, 2 minutes or just until firm; remove the oysters with a slotted spoon and reserve. Pour the liquid from the canned oysters into a saucepan.
2. Stir the soup, cream or milk and lemon juice into the oyster liquid until smooth. Simmer 5 minutes. Stir in the oysters. Ladle into a heated soup tureen. Serve with the TOAST POINTS.

Toast Points: Trim the crusts from very thinly sliced white bread; cut into triangles with a very sharp knife. Arrange in a single layer on a cookie sheet. Bake in a preheated slow oven (300°) for 20 minutes, turning cookie sheet if bread is not browning evenly; cool; store in a metal tin with a tight-fitting lid.

Royal Roast Goose

In Victorian days, a roast goose was the festive bird of Christmas. Today it's enjoyed year-round.

Roast at 325° for 2½ hours.
Makes 8 servings, plus leftovers.

1   frozen goose (8 to 10 pounds), thawed
     Salt and pepper
1   small onion, chopped (¼ cup)
2   large carrots, pared and diced
2   stalks celery, diced
     Royal Gravy (recipe, page 142)
     Vegetable Della Robia (recipe, page 142)

1. Preheat the oven to slow (325°).
2. Remove the neck and giblets from the goose and cook immediately for goose broth. Remove the excess fat from the body cavity and neck skin. Season with salt and pepper; stuff with the chopped onion, carrot and celery; truss the goose with string.
3. Place the goose, breast-side up, on a rack in a large roasting pan. Insert a meat thermometer into the inside thigh muscle, if you wish.
4. Roast in the preheated slow oven (325°) for 2½ hours, pricking with two-tined fork often while roasting to remove fat, or until the temperature on the meat thermometer reaches 165° and the drumstick moves easily. Serve with the ROYAL GRAVY; garnish the platter with the VEGETABLE DELLA ROBIA.

TIP: Don't waste the goose fat, but keep it to use in making leftover goose dishes or for a flavorful cooking fat. Melt down solid pieces of goose fat and add to the fat accumulated during roasting; strain through cheesecloth into a glass jar with a screw top; refrigerate and use within 1 month or pour into plastic containers and freeze up to 6 months.

Royal Roast Turkey

The festive bird is brushed with a spicy baste for golden color.

Roast at 325° for 2 hours, 30 minutes.
Makes 8 servings, plus leftovers.

1   fresh or frozen turkey (about 12 pounds)
     Apple-Cornbread Stuffing (recipe follows)
2   large onions, chopped (2 cups)
2   cups chopped celery
½   cup (1 stick) butter or margarine, melted
1   tablespoon Worcestershire sauce
1   teaspoon bottled aromatic bitters
1   teaspoon leaf marjoram, crumbled
     Royal Gravy (recipe, page 142)

1. Thaw the turkey, if necessary, following label directions; remove the giblets and neck; reserve for gravy.
2. Preheat the oven to slow (325°).
3. Lightly stuff neck and body cavities of the turkey with APPLE-CORNBREAD STUFFING. Skewer the neck skin to the back of the bird. Secure the wing tips with skewers or kitchen string. Secure the legs under the band of skin or metal clamp, or tie with kitchen string. Turn the remaining stuffing into a buttered 4-cup casserole. Cover the casserole with aluminum foil.
4. Sprinkle the chopped onion and celery in the bottom of a shallow roasting pan. Place the stuffed turkey on the vegetables in the pan. Brush part of the melted butter or margarine over the turkey. Make a tent of heavy-duty aluminum foil; place over the turkey with edges inside pan, not touching bird.
5. Roast the turkey in the preheated slow oven (325°), basting several times with drippings, for 2 hours. Stir the Worcestershire sauce, aromatic bitters and marjoram into the remaining melted butter or margarine. Brush part over the turkey.
6. Continue roasting, basting several times with the remaining butter mixture for 30 minutes longer, or until the meat thermometer registers 185° and the leg joint moves freely. About 1 hour before the turkey is done, place the extra casserole with stuffing in the oven. Bake until heated through. Remove the turkey to a heated serving platter. Remove string and skewers and keep warm. Let stand for 20 to 30 minutes before carving. Prepare ROYAL GRAVY, if you wish. Garnish with the DELLA ROBIA VEGETABLES, if you wish.

Apple-Cornbread Stuffing

Never stuff a goose before roasting because it is too fatty. If you want to serve this with goose, bake it in a casserole.

Makes about 10 cups.

½ cup (1 stick) butter or margarine
2 large onions, diced
2 cups diced celery
2 large apples, quartered, cored and chopped
1¼ cups water
2 packages (8 ounces each) cornbread stuffing mix
½ cup chopped parsley

1. Melt the butter or margarine in a large saucepan; stir in the onion, celery and apple; sauté until soft. Stir in the water; bring to boiling.
2. Pour mixture over the cornbread stuffing and mix in a large bowl; add the parsley; toss lightly to moisten.

Royal Gravy

To make gravy with a turkey, follow the same recipe, substituting turkey for goose.

Makes about 4 cups.

Goose giblets
1 medium-size onion, chopped (½ cup)
Few celery leaves
1 teaspoon salt
1 bay leaf
4 cups water
½ cup fat from roast
½ cup sifted all-purpose flour
Salt and pepper

1. Combine the giblets (except liver), onion, celery leaves, 1 teaspoon salt, bay leaf and 4 cups water in a large saucepan. Simmer for 1 hour, 40 minutes; add the liver, simmer 20 minutes longer, or until the meat is tender.
2. Strain the broth into a 4-cup measure; add the water if necessary, to make 4 cups. Reserve the liquid.
3. Finely chop the giblets and combine them with the liquid in a medium-size bowl. Cool, then cover with plastic wrap and refrigerate until ready to make the gravy.

4. After the goose has been removed from the roasting pan, remove the rack, if used; tip the pan and let the fat rise in one corner. Pour all the fat into a cup, leaving the juices in the pan. Measure ½ cup fat and return to the pan; blend in the flour with a wire whisk. Cook, stirring constantly, just until bubbly.
5. Stir in the giblet broth and giblets; continue cooking and stirring, scraping baked-on juices from the bottom and sides of the pan, until the gravy thickens and bubbles for 3 minutes.
6. Taste and season with salt and pepper and add a little bottled gravy coloring, if you wish.

Vegetable Della Robia

Beautifully presented vegetables add a festive touch to Christmas dinner.

Makes 8 servings.

1 bag (1 pound) fresh or frozen baby carrots
1 large cauliflower
1 large bunch broccoli
Boiling water
2 teaspoons salt
6 peppercorns
1 pound mushrooms, halved if large
1 cup (2 sticks) butter or margarine
1 pint cherry tomatoes, stemmed
1 teaspoon leaf tarragon, crumbled
Salt and pepper

1. Pare the fresh carrots, if used; cook in a small amount of salted boiling water in a large skillet for 10 minutes, or until crisply tender; remove with a slotted spoon to a heated large glass or ceramic platter and keep warm.
2. Trim the cauliflower and broccoli, then separate into flowerets; soak separately in warm salted water for 5 minutes; drain.
3. Place the broccoli in one large saucepan and the cauliflower in a second large saucepan. Add ½ cup boiling water, 1 teaspoon salt and 2 peppercorns to each; cover.
4. Steam for 15 minutes, or until crisply tender; drain. Arrange on the heated platter with the carrots.
5. Sauté the mushrooms in ¼ cup (½ stick) of the butter or margarine in a large skillet for 10 minutes, or until tender, but not brown. Remove

with a slotted spoon to the platter.

6. Melt another ¼ cup of the butter or margarine in the same skillet. Sauté the cherry tomatoes until tender. Remove to the platter.

7. Melt the remaining ½ cup (1 stick) butter or margarine in a small saucepan. Stir in the tarragon and salt and pepper to taste. Pour over the vegetables; toss to coat well. Serve hot, surrounding the ROYAL ROAST GOOSE or ROYAL ROAST TURKEY.

MICROWAVE TIP: If you wish to cook the carrots, cauliflower and broccoli in a microwave oven, prepare the vegetables according to the recipe above; arrange in separate piles in a large shallow microwave-safe casserole; add ½ cup water. Cover with plastic wrap. Microwave on high power for 10 minutes, turning the casserole one-half turn after 5 minutes, or until the vegetables are crisply tender.

Note: For a lo-cal version, reduce butter by half.

$ 🍴

Savory Red Cabbage

A hearty favorite with better-than-ever flavor.

Makes 8 servings.

1   medium-size red cabbage (about 1½ pounds)
2   large tart red apples, quartered and cored
¼   cup goose or bacon drippings
        OR: ¼ cup vegetable oil
1   medium-size onion, chopped (½ cup)
1½   teaspoons salt
¼   teaspoon pepper
¾   cup water
⅓   cup firmly packed brown sugar
3   tablespoons unsifted all-purpose flour
⅓   cup cider vinegar

1. Quarter, core and shred the red cabbage (a food processor does a quick job); dice the apple with the skin left on.

2. Heat the drippings or oil in a Dutch oven or heavy kettle; sauté the onion until soft; stir in the shredded cabbage and cook, stirring constantly, for 5 minutes.

3. Add the diced apples, salt, pepper and water; bring to bubbling; reduce heat to simmering; cover the pan.

4. Cook for 15 minutes for crisply tender cabbage or 1 hour for well done.

5. Combine the brown sugar and flour in a small bowl; stir in the vinegar to make a smooth paste, stir into the bubbling cabbage mixture; cook, stirring constantly, for 5 minutes, or until the mixture thickens. Serve on a heated platter with GLAZED SWEET POTATOES.

TIP: This vegetable dish can be made the day before: Spoon into a glass or ceramic heatproof dish; cover; cool and refrigerate. Reheat in a preheated slow oven (300°) for 30 minutes while the ROYAL ROAST GOOSE or TURKEY is resting.

$

Glazed Sweet Potatoes

No festive dinner is complete without a dish of golden sweet potatoes.

Bake at 325° for 30 minutes.
Makes 8 servings.

2   cans (1 pound, 8 ounces each) sweet potatoes
¼   cup (½ stick) butter or margarine
1   cup firmly packed dark brown sugar
2   teaspoons ground cinnamon

1. Preheat the oven to slow (325°).

2. Drain liquid from the sweet potatoes. Place sweet potatoes in a single layer in a shallow glass baking dish.

3. Heat the butter or margarine with the brown sugar and cinnamon in a large heavy skillet over low heat, stirring until sugar dissolves. Drizzle the mixture over the sweet potatoes.

4. Bake in the preheated slow oven (325°) for 30 minutes, basting with the glaze to coat evenly. Arrange on a heated platter with SAVORY RED CABBAGE.

Minted Peas

For a festive touch, stir in pimiento strips or diced red pepper.

Makes 8 servings.

3   *tablespoons butter or margarine*
1   *small onion, chopped ($\frac{1}{4}$ cup)*
2   *bags (1 pound each) frozen peas*
$\frac{1}{4}$ *cup hot water*
1   *teaspoon sugar*
    Salt and freshly ground pepper
    Butter or margarine
    Fresh mint

1. Melt the butter or margarine in a large saucepan; sauté the onion for 5 minutes, or until soft.
2. Add the peas, hot water and sugar; toss to mix well with a wooden spoon; cover.
3. Bring to boiling; lower heat; steam for 5 minutes. Season with salt and pepper to taste. Spoon into a heated serving bowl. Top with a large pat of butter or margarine. Garnish with fresh mint, if you wish.

Buttered Brussels Sprouts

Chestnuts add seasonal flair to a favorite winter vegetable.

Makes 8 servings.

1   *container (1 pint) Brussels sprouts*
    OR: 2 packages (9 ounces each) frozen Brussels sprouts
1   *cup chicken broth*
2   *tablespoons butter or margarine*
1   *teaspoon salt*
$\frac{1}{4}$ *teaspoon freshly ground pepper*
$\frac{1}{4}$ *teaspoon ground mace*
1   *can (15 ounces) whole chestnuts, drained*

1. Remove only the bruised leaves from the fresh Brussels sprouts; cut a cross in stem end; wash in salted warm water.
2. Bring the chicken broth and butter to boiling in a large saucepan; add the fresh or frozen sprouts, salt, pepper and mace; bring to boiling; lower heat to simmering and break apart the frozen sprouts, if used, with two forks; stir in the drained chestnuts and cover the pan.
3. Cook for 5 minutes for frozen or 20 minutes for fresh, or until the Brussels sprouts are crisply tender; remove with a slotted spoon to a heated

vegetable bowl, reserving the cooking liquid for soup making.
TIP: You can trim and soak fresh sprouts for cooking the day before and store them in a plastic bag in the refrigerator.

Tangy Cranberry Conserve

A cranberry relish is a traditional part of the holiday feast.

Makes 8 servings.

2   *cans (16 ounces each) cranberry sauce*
1   *cup celery crescents*
$\frac{1}{2}$ *cup chopped walnuts*

Place the cranberry sauce in a large serving bowl. Stir in the celery and nuts.

Tip: To make celery crescents, cut the celery into thin slices at a 45° angle with a sharp paring knife. Also, see page 145 for cranberry pointers.

Christmas Plum Pudding

A treasured family holiday dessert. The recipe makes two, so you can share one with a friend.

Steam for 3 hours.
Makes two 8-cup molds.

1   *cup firmly packed dark brown sugar*
2   *cups ground suet*
1   *cup soft bread crumbs (2 slices)*
1   *cup dried currants*
1   *cup raisins*
1   *cup mixed candied fruits*
$\frac{1}{2}$ *pound soft figs, cut up*
1   *cup halved pitted dates*
1   *cup finely chopped peeled tart apple*
1   *cup unsifted whole-wheat flour*
1   *cup unsifted all-purpose flour*
1   *teaspoon ground cinnamon*
$\frac{1}{2}$ *teaspoon ground cloves*
$\frac{1}{2}$ *teaspoon ground nutmeg*
$\frac{1}{2}$ *teaspoon salt*
2   *eggs, beaten*
1   *cup molasses*
1   *tablespoon baking soda*
$\frac{1}{2}$ *cup boiling water*
$\frac{1}{2}$ *cup warm brandy*
    Unseasoned dry bread crumbs

2 cups heavy cream, whipped
Red candied roses (optional)
Hard Sauce (recipe follows)

1. Combine the brown sugar with the suet, crumbs, currants, raisins, candied fruits, figs, dates and apple in a very large bowl until well blended.
2. Add the whole-wheat and all-purpose flours, cinnamon, cloves, nutmeg and salt, mixing well.
3. Combine the beaten eggs and molasses in a small bowl, blending well. Dissolve the baking soda in the boiling water in a 1-cup measure and stir into the eggs; add to the fruit mixture along with the warm brandy; toss to mix well.
4. Liberally grease two 8-cup molds with vegetable shortening. Coat generously with the unseasoned dry bread crumbs. Spoon the batter into the prepared molds. Cover with a double thickness of aluminum foil and tie with string.
5. Place the molds on a trivet in the bottom of a large deep kettle; pour boiling water to two-thirds the depth of the molds; cover the kettle.
6. Steam for 3 hours, adding more boiling water, if necessary, or until a wooden skewer inserted near the center comes out clean. Cool in the molds on a wire rack for 15 minutes. Loosen around edge of the molds; invert onto a wire rack; cool completely.
7. Drizzle the cakes with additional brandy; wrap separately in plastic bags; seal the bags; store in the refrigerator for at least 2 weeks to blend flavors, or wrap in heavy-duty aluminum foil and freeze for up to 2 months. Thaw for one day.
8. To serve: Reheat by placing the pudding on a wire rack over a pan of hot water on the rack of the oven. Bake in a preheated slow oven (300°) for 30 minutes, or until heated through. Place the pudding on a serving plate. Fit a pastry bag with a large star tip and fill with the whipped cream; pipe around the side and across the top of the pudding; garnish wth the red candied roses. Serve with the HARD SAUCE.

Hard Sauce: Makes about 2 cups. Beat ½ cup (1 stick) butter or margarine in a medium-size bowl with an electric mixer at high speed until fluffy. Beat in 1½ cups 10X (confectioners' powdered) sugar and 1 tablespoon boiling water until well blended. Stir in 1 tablespoon brandy, or sherry.

THE CRANBERRY CONNECTION

● *To avoid overcooking cranberries, remove them from the heat the minute they've popped.*
● *Have any leftovers? Simply freeze the raw berries as they are. The can be ground or chopped while still frozen, and used in batters and sauces without being thawed first.*
● *For a festive touch, use cookie cutters to make decorative shapes from sliced cranberry jelly.*

Victorian Lace Cake

A royally decorated cake—just perfect for the festive day.

Bake at 350° for 30 minutes.
Makes one 9-inch layer cake.

3 cups unsifted all-purpose flour
1 tablespoon baking powder
½ teaspoon salt
1½ cups sugar
⅔ cup vegetable shortening
6 egg yolks
1 teaspoon vanilla
1 cup milk
Rich Fudge Frosting (recipe follows)
Cake Lace (recipe follows)

1. Preheat the oven to moderate (350°).
2. Sift the flour, baking powder and salt onto wax paper.
3. Beat the sugar, shortening, egg yolks and vanilla in the large bowl of an electric mixer at high speed, 3 minutes, or until creamy smooth.
4. Turn mixer speed to low; add the flour mixture alternately with the milk, beating after each addition, just until batter is smooth. Pour the batter into two greased and floured 9-inch layer-cake pans, dividing evenly.
5. Bake in the preheated moderate oven (350°) 30 minutes, or until centers spring back when lightly pressed with fingertip.
6. Cool the layers in the pans on wire racks for 10 minutes; loosen around edges with a knife; turn out onto wire racks; cool completely.
7. To make this cake ahead, wrap each layer in heavy-duty aluminum foil, plastic wrap or a plastic

Lace Cake

bag; label date and freeze. The day you serve it,
thaw at room temperature for 1 hour.
8. Put the layers together and frost with the RICH
FUDGE FROSTING, garnish with the ROYAL FROSTING
and CAKE LACE.

Rich Fudge Frosting

Makes enough filling and frosting for two 9-inch layers.

$\frac{1}{2}$ cup (1 stick) butter or margarine
$\frac{1}{2}$ cup cocoa powder (not a mix)
$\frac{1}{4}$ cup water
1   package (1 pound) 10X (confectioners'
    powdered) sugar, sifted
    Dash salt
2   tablespoons brandy

Melt the butter or margarine with the cocoa in a large saucepan over low heat, stirring often, until the mixture is smooth; remove from heat. Beat in the 10X sugar, salt and brandy until smooth with electric mixer at high speed.

TIP: If the mixture becomes too thick while frosting the cake, add a few drops of hot water and beat.

Cake Lace

The perfect finish to a party cake. It looks much more difficult to do than it really is.

Place a 6 x 3-inch piece of wax paper over one of the designs in FIG. 3 with magazine on a flat surface. Fill a pastry bag fitted with a #3 writing tip with ROYAL ICING (recipe follows). Follow the design outline with the icing, then fill in the shaded areas with the icing. Fill the centers last, mounding the centers as for making a dot. Remove the wax paper with a large pancake turner and place on a cookie sheet. Repeat to use up the icing. Allow the icing to dry undisturbed overnight. When ready to decorate the cake, frost the cake, then carefully peel the "lace" off the wax paper and arrange in a decorative pattern on the cake. DO NOT TRY THIS PROJECT IN HUMID OR RAINY WEATHER.

FIG. 3 CAKE LACE

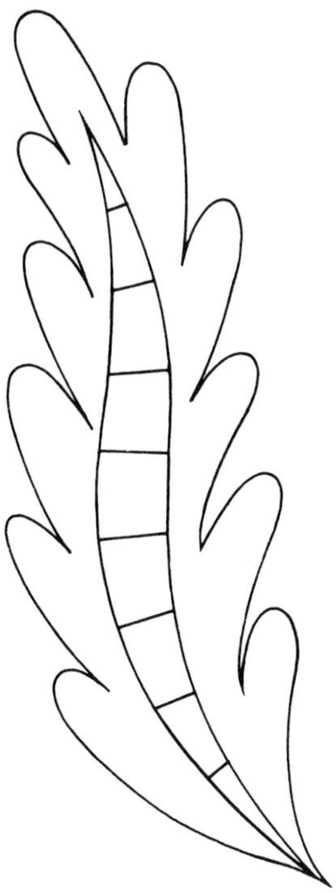

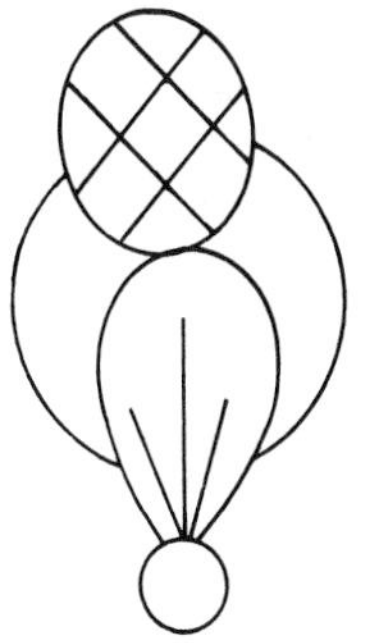

Royal Frosting

Makes enough to decorate one cake.

1   **egg white, at room temperature**
     Dash cream of tartar (optional)
1½ cups sifted 10X (confectioners' powdered) sugar

Beat the egg white with the cream of tartar, if used, in a small deep bowl with the electric mixer at high speed until foamy white and double in volume. Add the 10X sugar, a tablespoon at a time, beating constantly until the mixture is the consistency of sour cream and form's peaks when the beater is removed. Pack onto the pastry bag, or keep the bowl covered with a damp paper towel to keep the frosting from drying before it is piped out in the design.

Tip: If the icing is too stiff, add a tiny amount of unbeaten egg white; if the frosting is too soft, add a small amount more of 10X sugar.

Choose any of the designs shown here, using a longer spray for the top and a shorter pattern for the side of the cake; or design patterns of your own, using these designs for scale.

Different—and ingenious!—Cactus Christmas "Tree"

Who says Christmas has to be snowy? Celebrate a warm, sunshiny December 25th with a feast that salutes Mexico and decorations native to the Southwest. And whether you're basking in sun (or just *wish* you were)—Feliz Navidad!

SOUTH OF THE BORDER

Taco Wreath

SOUTHWEST FLAVOR

- Use colorful peppers, amaryllis and other native flowers to make wall decorations, wreaths and centerpieces.
- Tie red ribbon or red and green grosgrain around your outdoor lawn "pets".
- Tuck ferns into an amaryllis plant and tie the pot with a lavish red velvet ribbon bow.
- Line your driveway with potted poinsettia plants.
- Create a festive outdoor patio for Christmas breakfast: Use red and green calico mats and napkins, and choose bright red flowers for the centerpiece, interlaced with baby's breath or silver ribbon ties.
- For a still-life with a real South-of-the-Border touch, fill a large clay saucer with white candles of varying heights; surround them with marble chips or pebbles.

CACTUS CHRISTMAS TREE

DIRECTIONS:
Paint coffee cans dark green. Place one cholla (prickly pear) cactus plant in each; tie on a bright red bow made of bandana fabric. Stack the coffee cans on blocks of wood to form a Christmas tree shape.

Pepper Centerpiece

TACO WREATH

EASY: Achievable by anyone.
MATERIALS: 18″-dia. Styrofoam® wreath base; taco shells; hot-glue gun; fresh red and green chili peppers; sphagnum moss; gingham bow; floral wire; lotus pods (available at florist shop); more peppers for decoration.

DIRECTIONS:
1. Place wreath on a hard, flat surface and begin at the top to cover with taco shells, working from left to right. With folded edge down, open edges facing top of wreath. Using a hot-glue gun, apply glue to edges of "bottom" half of shell which will lie flat against the wreath form. Put next shell below, so open edge of the second shell touches the folded edge of the first shell. Continue around form.
2. For trim, add red and green chili peppers glued inside and at edges of shells. (Use fresh peppers—they will dry while on the wreath.)
3. With sphagnum moss, fill in between and behind shells to cover any visible parts of wreath form.
Note: To prevent taco shells from breaking, use shells as fresh as possible. If shells aren't fresh, they may be made more manageable by heating on a cookie sheet in a slow oven over an open pan of water placed on the oven rack below. Heat shells until *slightly* softer.
4. Tie gingham bow at top with floral wire and wire a cluster of three lotus pods, interspersed with peppers, to bow. Let wreath dry thoroughly before hanging.

PEPPER CENTERPIECE

EASY: Achievable by anyone.

DIRECTIONS:
Banana peppers in different tones of green and bright red are as colorful Christmas ornaments. Show them on a simple plate with a nosegay of laurel leaves in the middle.

r Ornament

💲 STAR ORNAMENT

EASY: Achievable by anyone.
MATERIALS—for 1 Star: Chenille: 1 emerald chenille stem, 8 white 3″ chenille bumps, 8 red 2″ chenille bumps, 1 yellow jumbo chenille stem, ½ gold tinsel stem (*see Materials Shopping Guide, page 272*); white glue in a tube; wire cutting pliers.

DIRECTIONS:
1. Shape one end of emerald stem as a 2″ diameter circle, twisting a small part of stem on circle to fasten it. This is basis for flower. Bend remaining stem at right angle to circle to make stem of flower. Cut all bumps apart, always cutting a midpoint of narrow part.
2. Hook (turning ½″ under) ends of white bumps to previously made circle. This will give a flower shape with petals of loops of chenille bumps.
3. Place one red bump lengthwise to cover open space at center of each white loop, hooking one end of red bump to outer end of loop and other end to emerald circle.
4. Shape yellow jumbo stem as tight flat coil. Make tight flat coil of gold half-stem and glue to center of yellow coil. Glue yellow coil to flower center.
5. Attach flower, upright, to branch using chenille stem as fastener.

Sunburst Afghan

NBURST AFGHAN
x 72")

ALLENGING: Requires more ex-
ence in knitting. (*Note:* Assem-
g the afghan is quite challenging.)
TERIALS: Fingering-weight yarn
gram ball);—12 balls White, 4
s Red, 2 balls each of Green and
k Blue, 1 ball Yellow; knitting nee-
, 1 pair No. 2, or ANY SIZE NEEDLES
T WILL OBTAIN THE STITCH GAUGE
OW.
JGE: St st - 7 sts = 1"; 9 rows = 1".
ASUREMENTS:
ITER: 42 x 42"
H SIDE STRIP: 5 x 42"
OR BOTTOM STRIP: 15 x 52"
te: See size of each unit on chart;
h square on chart indicates 1 x 1".

DIRECTIONS:
CENTER: Center is formed by many
different units sewn together.
1. UNITS: A—Diamonds (*Make 8
Red, 16 Yellow, 24 Blue, 32 Green, 16
White*): Starting at a side edge, cast on
30 sts. **Row 1:** K 1, *k in front and back of
next st*—**inc made;** k across to within
last 3 sts, *k 2 tog, k 1*—**dec made. Row
2:** Sl 1, p across. **Row 3:** Sl 1, inc in
next st, k across to within last 3 sts, k 2
tog, k 1. **Rows 4 through 29:** Rpt last
2 rows (Rows 2 and 3) alternately 13
times. Bind off, purling sts.
2. UNITS B—Triangles (*Make 24
White*): Starting at one side edge, cast
on 21 sts. **Row 1:** Sl 1, k across to
within last 3 sts, k 2 tog, k 1. **Row 2:** Sl
1, p across to end of row. **Row 3:** Sl 1,
k across to within last 3 sts, k 2 tog, k 1.
Rows 4 through 7: Rpt last 2 rows
(Rows 2 and 3) alternately 2 times.
Row 8: Sl 1, p 2 tog, p across— 16 sts.
Rows 9 through 24: Rpt Rows 1
through 8, twice. **Rows 25 through
29:** Rpt Rows 1 and 2, twice, then
Row 1 once more. **Row 30:** P 3 tog.
Bind off.

3. UNITS C (*Make 8 White*): Starting
at long edge, cast on 30 sts. **Row 1:** Sl
1, k across to within last 3 sts, *k 2 tog*—
dec made at end of row; k 1. **Row2:** Sl
1, p across. **Row 3:** Sl 1, K across to
within last 3 sts, k 2 tog, k 1. **Rows 4
through 7:** Rpt last 2 rows (Rows 2 and
3) alternately, 2 times. **Row 8:** Sl 1, p
2 tog, p across — 25 sts. **Rows 9
through 24:** Rpt first 8 rows (Rows 1
through 8) 2 times—there are 10 sts
less than on row 7. **Rows 25 through
29:** Rpt Rows 1 and 2 twice; then Row
1 once more—12 sts. Bind off.
4. UNITS D (*Make 8 White*): Starting
at long edge, cast on 40 sts. Work same
as for Unit C, having 35 sts on Row 7
and 22 sts on last row. Bind off rem 22
sts.
5. UNITS E (*Make 8 White*): Starting
at long edge, cast on 30 sts. **Row 1:** Sl
first st, *sl, 1, k 1, psso*—**dec made at beg
of row;** k to end of row. **Row 2:** Sl 1, p
across. **Row 3:** Sl first st, sl 1, k 1, psso,
k to end of row. **Rows 4 through 7:**
Rpt last 2 rows (Rows 2 and 3) alternately, 2 times—25 sts. **Row 8:** Sl 1, p
across to within last 3 sts, p 2 tog
through back of sts, p 1. **Rows 9
through 24:** Rpt first 8 rows (Rows 1
through 8) 2 times. **Rows 25 through
29:** Rpt first 2 rows (Rows 1 and 2) 2
times; then Row 1 once more — 12sts.
Bind off.
6. UNITS F (*Make 8 White*): Starting
at long edge, cast on 40 sts. Work same
as for Unit E, having 35 sts on Row 7
and 22 sts on last row. Bind off rem sts.
7. UNITS G—5"-Wide Strip (*Make 2
White*): Starting at one end, cast on 35
sts. Work even in st st (k 1 row, p 1
row) until strip measures 42" long,
ending with a p row. Bind off.
8. UNITS H—15"-Wide Strip (*Make
2 White*): Starting at one narrow edge,
cast on 105 sts. Work even in st st (k 1
row, p 1 row) until strip measures 52"
long, ending with a p row. Bind off.
9. UNITS I—2¼" Strip For Binding
(*Make 2 Red*): Starting at one end, cast
on 16 sts. Work even in st st until strip
measures 52", ending with a p row.
Bind off.

**FIG. 4 SUNBURST AFGHAN
(¼ CENTER SECTION)**

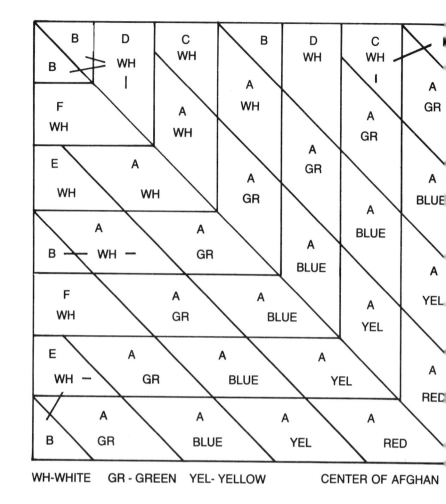

WH-WHITE   GR - GREEN   YEL- YELLOW   CENTER OF AFGHAN

10. UNITS J—2¼" Strip For Binding: Work same as for Unit I until strip measures 72". Bind off.

11. To Assemble Afghan: Pin each unit to padded surface; cover with a damp cloth and stream-press very lightly; allow to dry. FIG. 4 shows ¼ of center of Afghan. Following pattern for placement of units, with a darning needle and matching colors, sew units together, being careful to match corners and adjacent edges exactly. Repeat pattern 3 more times to complete center. Sew one 5"-wide strip to each side edge of center. Sew one 15"-wide strip across entire top edge and one 15"

strip across bottom edge. Sew one edge of a 52"-long Red strip to right side of a short edge of afghan. 1" below outer edge of White strip as in binding; fold Red strip in half to wrong side, over afghan edge and stitch in place. Sew other 52"-long Red strip to opposite edge in same manner. Working as before, bind long edges of afghan (including ends of previous binding) with the 72"-long Red strips.

12. SMALL RED DIAMONDS FOR STARS (*Make 32*): Starting at a side edge, cast on 18 sts. Work same as for Unit A until Row 3 has been completed. **Rows 4 through 17:** Rpt Rows

2 and 3 of Unit A, 7 times. Bind purling sts.

Arrange 8 diamonds as for ce Red areas of center of afghan; pieces together, using Red and a d ing needle. Sew one star over each ner of afghan approximately 4" in f long edge and 8" in from short e

POINSETTIAS: EASY-CARE YEAR-ROUND PLANTS

Poinsettias, native to Mexico, are a natural addition to a South-of-the-Border celebration.

Caring for a poinsettia is easy. As long as the plant is in bloom, keep it in a well-lighted spot (direct sun isn't necessary once it is past blooming), with evenly moist (not soggy) soil. Feed the poinsettia every two weeks, year-round, with a complete fertilizer, such as 10-15-10.

Follow this "holiday" schedule for poinsettia care:

● Cut bracts (the large, brightly colored modified leaves that are often mistakenly called flowers) back on St. Patrick's Day.

● Repot the plant into a larger container on Memorial Day, and put the plant outdoors for the summer.

● Cut stems back by six inches on Independence Day.

● Move the plant back indoors to a sunny window on Labor Day.

● On Columbus Day, start giving plant 14 hours of darkness daily. It is a photoperiodic plant, setting colorful bracts and blooms (the small yellow berries in the center of the bracts) in response to shorter daylight periods. Cover it with a large cardboard box if you don't have a light-tight closet—it must have absolute darkness. Continue the darkness treatment for 8-10 weeks, putting the plant in a window during the day where it will receive four to six hours of direct sun. Water and feed as usual. As soon as the poinsettia comes into bloom, discontinue the closet procedure.

With this care—and a bit of luck—you'll have a colorful plant again for Christmas.

Did You Know . . .

In Mexico, Christmas is often marked by a celebration called a posada, a pilgrimage symbolic of the journey to Bethlehem. On each of the nine nights before Christmas, a couple dressed as Mary and Joseph go from house to house in their village neighborhood. Only at the last house are they and the neighbors parading with them invited in for supper.

THE "POP"ULAR PIÑATA

The piñata is a gaily decorated earthenware pot filled with goodies and suspended from a ceiling or tree. For an American version of a piñata, decorate a strong paper bag with streamers, ribbons and crepe paper, then fill it with confetti, candy canes and small unbreakable toys. Tie the bag at the top and suspend it from the ceiling (or beam or banister). Let children "pop" it with a broom.

South-of-the-Border Christmas Eve Buffet

SOUTH-OF-THE-BORDER CHRISTMAS EVE BUFFET
(FOR 12)

Pernil Asado (Roast Pork) *
Beans with Rice *
Fried Plantains *
*Salsa Cruda (Uncooked
Tomato Relish)* *
Holiday Vegetable Bowl *
Avocado-Orange Salad *
Classic Flan *
*Mexican Pastry Buffet:
Bunuelos* *
Mexican Wedding Cakes *
Molasses Spice Cookies *

*Recipe follows

WORK PLAN

Two months To 1 Week Before
- Prepare MEXICAN WEDDING CAKES and MOLASSES SPICE COOKIES; freeze for up to 2 months or store in an airtight container for up to 1 week.

Two days before
- Buy fresh ham; refrigerate.
- Soak beans for BEANS WITH RICE.

Day before
- Marinate fresh ham for PERNIL ASADO.
- Cook beans for BEANS WITH RICE.
- Prepare SALSA CRUDA.
- Wash lettuce for AVOCADO-ORANGE SALAD: wrap in paper toweling, then in plastic bags, and refrigerate.
- Prepare CLASSIC FLAN; refrigerate.

Early in the day
- Prepare BUNUELOS.
- Slice plantains.
- Cut up vegetables for HOLIDAY VEGETABLE BOWL.
- Marinate oranges for AVOCADO-ORANGE SALAD.

Three hours before
- Roast PERNIL ASADO.

One hour before
- Assemble AVOCADO-ORANGE SALAD; refrigerate until dinnertime.
- Slowly reheat beans.
- Prepare RICE RING; allow to stand 5 minutes before unmolding.
- Fry plantains; keep warm.
- Prepare HOLIDAY VEGETABLE BOWL.
- Unmold CLASSIC FLAN; refrigerate.

Pernil Asado (Roast Pork)

In Cuba, the tradition at Christmas is to barbecue a whole roast pig. In America, a fresh ham is often substituted.

Roast at 325° for 3-3½ hours.
Makes 12 servings.

1	fresh ham, about 10 pounds
2	teaspoons salt
1	teaspoon pepper
1	teaspoon leaf oregano, crumbled
6	cloves garlic, chopped
2	tablespoons olive or vegetable oil
2	tablespoons lemon juice
1	tablespoon white vinegar
	Limes
	Whole pimientos
	Black olives

1. Prick the meat with a 2-tined fork and slash the skin with a sharp knife.
2. Combine the salt, pepper, oregano, garlic, oil, lemon juice and vinegar in a large plastic bag; add the fresh ham. Close the bag securely and turn the meat in the marinade several times; place in a shallow pan and refrigerate for at least 8 hours, or overnight, turning several times.
3. Preheat the oven to slow (325°).
4. Place the ham in a shallow roasting pan; pour the marinade over.
5. Roast in the preheated oven (325°) 3 hours to 3½ hours, or until a meat thermometer reaches 170°. Every half hour while the meat is roasting, remove the fat from the bottom of the pan to a cup. Remove the roast to a platter and let rest for 30 minutes; pour the drippings from the roasting pan into a cup; skim off the fat. Pour liquid into a small saucepan and heat until bubbly hot.
6. Garnish the platter with the lime slices and wedges, pimiento pieces and olives; pour sauce over and slice.

💲 🔢
Beans With Rice

If you can't get black beans, substitute red kidney beans.

Makes 12 servings.

1½ pounds black turtle beans or dried red kidney
    beans
1   bay leaf
½   teaspoon leaf oregano, crumbled
1   large onion, chopped (1 cup)
1   large green pepper, halved, seeded and chopped
3   cloves garlic, minced
3   tablespoons olive or vegetable oil
1   teaspoon salt
1   teaspoon ground cumin
½   teaspoon pepper
2   tablespoons red wine
    Rice Ring (recipe follows)
    Whole pimientos

1. Wash and pick over the beans; place in a large ceramic or glass bowl; add water to cover; top with plastic wrap and let stand several hours, or overnight.
2. Drain the water from the beans and place the beans in a large kettle; cover with cold water; add the bay leaf and oregano.
3. Bring the water to boiling; lower heat; cover. Simmer for 2 hours, or until the beans are tender.
4. Sauté the onion, green pepper and garlic in the oil in a medium skillet, until soft. Stir this mixture into the beans with the salt, cumin, pepper and red wine. Simmer for 5 minutes, or until the beans are tender.
5. To serve: Spoon part of the beans into the center of the RING RING and place the remaining beans in a heated serving dish. Garnish the RICE RING with strips of pimiento.

Tip: The beans can be cooked a day ahead. Cool, then refrigerate. At serving time, heat slowly, just until bubbly.

💲
Rice Ring

Pack hot rice into a ring mold, which then becomes the container for the black beans.

Makes 12 servings.

2¼ cups uncooked long-grain rice
1   large onion, chopped (1 cup)

3   cloves garlic, minced
¼   cup (½ stick) butter or margarine
¼   cup olive or vegetable oil
5   cups chicken broth
    Pinch sugar

1. Rinse the rice in a strainer under cold running water; drain well.
2. Sauté the onion and garlic in the butter or margarine and oil in a large skillet until soft; add the rice and sauté slightly.
3. Add the chicken broth and sugar to the rice in the skillet; bring to boiling; lower heat; cover the skillet; simmer for 20 minutes, or until the liquid is absorbed and the rice is tender.
4. Pack the rice into a well-oiled 8- or 9-cup ring mold; cover with aluminum foil and allow to stand for 5 minutes. Shake mold gently and invert onto the heated platter. Fill the center with part of the hot beans.

💲
Fried Plantains

Plantains, members of the banana family, are a delightful staple of Caribbean cuisine.

Makes 12 servings.

6   hard, green plantains (about 4½ pounds)
    Vegetable oil
    Garlic salt

1. Peel the plantains with a sharp paring knife; cut into ¼-inch-thick slices.
2. Pour the oil to a depth of 1 inch in an electric frypan; heat to 250°.
3. Fry the plantain slices in batches, 2 minutes per side, or until golden but still soft; remove from the oil with a slotted spoon.
4. Drain the slices on paper towels; let cool for 1 or 2 minutes; flatten with the bottom of a glass.
5. Increase the temperature of the oil in the frypan to 400°; refry the plantain slices for 1 minute, or until they are crisp; remove from the oil with a slotted spoon; place on a paper towel-lined cookie sheet; sprinkle with the garlic salt and keep warm until ready to serve.

💲 🔊 🌊

Salsa Cruda (Uncooked Tomato Relish)

Sweet and hot peppers plus tomatoes and onions make a classic Latin relish that's color-coordinated with the holiday season.

Makes two cups.

2   medium-size ripe tomatoes
1   small red pepper
1   small green pepper
1/2 cup sliced green onion
1   canned serrano chile, seeded and chopped
     OR:
1   canned jalapeño chile, seeded and chopped
1   tablespoon chopped fresh coriander (optional)
     Dash pepper
     Dash sugar

1. Peel and seed the tomatoes; chop finely and place in a medium-size glass or ceramic bowl.
2. Halve, seed and chop the red and green peppers and add to the bowl with the green onion, serrano or jalapeño chile, coriander, if used, salt, pepper and sugar; stir to blend well. Cover the bowl with plastic wrap.
3. Refrigerate for at least 2 hours, or overnight. Spoon into a serving dish.

🌊

Holiday Vegetable Bowl

Pieces of corn on the cob plus zucchini, yellow squash and tomatoes create a colorful vegetable dish.

Makes 12 servings.

1   large onion, chopped (1 cup)
3   cloves garlic, minced
4 1/2 tablespoons olive or vegetable oil
6   medium zucchini, trimmed and sliced
6   medium yellow squash, trimmed and sliced
6   large ears corn, shucked and cut into 2-inch pieces
1   can (1 pound, 12 ounces) whole tomatoes
2   teaspoons salt
1 1/2 teaspoons leaf basil, crumbled
1/2 teaspoon leaf oregano, crumbled
1/2 teaspoon pepper

1. Sauté the onion and garlic in the oil in a large kettle until tender; add the zucchini, yellow squash and corn; toss to coat with oil.
2. Drain the liquid from the tomatoes into the kettle and add salt, basil, oregano and pepper; bring to boiling; lower heat; cover the kettle; simmer for 10

> ### "HOT TIP" TOMATOES
>
> ● *To peel tomatoes, plunge them, one at a time, into boiling water for 1 minute. Then, immediately plunge them into ice and water. Peel off skin with a sharp paring knife.*
> ● *To seed tomatoes, cut peeled tomatoes in half, crosswise, and squeeze gently to extract seeds.*

minutes, or until the vegetables are crisply tender. Add the tomatoes and cook for 5 minutes longer, or until tomatoes are heated through. Spoon into a heated vegetable dish.

Avocado-Orange Salad

Two tropical fruits—the avocado and orange—give this salad a unique, refreshing flavor. The dish is enhanced by the mild tang of red onion slices.

Makes 12 servings.

3   large ripe avocados
3/4 cup peanut or vegetable oil
1/3 cup cider vinegar
1   teaspoon salt
1/2 teaspoon pepper
6   small California oranges
1   large red onion
1   large head leaf or Boston lettuce, washed and dried

1. Halve and seed the avocados; peel and cut into lengthwise slices; arrange in a single layer in a glass utility dish.
2. Combine the oil, vinegar, salt and pepper in a 1-cup jar with a screw top; shake to blend. Drizzle part over the avocado slices and baste to coat all the slices; cover with plastic wrap and refrigerate for at least 1 hour to blend flavors.
3. Pare the oranges and cut into thin slices; slice the red onion.
4. Line a large platter with the leaf or Boston lettuce leaves and arrange the onion and orange slices in a pretty pattern over the lettuce. Cover with plastic wrap and refrigerate.
5. At serving time: Arrange the avocado slices on the prepared salad and pass the remaining dressing in a serving dish.

Classic Flan

A delicate blending of eggs and milk, crowned with caramelized sugar.

Bake at 325° for 1 hour.
Makes 12 small servings.

1   envelope unflavored gelatin
3¾ cups cold milk
1   two-inch piece stick cinnamon
1   piece lemon rind
4   eggs
¾   cup sugar
1   teaspoon vanilla
     Dash salt

1. Preheat the oven to slow (325°).
2. Sprinkle the gelatin over the cold milk in a medium-size saucepan; stir in the cinnamon and lemon rind. Heat slowly until the milk is hot, but not boiling. Let cool for 5 minutes; remove the cinnamon stick and lemon rind.
3. Beat the eggs with a wire whisk until foamy in a large bowl; beat in ¼ cup of the sugar until fluffy. Stir in the milk until well blended.
4. Sprinkle the remaining ½ cup sugar in the bottom of a large heavy skillet. Place over medium heat, shaking pan often, until the sugar melts and turns golden. Immediately pour the caramel into the bottom of a 4-cup soufflé dish or straight-sided baking dish.
5. Pour the custard mixture into the prepared dish. Center the dish in a larger baking dish and place on the center shelf of the oven; add boiling water to half the depth of the baking dish.
6. Bake in the preheated oven (325°) for 1 hour, or just until the center sets; cool in the baking dish on a wire rack for 1 hour; cover with plastic wrap; refrigerate overnight.
7. To serve: Loosen the custard around the edge of the dish with a small, sharp knife; dip the dish into a bowl of hot water for 30 seconds. Invert onto a serving dish with a raised edge. Refrigerate until serving time.

Bunuelos

In Mexico, these fried pastries are often broken up into a bowl, topped with syrup and eaten with a spoon.

Makes 2 to 4 dozen.

4   cups unsifted all-purpose flour
1   tablespoon sugar
1   teaspoon baking powder
1   teaspoon salt
4   eggs, lightly beaten
1   cup milk
¼   cup (½ stick) butter or margarine, melted
½   cup water (approximately)
     Vegetable shortening
     Vegetable oil for deep frying
     Cinnamon Sugar (recipe follows)
     OR: Brown Sugar Syrup (recipe follows)

1. Sift the flour, sugar, baking powder and salt together into a large bowl. Add the eggs, then the milk and melted butter or margarine. Beat the mixture well, adding as much water as needed to make a dough that can be easily handled without being sticky.
2. Knead the dough until smooth. Divide it into walnut-size pieces (or smaller, if you prefer); roll into balls, rubbing each ball with the shortening to prevent them from sticking. Cover the ball with a cloth; let stand for 20 minutes.
3. Flour a pastry board lightly; flatten each ball into a round, spreading with your hand to make them very thin. Let stand for 5 minutes.
4. Fry the rounds, a few at a time, in deep hot vegetable oil (375°) until golden. Drain on paper towels. Serve whole, sprinkled with the CINNAMON SUGAR, or break up and serve with the BROWN SUGAR SYRUP.

Cinnamon Sugar: Makes 1 cup. Combine 1 cup granulated sugar with 1 to 2 teaspoons ground cinnamon in a small bowl.

Brown Sugar Syrup: Makes enough for 1 batch of BUNUELOS. Combine 1½ cups firmly packed light brown sugar, 1 cup water and 1 cinnamon stick in a medium saucepan. Simmer over very low heat for 30 minutes, stirring occasionally.

Mexican Pastry Buffet

Mexican Wedding Cakes

For a festive touch, place these in tiny paper cups to serve at Christmas.

Bake at 350° for 30 minutes.
Makes 2 dozen.

2 cups unsifted all-purpose flour
1 cup pecans, finely chopped
½ cup sifted 10X (confectioners' powdered) sugar
   Pinch of salt
1 cup (2 sticks) unsalted butter, softened
1 teaspoon vanilla
   10X (confectioner's powdered) sugar

1. Preheat the oven to moderate (350°).
2. Combine the flour, nuts, sugar and salt in a medium-size bowl. Stir in the vanilla. Cut in the butter with a pastry blender; stir until mixture forms a ball.
3. Divide the dough into 24 even pieces; gently shape into balls between hands. Place on an ungreased cookie sheet.
4. Bake in the preheated moderate oven (350°) 30 minutes, or until the cookies are delicately browned. Remove from cookie sheets to wire racks; cool slightly. Dust thickly with the 10X sugar.

Tip: Butter really does give better flavor to these cookies. However, if you choose to use margarine, omit the pinch of salt.

Molasses Spice Cookies

Spice cookies with a definitive molasses flavor.

Bake at 350° for 12 to 13 minutes.
Makes about 3 dozen.

2¼ cups unsifted all-purpose flour
2 teaspoons baking soda
2 teaspoons ground ginger
1 teaspoon ground cinnamon
¼ teaspoon ground cloves
¼ teaspoon salt
½ cup (1 stick) butter or margarine
½ cup firmly packed light brown sugar
1 egg
½ cup molasses

⅓ cup strong, hot coffee
   Grated rind of ½ orange
   Grated rind of ½ lemon
1 tablespoon whole anise seed, crushed
1 teaspoon coriander seeds, crushed
   Snowy Icing (recipe follows)
   Pecan halves

1. Preheat the oven to moderate (350°).
2. Sift together the flour, baking soda, ginger, cinnamon, cloves and salt.
3. Beat the butter or margaine until light and fluffy in a large bowl with an electric mixer at high speed; gradually beat in the sugar, then the egg. Gradually beat in the molasses, scraping the bowl with a rubber spatula. Lower mixer speed to slow.
4. Gradually beat in half of the sifted ingredients, continuing to scrape the bowl and beating only until mixed. Beat in the coffee, then the remaining sifted ingredients, beating only until smooth. Stir in the grated orange and lemon rinds, the anise seed and the coriander.
5. Place heaping teaspoonfuls of the dough, 2 inches apart, on two aluminum foil-covered cookie sheets.
6. Bake on both racks of the preheated moderate oven (350°), reversing the position once, for 12 to 13 minutes, or until the tops spring back when lightly pressed with fingertips. Remove from the cookie sheets to wire racks with a wide metal spatula. Cool completely.
7. Place a teaspoonful of the SNOWY ICING on top of each cookie, spread it with the back of a spoon, leaving a ½- to ¾-inch margin un-iced. Place a pecan half on top of each cookie. Let the icing set before storing the cookies in an airtight container.

Snowy Icing: Makes enough for 3 dozen cookies. Beat together 3 cups sifted 10X (confectioners' powdered) sugar, 5 tablespoons milk and 2 teaspoons vanilla until smooth in a small bowl, using a rubber spatula. Add more sugar or milk, if necessary, to make icing of soft spreading consistency.

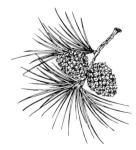

Wheat Tree; Braided Wheat Wreath

Do you yearn for a simpler time, when Christmas wasn't so commercial? This year, treat yourself to an old-fashioned yule: Start with decorations made from natural materials, then enjoy a dinner that's as hearty as it is soul-satisfying.

HOMESPUN HOLIDAY

Pine Cone Wreath

NATURAL TOUCHES:

● Arrange oranges and kumquats with fresh holly leaves in a bowl for a cheery holiday centerpiece.
● For a simple yet lovely arrangement, heap pine cones on a brass scale; hide the bracket with running cedar.
● A natural setting for punch: Surround a punchbowl or large porcelain bowl with a "wreath" of fresh fruit, pine cones, seeds and berries on a bed of large, glossy leaves.

TABLE TREE

EASY: Achievable by anyone.

DIRECTIONS:
Cut a block of Oasis® into a cone shape. Soak Oasis in water, then insert cuttings of boxwood into it to form the tree. *Alternate method:* Using a Styrofoam® cone as a base, wrap the cone with moistened sphagnum moss. To keep the moss in place, either wrap chicken wire around it, or tie florist's wire around cone at 2-3″ intervals. Then insert boxwood into cone. Decorate with BRAIDED WHEAT WREATHS (*below*).
Note: Place tree on water-resistant base.

BRAIDED WHEAT WREATHS

EASY: Achievable by anyone.
MATERIALS: Cleaned wheat; wire.

DIRECTIONS:
Soak wheat overnight. While it is still damp, pick up a bundle (1 or 2 inches thick) of straight strands and twist wire around one end. Divide into three parts and braid tightly, shaping a curve as you work. About 2 inches from the ends, add a similar bundle (overlapping), and continue braiding. When the circle is about 6″ in diameter, cross ends and wire them together. Air dry.

PINE CONE WREATH

EASY: Achievable by anyone.
MATERIALS: 15x15″ wire star (*see Materials Shopping Guide, page 272*); assorted pine cones, such as Norway Spruce, White or Red Spruce, Beechnut pods, Pinyon Pine or any other cones large and small; 1 large pine cone cut in half; 18″ square of brown fabric; glue gun; clear plastic spray.

DIRECTIONS:
1. Cover wire star with brown fabric, turning edges of fabric to back of frame and gluing edges.
2. Select 10 long pine cones equal in length such as Norway Spruce. Glue each pine cone to the side of each point on the star. Fill in star points with small thin pine cones.
3. Cut one large pine cone in half with heavy pruning shears. Turn bottom side of cone up and glue to center of star. Fill in around center cone with small cones. Add small decorative round cones on end of each star point.
4. Spray star with clear plastic to seal and add shine.

PINE CONE POINTERS

● *For a neat look, select pine cones that are uniform in size. For a more natural, free form effect, choose a variety of sizes and shapes.*
● *Before using pine cones for your wreaths or any other Christmas decorations, place them in a warm oven for about an hour. They will open up very nicely.*

PATCHWORK WALL HANGING (48½ x53″)

AVERAGE: For those with some [ex]perience in quilting.
NOTE: The quilt illustrated is basic[al]ly one color with small amounts of o[th]er colors introduced in various part[s] the design. Within your chosen co[lor] family you will need fabrics in to[ne] ranging from dark through medi[um] dark, medium light to light. Natu[ral] fiber material or blends, all solid co[lor] pieces, all patterned pieces or a m[ix]ture of solids and patterns may be us[ed]. "A" on the pattern represents the d[eep] value of the basic color. White or o[ff] white and black or off-black can [be] used for accents. It will be helpful[to] make a paper pattern and plan co[lor] placement before cutting your mate[ri]als. The pattern that is given illustra[tes] one-fourth of the quilt. The f[our] blocks sewn together will form the c[en]ter "medallion" or design.
MATERIALS: One yd. fabric for b[or]ders and bias tape to bind edges, ¼ [yd.] of other fabrics; 2 yds. fabric to co[ver] back of quilt (Choose a color to harm[o]nize with those on front, perhaps [the] same as one of the minor ones in [the] pattern); paper; pencil; ruler; color[ed] pencils or crayons; quilt batting; sc[is]sors; pins; needle; thimble; quilt[ing] thread; iron; sewing machine (this [is] optional).

tchwork Wall Hanging

FIG. 5 PATCHWORK WALLHANGING (¼ design)
1 SQ. = 2″

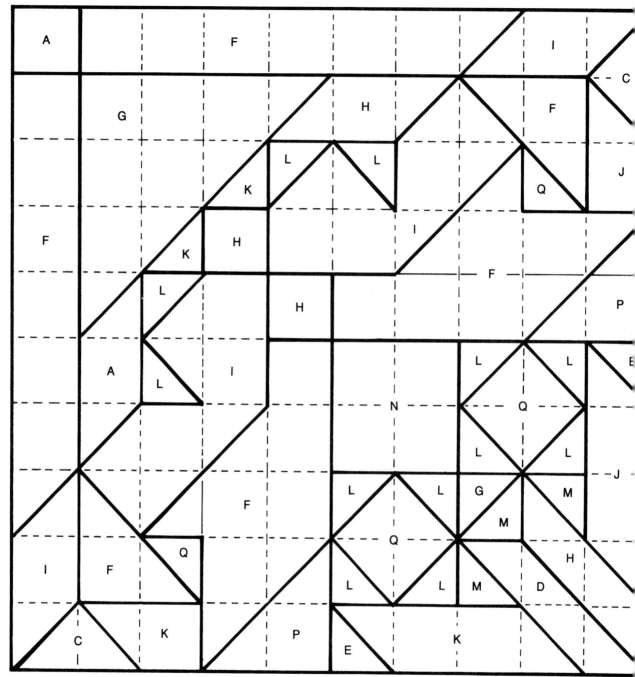

RECTIONS:

Prewash all fabrics to remove siz-
, assure color fastness and to pre-
ink. Iron.

Enlarge the quarter pattern in FIG.
 following the directions on page
.

Mark and cut fabric carefully, re-
mbering to allow ¼″ extra all
und for seams. Stitch the pieces to-
her to make four identical blocks
-20″ square. Sew these blocks to-
her to form central design. Add bor-
s if desired. Three border strips are
 the sides and five are on the top and
ttom of the hanging shown.

When top is finished, lay it right
e down on a large flat surface, cover
h quilt batting and fabric chosen for
ck. Baste the three layers together in
rid pattern and then either quilt or
 the layers together.

Bind the edges with bias strips to
ish. Make bias strips by folding a
are of fabric in half diagonally.
easure 1⅝″ strips, cut carefully and
 strips together. Place along edge
 front side of quilt, right sides to-
her, and stitch ⅛″ from edge.

Turn to back, turn under ⅛″ seam
d hand-stitch to back.

For hanging, sew a strip of fabric 1″
de to top back to make a sleeve for
wel or rod.

NATURAL MATERIALS: KEEP THEM LOOKING FRESH FOR THE HOLIDAYS

Woody greens Hammer stems to crush bark and fibers, then place stems in water immediately. In a bucket, combine 2½ gallons luke-warm water with either 1 (liter) bot-tle lemon-lime soft drink or ½ cup sugar or 1 cup corn syrup; mix well. Place stems in bucket until ready to use.

Magnolias Soak cut stems in 2 gal-lons hot water mixed with 3 table-spoons laundry bleach until ready to use. To shine leaves, rub on vegeta-ble oil with a soft cloth. *Note:* Keep fresh indoor arrangements, such as woody greens and magnolias, in a cool place and far away from radia-tors, fireplaces, etc.

Christmas trees As soon as you get the tree home, remove ½ inch of the trunk and place the tree in wa-ter. Keep the tree-stand container filled with water until you're ready to discard the tree.

Roping Keep in a cool place. Spray roping and other cut greens with water every other day; spray box-wood roping with "Wilt Proof."

Evergreens Spray with acrylic floor wax—this traps moisture inside greens. *Note:* Do not get wax on furniture or other wood surfaces.

Leafy Greens To add a glossy fin-ish, spray or rub on "Green Glow," "Plant Shine" or "Leaf Polish."

Fruits Purchase as green and firm as possible, and refrigerate immediate-ly. *To prepare for use:* ● Whole fruit (except citrus). Dip in bowl of "Klear." Next, dry fruit: Push wire through fruit *(see Figs. 7a-c on page 171)* and suspend from hanger or broom handle. ● Halve fruit. Dip cut side into melted paraffin. Let dry; repeat dipping process and dry. *To mount a whole or half pineapple on a wreath or Styrofoam® plaque:* Wrap a "noose" of heavy-gauge wire around the pineapple, just below its leaves. Push wire through plaque and around floral picks or tooth-picks (or twist around back of wreath). Twist ends of wire up and around hanger at top back *(see Fig. 7d).*

Nuts and cones Dip nuts in "Klear." Let dry, then drill a small hole approximately ½ inch into ends of nuts or backs of cones. In-sert heavy floral wire, approximate-ly the same diameter as the hole, and apply drop of glue with hot-glue gun at opening. Let dry thoroughly. Attach wire end to the wreath or decoration.

Note: Nuts, cones and dried fruits can be reused if you keep them in airtight plastic bags containing moth flakes. Store in a cool, dry place.

Balsa Wood Angel

℈LSA WOOD ANGEL

⸱Y: Achievable by anyone.
⸱TERIALS: Balsa wood 4x5x1/32″
⸱k; craft knife; fine sandpaper and
⸱ry board; cord to hang; heavy
⸱e paper.

⸱RECTIONS:

⸱n folded tracing paper, trace angel
⸱-pattern in FIG. 6, including inner
⸱nings. Cut out shape, then inner
⸱ning. Open paper for full 4x4¼″
⸱ern.
⸱race the shape and openings on
⸱a; cut out with a craft knife. Make a
⸱ cut first, then a second pass to
⸱d splintering. Sand edges; use an
⸱ry board on cutout edges. Add
⸱ger cord.

**FIG. 6
HALF PATTERN
ACTUAL SIZE**

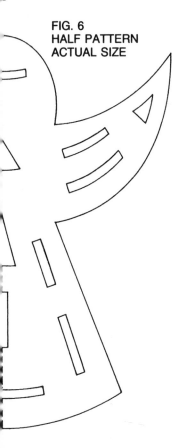

GENERAL DIRECTIONS FOR PREPARING FRUIT FOR HANGING DECORATIONS

DIRECTIONS: Medium-Size Fruit (*about the size of an apple*) should be wired to a floral pick:

1. Cut two 5″-long pieces of No. 22 or No. 24 gauge wire.
2. Insert one wire through apple near bottom end (*see* FIG. 7a). At the same level, insert the second wire, at right angles to the first (*see* FIG. 7b).
3. Twist the wires around a floral pick; don't puncture the fruit with the pick (*see* FIG. 7c).

FIG. 7 TO WIRE FRUIT

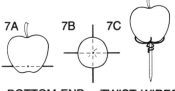

7A   7B   7C

BOTTOM END   TWIST WIRES AROUND FLORAL PICK

Smaller Fruit (*like a crab apple*) would need only one wire.
Very Small Fruit (*like cranberries*) need a wire stem:
1. At one end of a piece of green floral wire, bend a U-shaped "shepherd's crook." Push its straight end through a cranberry, so the "crook" goes into the berry top.
2. To make a string of berries, wire the first berry (*see* Step 2, above), push the wire through the rest of the berries and twist the wire against the last berry to serve as a knot.

A Hearty Buffet

A HEARTY BUFFET
(FOR 12)

Cream of Carrot Soup*
Crumb-Topped Muffins*
Beef Burgundy*
with Parsley Noodles*
Glazed Chicken Breasts*
with Wild Rice Pilaf*
Curried Vegetables*
White Burgundy
Mountain Rhine
Red Burgundy   Pouilly-Fuissé
Gorgonzola Salad*
Garlic Bread
Cheese Board* with Crackers
Baked Fruit Salad*
Mocha Silk Pie* OR:
Crunchy Walnut Pie*
Brandy Demitasse
Coffee Liqueur

*Recipe follows

WORK PLAN

Up to two months ahead
- Prepare CRUMB-TOPPED MUFFINS; freeze.

Day before
- Prepare CREAM OF CARROT SOUP; chill.
- Prepare BEEF BURGUNDY; chill.
- Wash lettuce and make ITALIAN DRESSING for GORGONZOLA SALAD; refrigerate.
- Prepare CRUNCHY WALNUT PIE.

Early in the day
- Prepare GLAZED CHICKEN BREASTS; chill.
- Cut up vegetables for CURRIED VEGETABLES.

Three hours ahead
- Thaw CRUMB-TOPPED MUFFINS.
- Prepare BAKED FRUIT SALAD, but do not bake it yet.

1½ hours ahead
- Make WILD RICE PILAF.

One hour ahead
- Arrange CHEESE BOARD.
- Heat BAKED FRUIT SALAD.
- Reheat BEEF BURGUNDY, GLAZED CHICKEN BREASTS and CREAM OF CARROT SOUP.
- Warm CRUMB-TOPPED MUFFINS.
- Prepare CURRIED VEGETABLES.
- Arrange GORGONZOLA SALAD; chill.
- Garnish MOCHA SILK PIE; refrigerate.
- Make PARSLEY NOODLES.
- Prepare DEMITASSE; keep warm in a thermos.

Cream Of Carrot Soup

Warm winter-chilled guests with a delicate soup that's more flavorful if made ahead and reheated.

Makes 12 servings.

10	cups water
10	envelopes or teaspoons instant chicken broth
1	package (1 pound) carrots, pared and thinly sliced
½	cup (1 stick) butter or margarine
1	large onion, chopped (1 cup)
2	cups sliced celery
1	cup unsifted all-purpose flour
4	egg yolks
4	cups light cream
¼	teaspoon white pepper
¼	teaspoon ground mace
	Popcorn

1. Combine the water and instant broth in a large kettle and bring to boiling; add the carrots. Simmer for 15 minutes, or until the carrots are tender when pierced with a two-tined fork.
2. Melt the butter or margarine in a large skillet; sauté onion until soft; stir in the celery and cook for 5 minutes; sprinkle flour over. Cook, stirring constantly, until the flour bubbles and cooks for 3 minutes.
3. Ladle about 4 cups of the chicken broth into the skillet. Cook, stirring constantly, until the mixture thickens and bubbles for 3 minutes.
4. Pour the onion sauce into the kettle and stir to blend well. Lower the heat and simmer, stirring often, for 30 minutes. Remove the kettle from heat and cool.
5. Process the mixture, 3 cups at a time, in the container of an electric blender or food processor on high speed until smooth. Pour into a very large ceramic bowl; cover with plastic wrap. Chill until party time.
6. Reheat the soup mixture just to boiling in a large kettle. Beat the egg yolks in a medium-size bowl with a wire whip; blend in the light cream, pepper and ground mace until smooth.
7. Ladle about 3 cups of the hot liquid into the bowl; return to the kettle and heat slowly but *do not allow soup to boil.* Float the popcorn on top.

💲 📧

Crumb-Topped Muffins

These pumpkin muffins have an almond and brown sugar crown.

Bake at 400° for 20 minutes.
Makes 1 dozen muffins.

Crumb topping
1/3 cup all-purpose flour
1/4 cup diced almonds, toasted
3 tablespoons brown sugar
2 tablespoons melted butter or margarine
1/4 teaspoon almond extract

Muffins
2 cups unsifted all-purpose flour
1/3 cup sugar
1 1/2 teaspoons baking powder
1 teaspoon salt
1/2 teaspoon pumpkin pie spice
1/3 cup vegetable shortening
1 cup pumpkin (from a 1-pound can)
1/2 cup milk
1 egg
1/2 cup diced almonds, toasted

1. Preheat the oven to hot (400°).
2. Make the topping: Combine the flour, almonds and brown sugar in a small bowl; toss with a fork until well blended. Stir in the melted butter or margarine and the almond extract to make a crumbly mixture.
3. Make the muffins: Sift the flour, sugar, baking powder, salt and pumpkin pie spice into a large bowl.
4. Cut in the shortening with a pastry blender to make a crumbly mixture.
5. Add the pumpkin, milk, egg and almonds and stir 20 times with a wooden spoon, or just until blended.
6. Divide the batter among 12 well-greased large muffin-cups; sprinkle with the crumb mixture topping.
7. Bake in the preheated hot oven (400°) for 20 minutes, or until the topping is golden. Cool in the muffin-cups on a wire rack for 5 minutes; carefully loosen muffins around the edges with a sharp knife. Serve warm or cool completely. Place on a cookie sheet and freeze, just until firm. Transfer to a large plastic freezer container with tight-fitting lid; label, date and freeze.
8. At party time: Remove the muffins from the freezer container and thaw several hours ahead. Arrange on a cookie sheet. Warm in a preheated moderate oven (350°) for 10 minutes, or until heated through.

THE PERFECT MUFFIN

- *Always sift the dry ingredients together.*
- *Cool the melted shortening slightly before you use it, to prevent cooking the egg when you mix the batter together.*
- *Stir liquid into the dry ingredients just until mixed. (Batter should be lumpy.) Overmixing causes tough, coarse-textured results.*
- *Fill greased muffin-pan cups only two-thirds full.*
- *An ice cream scoop is ideal for evenly dividing the muffin batter into muffin-pan cups.*

💲 🎴

Beef Burgundy

Hearty and delicious, this dish is even better reheated!

Bake at 325° for 1½ hours.
Makes 12 servings.

½   pound thickly sliced bacon
3   pounds lean boneless beef chuck, cubed
1   large onion, chopped (1½ cups)
1½ cups finely chopped carrot
1½ cups finely chopped celery
3   cloves garlic, minced
2   teaspoons salt
1½ teaspoons leaf thyme, crumbled
1   bay leaf
½   teaspoon pepper
3   cups dry red wine
⅓   cup unsifted all-purpose flour
1½ pounds mushrooms
1   bunch carrots
⅓   cup butter or margarine
2   envelopes or teaspoons instant chicken broth
¾   cup water
    Parsley Noodles (recipe follows)

1. Preheat the oven to slow (325°).
2. Cut the bacon into 1-inch pieces; place in a saucepan; cover with water. Bring to boiling; lower heat; simmer for 10 minutes. Dry the bacon on paper towels. Fry until crisp in a large flameproof casserole or kettle. Remove to paper towels and reserve; pour off all but 2 tablespoons of the fat into a cup.
3. Brown the beef, a few pieces at a time, in a casserole or kettle; remove and reserve. Sauté the onion, chopped carrot, celery and garlic in the pan drippings, adding more bacon fat, if needed, until soft; stir in the salt, thyme, bay leaf and pepper; return the beef to the casserole; add the wine; bring slowly to boiling; cover. (If using a kettle, spoon the mixture into a large casserole; cover.)
4. Bake in the preheated slow oven (325°) for 1½ hours or until the beef is very tender; remove the bay leaf. Remove the beef from the liquid with a slotted spoon; keep warm.
5. Pour half of the liquid into the container of an electric blender or food processor; add half of the flour; cover the container; process at high speed for 1 minute, or until smooth. Process the remaining liquid and flour. Return all the liquid to the flameproof casserole or a large saucepan; bring to boiling. Cook, stirring constantly, until the sauce thickens and bubbles for 3 minutes longer.
6. While the beef cooks, wipe the mushrooms with a damp paper towel; quarter the mushrooms and cut the carrots into 5-inch pieces.
7. Sauté the mushrooms in the butter or margarine in a large skillet; remove; sauté the carrots for 5 minutes; add the instant chicken broth and water to the skillet; cover and simmer for 15 minutes, or until the carrots are almost tender; push to one side. Return the mushrooms to the skillet. Cover; simmer for 5 minutes, or until the vegetables are just tender.
8. Return the beef and sauce to the casserole. Surround with the vegetables and the cooking liquid; sprinkle the beef with the cooked bacon. Serve with PARSLEY NOODLES.

Tip: The finished dish can be held in a preheated, very slow oven (275°) for 1 hour before serving. Or, cook the beef and make the sauce the day before. Cool, then cover and refrigerate. One hour before serving, place the casserole in the oven. Set the oven to moderate (350°) and bake for 1 hour, or until bubbly-hot, while preparing the vegetables. Serve with the PARSLEY NOODLES.

💲

Parsley Noodles

A colorful, as well as flavorful, addition to a buffet.

Makes 12 servings.

1½ packages (1½ pounds total) medium noodles or fettuccine
⅓   cup butter or margarine
⅓   cup chopped parsley
¾   teaspoon freshly ground pepper

1. Cook the noodles or fettuccine in boiling salted water in a large kettle, following the label directions; drain and return to the kettle.
2. Add the butter or margarine, cut into pieces, the chopped parsley and pepper. Toss gently with a long wooden spoon until well blended. Keep warm over *very low heat*; spoon into a heated serving bowl just before serving.

§

Glazed Chicken Breasts

Apricot preserves make a tangy topping for oven-baked chicken.

Bake at 350° for 1 hour.
Makes 12 servings.

1/3 cup butter or margarine
1   tablespoon garlic salt
1/2 teaspoon seasoned pepper
6   whole chicken breasts, split (about 12 ounces
     each)
1 1/4 cup apricot preserves
     Wild Rice Pilaf (recipe follows)
     Canned mandarin orange sections

1. Preheat the oven to moderate (350°).
2. Melt the butter or margarine with the garlic salt
   and pepper in a large roasting pan in the oven
   while the oven preheats.
3. Coat the chicken breasts with the melted butter
   and arrange, skin-side up, in the pan.
4. Bake in the preheated moderate oven (350°) for 45
   minutes, basting several times with pan drippings.
   Spoon the apricot preserves over the chicken
   breasts.
5. Bake for 15 minutes longer, or until well glazed.
   Arrange over the WILD RICE PILAF on a heated
   serving platter. Garnish with the mandarin orange
   sections.

Tip: This recipe can be prepared ahead of time. Cool,
then cover the pan with plastic wrap and refrigerate.
At party time, remove plastic and heat in a preheated
moderate oven (350°) for 30 minutes, or until hot.

Wild Rice Pilaf

*Add various herbs for a different flavor: Rosemary, thyme and dill
are all good choices.*

Bake at 350° for 1 hour.
Makes 12 servings.

3   packages (6 ounces each) long grain and wild
     rice mix
1/2 cup (1 stick) butter or margarine
1   large onion, chopped (1 cup)
3 3/4 cups boiling water
1   bunch green onions, chopped
1/4 cup chopped parsley

1. Preheat the oven to moderate (350°).
2. Sauté the rice mix in the butter or margarine in a

large skillet until the white rice turns a light
brown; push to one side; add the onion and sauté
until soft.
3. Stir the seasoning mix packet into boiling water.
   Bring to boiling. Pour into a large casserole; cover.
4. Bake in the preheated moderate oven (350°) for 1
   hour, or until the liquid is absorbed and the rice is
   tender. Stir in the chopped green onions and
   chopped parsley.

§ ▓

Curried Vegetables

*A rainbow of vegetables adds splash, as well as flavor,
to a party buffet.*

Makes 12 servings.

1   medium eggplant
1   bunch broccoli
2   large green peppers
2   large zucchini
2   large yellow squash
3/4 pound mushrooms
1/3 cup vegetable oil
1   large onion, chopped (1 1/2 cups)
3   cloves garlic, minced
1   to 3 teaspoons curry powder
1/3 cup chicken broth
1   tablespoon salt
1/2 teaspoon seasoned pepper

1. Trim the eggplant; cut into 1-inch slices and cube;
   wash and trim the broccoli and cut into small
   flowerets; halve, seed and dice the green peppers;
   trim and slice the zucchini and the yellow squash;
   wipe and slice the mushrooms.
2. Heat the oil in a large kettle; sauté the onion and
   garlic until soft; stir in the curry powder and cook,
   stirring constantly for 2 minutes.
3. Add the prepared vegetables and toss until well
   coated with the curry butter; cook, stirring often,
   for 5 minutes.
4. Add the chicken broth, salt and pepper; bring to
   boiling; lower the heat; cover the kettle.
5. Cook for 5 minutes, or until the vegetables are
   crisply tender. Remove with a slotted spoon to a
   heated serving bowl.

Tip: All the vegetables can be prepared ahead of time
and refrigerated in a plastic bag; do not cook them
until serving time if you want to have crisply cooked
vegetables.

Gorgonzola Salad

Gorgonzola cheese is the Italian equivalent of Roquefort or blue cheese. Its extra-pungent flavor adds punch to a buffet menu with many flavors.

Makes 12 servings.

1   **head romaine**
1   **head leaf lettuce**
1   **head iceberg lettuce**
1   **head Boston lettuce**
4   **large ripe tomatoes, cored and cut into wedges**
1   **cup crumbled Gorgonzola cheese**
     Salt and freshly ground pepper
     Italian Dressing (recipe follows)

1. Wash the romaine, leaf, iceberg and Boston lettuces; drain well on paper toweling and break into bite-size pieces; place in a large plastic bag and tie securely; chill.
2. Arrange the salad greens in one or two large salad bowls and top with the tomato wedges and the crumbled cheese. Season with salt and freshly ground pepper. Serve with the ITALIAN DRESSING.

Italian Dressing: Makes 2 cups. Combine ⅔ cup olive oil, ⅔ cup vegetable oil, ⅔ cup red wine vinegar, 2 teaspoons salt, ¼ teaspoon freshly ground pepper and 1 bay leaf in a 2-cup jar with a screw top. Shake and chill until serving time.

Cheese Board

A well-selected platter of cheeses can make the perfect start, or ending, to a memorable party meal.

Makes 12 servings.

1   **round (8 ounces) Bonbel cheese**
1   **wedge (½ pound) Edam cheese**

1   **wedge (½ pound) Vermont Cheddar cheese**
1   **wedge (¼ pound) Roquefort or blue cheese**
1   **wedge (¼ pound) Camembert cheese**
1   **package (6 ounces) water crackers**
1   **package (6 ounces) sesame-seed wafers**

1. Remove the cheeses from their wrappings and let stand at room temperature for 1 hour before serving.
2. Arrange the cheeses and the crackers on one large or two smaller cheese trays. Serve with several sharp knives.

Tip: As soon as possible after the party, wrap any remaining cheeses individually in plastic wrap, then aluminum foil, and refrigerate. Store the crackers in a tin with a tight-fitting lid.

Baked Fruit Salad

Serve this with the entrées, topped with sour cream, or as a dessert with ice cream.

Bake at 350° for 45 minutes.
Makes 12 side dish (8 dessert servings).

1   **can (16 ounces) sliced peaches**
1   **can (16 ounces) sliced pears**
1   **can (16 ounces) apricot halves**
1   **can (16 ounces) pineapple chunks**
1   **cup pecan halves**
½   **cup maraschino cherries**
½   **cup (1 stick) butter or margarine**
2   **tablespoons cornstarch**
½   **cup firmly packed light brown sugar**
     Sour cream (optional)

1. Preheat the oven to moderate (350°).
2. Drain the peaches, pears, apricots and pineapple, reserving 1½ cups mixed fruit syrups; place the fruit in a shallow 10-cup casserole. Top with the pecans and cherries.
3. Melt the butter or margarine in a small saucepan. Stir in the cornstarch, mixing until well blended. Add the sugar and stir until well blended. Stir in the reserved fruit syrups.
4. Cook over moderate heat, stirring often, until the mixture thickens and bubbles for 3 minutes. Pour over the fruit.
5. Bake in the preheated moderate oven (350°) for 45 minutes, or until bubbly hot and golden. Spoon into a heatproof glass serving bowl. Top with the sour cream, if you wish.

Crunchy Walnut Pie

Crunchy Walnut Pie

A hint of lemon adds a pleasant touch.

Bake at 375° for 40 to 50 minutes.
Makes one 9-inch pie.

Pastry for single-crust 9-inch pie shell
3   eggs
½   cup firmly packed light brown sugar
1   cup light corn syrup
¼   cup melted butter or margarine
    Grated rind and juice of ½ lemon
1   teaspoon vanilla
½   teaspoon ground cinnamon
¼   teaspoon salt
2   cups walnut halves or pieces

1. Preheat the oven to moderate (375°).
2. Prepare the pastry from your favorite recipe (or use a packaged mix or frozen thawed piecrust); fit loosely into a 9-inch pie plate. Crimp or flute the edge decoratively to make a stand-up rim; place on a cookie sheet. Refrigerate while preparing filling.
3. Beat the eggs lightly in a medium-size bowl; add the brown sugar, corn syrup, melted butter, lemon rind and juice, vanilla, cinnamon and salt; mix until well blended.
4. Place the walnuts in an even layer in the bottom of the pastry shell; pour the filling over. Place the cookie sheet on the lowest shelf of the preheated moderate oven (375°).
5. Bake the pie for 40 to 50 minutes, or until the filling jiggles only slightly when the dish is gently shaken. Slide off the cookie sheet onto a wire rack; cool for at least 2 hours, preferably overnight. *Pie is best if made one day in advance, cooled, wrapped in foil and stored at room temperature until serving time.*

Mocha Silk Pie

Buttery-rich mousse complements a crunchy almond crust.

Makes one 9-inch pie.

Almond Crust (recipe follows)
½ cup (1 stick) butter or margarine, softened
¾ cup firmly packed light brown sugar
1 square (1 ounce) unsweetened chocolate, melted and cooled
2 teaspoons instant coffee powder
2 eggs
Amaretto-Coffee Cream (recipe follows)
Tiny almond macaroon biscuits

1. Make the ALMOND CRUST.
2. Cream the butter or margarine and the sugar until light and fluffy in the large bowl of an electric mixer at high speed. Beat in the chocolate and coffee powder until well blended.
3. Beat in the eggs, one at a time, beating for 5 minutes after each addition, or until all the sugar dissolves and the mousse is very smooth. Spoon into the prepared and cooled crust. Cover with plastic wrap. Refrigerate for 6 hours or overnight.
4. Make the AMARETTO-COFFEE CREAM. Spoon into a pastry tube or bag fitted with a star tip. Pipe rosettes in two circles on top of the pie. Top each rosette with a tiny almond macaroon biscuit. Refrigerate until serving time.

Amaretto-Coffee Cream: Makes 2 cups. Whip 1 cup heavy cream in a small deep bowl with an electric mixer at high speed until soft peaks form. Add 1 tablespoon Amaretto liqueur, 1 tablespoon cold strong coffee and 1 tablespoon 10X (confectioners') sugar; beat until stiff.

Almond Crust

Bake at 400° for 5 minutes.
Makes one 9-inch crust.

1¼ cups ground almond macaroon biscuits
½ cup finely chopped almonds
⅓ cup sugar
⅓ cup melted butter or margarine
½ square (1 ounce) unsweetened chocolate, melted

1. Preheat the oven to hot (400°).
2. Combine the almond macaroon biscuit crumbs, chopped almonds and sugar in a small bowl. Stir in the melted butter or margarine and chocolate.
3. Press over the bottom and side of a well-greased 9-inch pie plate.
4. Bake in the preheated hot oven (400°) for 5 minutes. Cool completely on a wire rack before filling.

TABLE TOP TREE

MATERIALS:

Boxwood branches; Styrofoam cone at least 12" high (boxwood sprigs will add at least 4" to the height of the cone when finished); green felt for base of cone; red velvet ribbon; heavy-duty plastic bag.

DIRECTIONS:

● *Clip boxwood sprigs into graduated lengths from 4" to 8". Place in a heavy-duty plastic bag, fill with water, tie securely and store in a cool (not freezing) place for about 48 hours. Boxwood branches will stay fresh for several weeks.*

● *Cut green felt into a circle to fit the base of the cone and glue it in place.*

● *Remove branches from the bag and place them on newspapers to absorb the water. Starting at the bottom edge of the cone, push the cut ends of the sprigs into the Styrofoam. Work up to the top where the shortest sprigs will be placed upright into tip of cone.*

● *Bows may be tied around the branches themselves, or fastened to the branches with a piece of spool wire. Add tiny balls or other decorations if desired.*

HYDRANGEA WREATH

Use a combination of red, blue and pink hydrangeas. Attach to straw wreath form (available from florist) with U-shaped floral pins, letting head of one flower cover the stem of another until the entire form is covered. Attach wine-red velvet ribbon with a strip of floral wire.

A FRAGRANT SETTING FOR CANDLES

Fresh cedar with berries, pine cones and dried seedpods form a "nest" for fat red candles grouped in different heights. (Make sure flames don't get too near the cedar.)

FOR A SIMPLE COUNTRY LOOK

Heap pine cones on a brass scale; hide the bracket with running cedar.

Nice and Easy Christmas: Make presents part of the decoration! Wrap them in coordinating paper, then place in an eye-catching spot.

The holidays are approaching and there's *still* so much to to do? Don't say, "Bah, humbug!" Instead, try these simple-to-make ornaments and finger foods. They'll ease the Christmas time crunch, and give you more time to enjoy the festivities!

NICE AND EASY

Colored Card Ornaments

CHRISTMAS IN AN INSTANT

● No time to make ornaments? Use candy canes bows and ribbons, with lace for hanging them (as well as for garlands).
● Group candles of different heights together. (Be careful to place them on a fireproof surface!)
● Pile citrus pomanders in an attractive bowl to make a fragrant centerpiece.
● Group poinsettias near your entryway table or by the fireplace. Set candles of the same color in groups by the table or mantel.

COLORED CARD ORNAMENTS

EASY: Achievable by anyone.
MATERIALS: Red, dk. green and lt. green poster board (one 22 x 28" piece in each color makes about 40 ornaments); lace edging (about $\frac{3}{8}$" wide); ribbon for bows ($\frac{1}{2}$" to 1" wide); white glue.

DIRECTIONS:
1. Trace actual-size half-patterns (*see Fig. 8, at right*) on folded tracing paper. Cut out and open for full pattern. Transfer or glue full patterns to cardboard. Also on cardboard, draw a 4"-dia. circle and 3 squares ($1\frac{1}{4}$", 2", $3\frac{1}{2}$").
2. Ornament Front: Glue lace edging behind and extending from a circle or large square. On top, glue a heart, a star or 2 smaller squares (*see photo*) over more lace edging.
3. Ornament Back: Fold $\frac{1}{2}$" yd. ribbon in half. Glue it to a circle or large square with loop extending about 2" above and tails crossed at center.
4. Glue ornament front to back (over ribbon). Tie a bow with 16"-long ribbon and glue it to the center top. Hang from tree or garland.

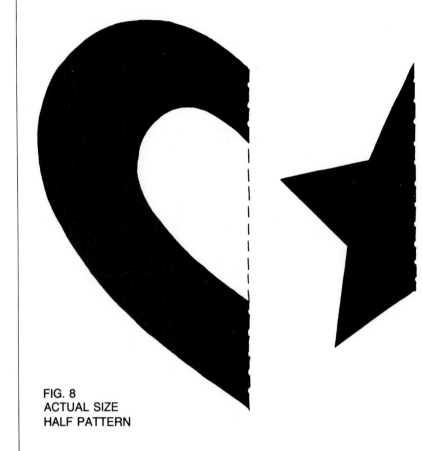

FIG. 8
ACTUAL SIZE
HALF PATTERN

Did You Know. . .

The average American household receives 26 holiday cards a year!

CANDY CANE WREAT

EASY: Achievable by anyone.

DIRECTIONS:
To create this sweet greeting for y door: Bind three $5\frac{1}{2}$" candy canes w invisible plastic tape (do 4 sets). each with thin satin ribbon; attach wreath with floral wire, secure 6 w picks filled with fresh miniature car tions and baby's breath. Add a s bow.

ndy Cane Wreath

STAR OF ROSES CENTERPIECE

EASY: Achievable by anyone.

DIRECTIONS:

1. Thoroughly soak floral foam in a bucket of water, then cut it to fit a bowl or casserole. (We used a silver bowl, but an ordinary casserole, mixing or salad bowl works fine, too.) Line the rim with galax leaves stuck into toothpick holes in the foam.

2. Place 6 fresh miniature roses, equally spaced at the rim, to set the star points. In between, insert fresh white carnations to make 6 white triangles (*see photo*). Fill the rest of the square with roses.

3. Tuck a sprig of leatherleaf fern at each inside corner of the star.

Star of Roses Centerpiece

GRANNY SQUARE AFGHAN & PILLOW TOP *(Afghan, 45″ x 60″; Pillow Top, 13″ x 13″)*

AVERAGE: For those with some experience in crocheting.

MATERIALS: Sport Weight yarn, 3-ply (3 oz. ball): 7 balls Vermilion (A) and 5 balls Ecru (B) crochet hook, Size F, OR ANY SIZE HOOK TO OBTAIN THE MOTIF MEASUREMENTS BELOW; 13″-square knife-edge ecru pillow.

GAUGE: Each motif measures 7½ x 7½″ square. **Be sure to check your gauge.**

DIRECTIONS:

1. Motif *(Makes 48)*: With A, ch 6. Join with sl st to form ring. **Rnd 1:** Ch 3, make 2 dc in ring, ch 3, * make 3 dc in ring, ch 3; rep from * 2 more times. Join to top of ch-3. **Rnd 2:** Sl st in next 2 dc, sl st in next sp, ch 3, in same sp make 2 dc, ch 3, 3 dc; * ch 1, in next sp make 3 dc, ch 3, 3 dc; * rep from * 2 more times; ch 1. Join. **Rnd 3:** Sl st in

next 2 dc, sl st in next sp, ch 3, in same sp make 2 dc, ch 3, 3 dc; * ch 1, 3 dc in next ch-1 sp, ch 1 in corner ch-3 sp make 3 dc, ch 3, 3 dc; rep from * 2 more times; ch 1, 3 dc in last ch-1 sp, ch 1. Join. Cut A and fasten. **Rnd 4:** Attach B with sl st in next ch-3 sp at beg of last rnd, ch 3, in same sp make 2 dc, ch 3, 3 dc; ** ch 1, 3 dc in next ch-1 sp; rep from ** to next corner ch-3 sp, ch 1, in corner ch-3 sp make 3 dc, ch 3, 3 dc. Work remaining 3 sides in same way, starting at **. Join last ch-1 to top of ch-3. Cut B and fasten. **Rnds 5-7:** Attach A with sl st in next ch-3 sp at beg of last rnd and rep Rnd 4. Cut A and fasten. **Rnd 8:** Attach B as before and rep Rnd 4. Fasten off.

2. Finishing: Pin each motif to measurements on a padded surface; cover with a damp cloth and allow to dry. Do not press.

To join motifs: From right side, sew motifs together working through back

lp *only* of each st and keeping sear elastic as crochet fabric, join moti gether from center of a ch-3 corn to center of next corner sp, matc sts. Join 8 rows of 6 motifs each.

3. Edging: Rnd 1: With wrong facing, attach B to any ch-3 corn ch 1, make 3 sc in same corner sp, in each st across to within next cor 3 sc in corner; rep from * around. **Rnd 2:** With right side facing, sl each st around. Join. Fasten off.

4. Pillow top: Work same as moti Afghan through Rnd 8. **Rnds 9** Attach A as before and rep Rnd 4. A and fasten. **Last Rnd:** Attach before and rep Rnd 4. Fasten off. **Edging:** Work same as Afghan.

5. Blocking: Block Pillow Top to r sure 13″ square. Slipstitch edges, r side up, to seamline of a 13″-sq knife-edge ecru pillow.

ranny Square Afghan and Pillow Top

CHRISTMAS IN AN INSTANT

● *No time to make ornaments? Use candy canes, bows and ribbons, with lace for hanging them. (Works well with garlands, too!)*

● *Group candles of different heights together. (Be careful to place them on a fireproof surface!)*

● *Show off your Christmas cards in unusual places—the kitchen, guest room, etc. Group them on a mantel or shelf; fill out the display with greenery, and tape a string of tiny lights overhead.*

● *For the kitchen, line a colorful tin or crock with a Christmas-y tea towel or napkin. Fill it with old-fashioned wood utensils such as spoons and spatulas.*

● *Pile citrus pomanders in an attractive bowl to make a fragrant centerpiece.*

● *Bake a batch of sugar or gingerbread cookies (with a hole in them for hanging) and use them as ornaments for the tree, or on your windows. Decorate or leave plain; hang with fishing wire or pretty ribbon.*

● *Group poinsettias near your entryway table or by the fireplace. Set candles of the same color in groups on the table or mantel.*

● *Don't forget your bedroom! Tartan plaid sheets or comforters will give the room instant holiday cheer. And bring in the poinsettias, too!*

● *Use flannel sheets for a cozy table setting. Cut a red sheet to size for the tablecloth. Cut a coordinating pattern sheet into napkins with pinking shears; gather with napkin rings.*

● *Quick mantel decor: Lay pine cuttings across the top of a mantel (make a garland if you have a bit more time) and decorate with 3 or 4 giant red bows.*

Hors d'oeuvres in Reserve: A make-ahead cocktail party

MAKE-AHEAD COCKTAIL PARTY

(FOR 16)

*Creole Nuts**
*Gingered Chicken**
*Savory Baked Goat Cheese**
*Tomato Lime Dip**
Vegetable Dippers
*Pita Chips**
Curried Beef Rolls with
*Chutney Dipping Sauce**
*Cherry Tomatoes with Hummus**
*Indonesian Satay**
*Chile Cheese Squares**

**Recipe follows*

WORK PLAN

Since this party is designed to be easy to prepare, it is really not necessary to freeze any of the hors d'oeuvres ahead of time. However, of the menu items, the Creole Nuts, Pita Chips, and Chile Cheese Squares can be prepared ahead and frozen successfully.

Several days before
● Make herbed crumbs for SAVORY BAKED GOAT CHEESE.

Day before
● Prepare CREOLE NUTS.
● Cut chicken and make marinade for GINGERED CHICKEN: refrigerate.
● Cut up pork for INDONESIAN SATAY; chill.
● Shred cheese and cut up jalapeño peppers for CHILI-CHEESE SQUARES; chill.
● Cut up goat cheese for SAVORY BAKED GOAT CHEESE; refrigerate.
● Make TOMATO-LIME DIP; chill.
● Prepare CHUTNEY DIPPING SAUCE for CURRIED BEEF ROLLS; chill.
● Prepare HUMMUS; chill.

Early in the day
● Cut up VEGETABLE DIPPERS; chill.
● Make herb butter for PITA CHIPS; refrigerate.

Two hours before
● Make GINGERED CHICKEN; cool and arrange on skewers.
● Coat goat cheese with crumbs and oil.
● Brush pita with herbed butter.
● Blanch lettuce leaves and prepare curried beef for curried beef rolls; assemble.
● Scoop out cherry tomatoes; fill with hummus.
● Marinate and skewer pork for INDONESIAN SATAY onto skewers; make peanut sauce.
● Prepare CHILI-CHEESE SQUARES.

15-30 minutes before
● Heat SAVORY BAKED GOAT CHEESE, PITA CHIPS; INDONESIAN SATAY.

Creole Nuts

These spicy nuts make a delicious accompaniment to cocktails.

Bake at 350° for 5 minutes.
Makes 3 cups.

2   tablespoons vegetable oil
1   teaspoon ground cumin
1   teaspoon curry powder
1/4   teaspoon cayenne pepper
1/8   teaspoon white pepper
1 1/3   cups whole unblanched almonds (about 7 ounces)
1 1/4   cups pecan halves (about 5 ounces)
3/4   cup walnut halves (about 4 ounces)
1/4   teaspoon salt, or to taste

1. Preheat the oven to moderate (350°).
2. Mix together the oil, cumin, curry powder, cayenne and white pepper in a large mixing bowl. Add the nuts; stir to coat evenly. Spread the nuts in a single layer on a baking sheet.
3. Bake in the preheated moderate oven (350°) for 5 minutes. Sprinkle the salt over the nuts. Let cool. Store completely cooled nuts in an airtight tin at room temperature.

Microwave Directions For Creole Nuts

650-Watt Variable Power Microwave Oven

INGREDIENT CHANGES:
Reduce the oil to 1 tablespoon and eliminate the white pepper.

DIRECTIONS:
Combine the oil, cumin, curry powder and cayenne pepper in a 10-inch microwave-safe pie plate; stir to mix well. Add the almonds, pecans and walnuts; stir to coat the nuts with the spice mixture. Microwave, uncovered, at full power for 4 1/2 to 5 minutes, stirring twice. Stir in the salt. Let the nuts cool in the pie plate.

Gingered Chicken

Use colorful combinations of vegetables to create a striking appetizer.

Makes 40 skewers.

- 2 tablespoons soy sauce
- 2 tablespoons water
- 1 teaspoon sugar
- 1/2 teaspoon grated, pared fresh gingerroot
- 1/2 teaspoon Oriental sesame oil*
- 1 1/2 pounds boneless, skinned chicken breast, cut into 1/2-inch cubes
- 1 tablespoon vegetable oil
- 30 red radishes, sliced
- 3 bunches large green onions, sliced
- 80 snow peas (6 ounces)

1. Mix the soy sauce, water, sugar, gingerroot and sesame oil in a medium-size bowl. Add the chicken; toss to coat evenly. Let stand for 5 minutes at room temperature.
2. Heat the vegetable oil in a heavy, large skillet. Drain the chicken, reserving marinade. Add the chicken to the hot skillet and brown quickly on all sides for about 1 1/2 minutes.
3. Add the reserved marinade; continue cooking, stirring frequently, until almost all of the liquid has evaporated.
4. Transfer the chicken to a bowl. When cool enough to handle, skewer on wooden skewers with the radish slices, green onion slices and snow peas. Serve at room temperature.

*Note: Oriental sesame oil has more flavor and is darker than regular sesame oil and can be found in the Oriental food section of your supermarket or in a specialty food store.

Savory Baked Goat Cheese

The smooth, melty cheese and the crunchy bread coating make this an unusual treat.

Bake at 400° for 10 minutes.
Makes 40 appetizers.

- 1/2 cup fresh bread crumbs
- 1/2 teaspoon leaf thyme, crumbled
- 1/8 teaspoon salt
- 1/8 teaspoon pepper
- 8 ounces firm goat cheese
- 2 to 3 tablespoons good-quality olive oil
- 5 slices Westphalian pumpernickel cut into 1-inch squares or triangles

1. Preheat the oven to hot (400°).
2. Blend the bread crumbs, thyme, salt and pepper in a blender or food processor for about 5 seconds. Pour into a shallow bowl. Set aside. (The blender crushes the thyme to release the flavor and also makes the bread crumbs finer.)
3. Cut the cheese into forty 1/2-inch cubes. Coat lightly with the olive oil; roll in the seasoned crumbs to coat evenly. Place each cube on a pumpernickel square. Arrange on a baking sheet.
4. Bake in the preheated hot oven (400°) for 10 minutes. Serve warm.

Tomato-Lime Dip With Vegetable Dippers

A fresh-tasting dip that's sure to be a hit at any party.

Makes 2⅔ cups.

1   *container (16 ounces) dairy sour cream*
1   *can (16 ounces) stewed tomatoes, well drained and chopped (about 1 cup)*
½   *cup chopped green onion*
2   *tablespoons chopped fresh dill*
12 *drops liquid red-pepper seasoning*
1½ *teaspoons grated lime rind*
¼   *teaspoon salt*
¼   *teaspoon white pepper*
    Assortment of raw vegetables for dipping: endive, carrots, celery, cucumber, zucchini, sweet red and green pepper, radishes, fennel, broccoli, etc.

1. Mix together the sour cream, tomatoes, green onion, dill, red-pepper seasoning, lime rind, salt and pepper in a large bowl. Cover and refrigerate for at least ½ hour to allow flavors to blend.
2. Choose vegetables for variety of color and cut into interesting shapes.
3. Garnish the dip with dill or lime zest, if you wish.

Pita Chips

Pita chips are a crunchy snack to enjoy at home or at a party. White and wheat pita breads can be mixed for a nice variation. Make ahead and store in an airtight container.

Bake at 350° for 10 to 12 minutes.
Makes 48 chips.

6   *tablespoons butter or margarine*
4   *tablespoons vegetable oil*
2   *cloves garlic, crushed in a press or very finely chopped*
½   *teaspoon cayenne pepper*
¼   *teaspoon black pepper*
12 *ounces pita bread (6 large or 12 small pita breads)*

1. Preheat the oven to moderate (350°).
2. Melt the butter with the oil in a small saucepan. Add the garlic, cayenne and black peper. Simmer over low heat until frothy, about 2 minutes. Remove from the heat.
3. Separate each pita bread into 2 halves. Lightly brush the "inside" of bread with the butter mixture. Cut each half into 4 wedges. (For small pitas, cut each half into 2 wedges.) Place the wedges on an ungreased baking sheet.
4. Bake in the preheated moderate oven (350°) for 10 to 12 minutes until lightly browned. Cool on the pan on a wire rack.

Curried Beef Rolls With Chutney Dipping Sauce

These attractive bundles feature a spicy beef mixture teamed up with a sweet sauce. The rolls and dipping sauce can be prepared a day ahead and refrigerated. Serve rolls at room temperature.

Makes 32 rolls.

1	pound lean ground beef
$\frac{1}{4}$	teaspoon salt
$\frac{1}{4}$	teaspoon black pepper
3	to 4 teaspoons curry powder
$\frac{1}{2}$	teaspoon cumin seeds
$1\frac{1}{8}$	teaspoon cayenne pepper
2	tablespoons fresh lemon juice

Chutney Dipping Sauce:

$1\frac{1}{2}$	cups dairy sour cream
3	tablespoons chutney, finely chopped
1	tablespoon fresh lemon juice
16	large romaine lettuce leaves

1. Brown the meat in a large skillet over low heat, breaking up meat with a wooden spoon. Season with the salt and black pepper. Carefully drain all but 1 tablespoon of the fat, if necessary.
2. Add the curry powder, cumin seeds and cayenne. Continue cooking and stirring for 2 to 3 minutes to cook the curry powder. Remove from the heat. Stir in the 2 tablespoons lemon juice. Set aside.
3. Prepare the Chutney Dipping Sauce: Stir together the sour cream, chutney and the 1 tablespoon lemon juice in a bowl. Add $\frac{1}{3}$ cup of this mixture to the meat; stir well. Store the remaining sauce in the refrigerator.
4. Blanch the lettuce leaves by plunging them in a large pot of boiling water for 5 seconds; then rinse under cold running water to stop cooking. Cut each lettuce leaf in half lengthwise and remove the thick center stem. You will need a piece, about 4 to 5 inches by $2\frac{1}{2}$ to 3 inches, for each roll.
5. Spoon $1\frac{1}{2}$ to 2 teaspoons of the meat filling onto a short end of each lettuce leaf. Roll up, tucking in sides. Place, seam-side down, on the serving plate. Serve with the remaining dipping sauce.

Microwave Directions For Curried Beef Rolls

650-Watt Variable Power Microwave Oven

DIRECTIONS:

Crumble the beef into a 10-inch microwave-safe pie plate. Microwave, uncovered, at full power for 4 minutes, stirring after 2 minutes. Pour off all of the liquid. Sprinkle the meat with the salt, black pepper, curry powder, cumin seeds and cayenne pepper. Microwave, uncovered, at full power for 30 seconds longer. Stir in the lemon juice and dipping sauce as directed in recipe at left. Set aside. Wash the romaine leaves; do not shake off water. Wrap 5 to 6 pieces of romaine loosely in paper toweling. Microwave at full power for 1 minute. Remove the toweling and rinse immediately under cold water to stop the cooking. Repeat with the remaining romaine. Proceed as in the recipe at left.

⑤ Cherry Tomatoes With Hummus

Makes 60 stuffed tomatoes.

2	pints small cherry tomatoes
1	can (16 ounces) garbanzo beans
1	to 2 cloves garlic
2	tablespoons sesame seeds, toasted
2	tablespoons fresh lemon juice
2	teaspoons Oriental sesame oil (see Note for Gingered Chicken, page 191)
	Parsley for garnish

1. Slice off the tops of the cherry tomatoes. Scoop out the pulp and seeds with a melon baller. Let the tomatoes drain, cut-side down, on paper toweling.
2. Drain the garbanzo beans, reserving 3 tablespoons of the liquid.
3. Finely chop the garlic in a food processor or blender, using several on/off pulses. Add the reserved bean liquid, sesame seeds, lemon juice and sesame oil. Whirl until smooth for about 30 seconds.
4. Fill each tomato, using a small spoon or a pastry bag. Garnish each with a small parsley leaf.

Indonesian Satay

Makes 40 skewers.

$\frac{1}{2}$ cup prepared teriyaki sauce
3   tablespoons sugar
1   tablespoon vinegar
2   teaspoons ground cumin
$\frac{1}{4}$ teaspoon cayenne pepper
1   pound boneless pork shoulder, trimmed of fat
    and cut into 80 cubes, $\frac{1}{2}$ to $\frac{3}{4}$ inch
2   teaspoons cornstarch
$\frac{3}{4}$ cup milk
2   tablespoons smooth peanut butter

1. Preheat the broiler. Mix together the teriyaki sauce, sugar, vinegar, cumin and cayenne in a large bowl. Add the pork cubes; stir to coat. Let stand for 5 minutes at room temperature.
2. Skewer 2 pork cubes onto each of 40 metal skewers. Reserve the marinade. Set aside.
3. Dissolve the cornstarch in the milk in a small bowl. Set aside.
4. To prepare the sauce, bring $\frac{1}{4}$ cup of the reserved marinade to boiling in a small saucepan. Cook for 1 minute. Add the cornstarch mixture and the peanut butter. Bring to boiling, stirring with a whisk. Lower the heat; simmer for 3 minutes. Set aside.
5. Broil the pork 4 to 5 inches from the source of heat for about 2 minutes on each side. Dip in the peanut sauce; arrange on a serving platter. Serve with additional peanut sauce.

Microwave Directions For Satay Sauce

650-Watt Variable Power Microwave Oven

DIRECTIONS:
Combine $\frac{1}{4}$ cup of the reserved marinade, milk and cornstarch in a 4-cup microwave-safe measure; whisk until smooth. Stir in the peanut butter until smooth. Microwave, uncovered, at full power for 3 minutes until mixture comes to a full boil, stirring well after $1\frac{1}{2}$ minutes. Remove from the microwave. Stir again.

Chili-Cheese Squares

Bake at 400° for 10 minutes; then at 325° for 10 minutes.
Makes 64 squares.

6   eggs
$\frac{1}{4}$ teaspoon salt
$\frac{1}{4}$ teaspoon white pepper
$\frac{1}{4}$ cup unsifted all-purpose flour
$\frac{1}{4}$ teaspoon baking powder
8   ounces Monterey Jack cheese, shredded
    (about 2 cups)
2   or 3 tablespoons chopped fresh cilantro*
3   to 4 teaspoons finely chopped, seeded jalapeño peppers, pickled or fresh

1. Preheat the oven to hot (400°).
2. Line a 9 x 9 x 2-inch-square baking pan with aluminum foil so the ends overhang. Generously grease the foil.
3. Beat together the eggs, salt and pepper in a large bowl until foamy. Add the flour and baking powder. Beat until smooth and no lumps remain.
4. Add the cheese, cilantro and jalapeño pepper; stir until well mixed. Pour into the prepared pan.
5. Bake in the preheated hot oven (400°) for 10 minutes. Lower the oven temperature to slow (325°). Bake for 10 minutes more.
6. Cool in the pan on a wire rack for 10 to 20 minutes. Remove the foil with the cheese mixture to a cutting board. Peel down the sides of the foil. Cut into 1-inch squares. Serve warm or at room temperature.

*Note: Cilantro, also known as fresh coriander or Chinese parsley, is a pungent herb used in southwestern, Mexican and Middle Eastern cuisines.

MORE QUICK HORS D'OEUVRES

● *Top round tortilla chips with a dab of canned refried beans and chopped jalapeño peppers, then with grated Monterey Jack cheese or queso bianco; broil until bubbly.*

● *Heat brie in a slow oven until it just begins to melt. (If you want, you can top the cheese with slivered blanched almonds and a sprinkling of sifted brown sugar before it goes into the oven.) Serve immediately with fresh fruit and crackers.*

● *Combine process cheese spread with some canned chili con carne. Cook in a heavy saucepan, stirring constantly, until the mixture is hot and bubbly. Dip tortilla chips and pepper strips.*

● *Stuff stemmed fresh mushrooms with garlic and herb cheese; dip mushroom bottoms in melted butter; bake in a moderate oven until the cheese is hot.*

● *Fill cucumber cups with tuna salad, spiced with curry powder or dillweed and lemon.*

● *Use cherry tomatoes as containers for canned deviled ham; simply hollow out with a small spoon.*

● *Make Italian herb sticks by trimming sliced white bread and brushing with a mixture of 1 stick butter, melted, $\frac{1}{4}$ teaspoon garlic powder, $\frac{1}{4}$ teaspoon salt, 1 teaspoon mixed Italian herbs and 1 tablespoon grated Parmesan cheese; toast until golden in the oven, then cut into sticks and serve warm.*

● *Wrap bread sticks in partially cooked bacon strips. Place on roasting pan rack and bake in a moderate oven (350°) until the bacon is crisp.*

● *Marinate canned mushrooms in bottled Italian dressing.*

Garnish with diced pimiento.

● *Buy frozen tortellini and cook al dente, following package directions. Thread onto skewers. Brush with prepared pesto or tomato sauce and sprinkle with grated Parmesan cheese. Serve immediately.*

● *Dip 2-inch cubes of boneless, skinless chicken breasts into melted butter or margarine, then into seasoned bread crumbs mixed with grated Parmesan cheese. Place in a single layer on foil-lined cookie sheets. Bake at 400° for about 10 minutes, or until golden and cooked inside.*

● *Oriental Crudités: Mix equal parts soy sauce, peanut oil and red wine vinegar. Use to marinate raw vegetables such as broccoli, mushrooms and red pepper strips. (Prepare marinade and vegetables ahead of time; mix $\frac{1}{2}$ hour before serving.)*

● *Super-Quick Crudités: Choose large pieces of vegetables, such as raw carrots, celery and cherry tomatoes, from your local salad bar. Serve with prepared creamy dressings of your choice as dips.*

● *Buy chopped chicken liver at your delicatessen; puree in the food processor to make extra-smooth. Pipe into raw mushroom caps, using a pastry bag fitted with a star tip. Garnish with sieved egg or pimiento strips.*

● *Mix equal amounts grated Cheddar cheese, all-purpose flour and butter until well blended. Chill dough 30 minutes. Roll out as for cookie dough; cut into strips with a pastry wheel. Place on a lightly greased cookie sheet. Brush with beaten egg. Bake at 350° until golden brown (watch for burning).*

American Country Tree

If your idea of a perfect Christmas is one brimming with country charm, look no further. These Early American-inspired decorations will win your heart—and the dinner will win raves from your whole family!

AMERICAN COUNTRY

Festive Duck Ornament

NOSTALGIC TOUCHES

Fill a set of ceramic bowls with lots of shiny red apples. Display on a table front, surrounded by greenery, pine cones and berries.

● For your table: Tie bunches of long cinnamon sticks with red ribbon; place at each setting. Sew stuffed hearts from old fabric and attach to fabric loops to make napkin holders.

● An easy way to dress up your kitchen: Place red, white and green pasta in glass storage jars; tie the knobs on jar tops with ribbon. (After the holidays, you can cook up a colorful plateful of pasta for dinner!)

FESTIVE DUCK ORNAMENT

EASY: Achievable by anyone.
MATERIALS: (for one duck) two 9 x 12" pieces white felt; ¼ yd. fusible web; thick yellow and black acrylic paints; fine artist's brush; white glue; one green chenille stem; one small yellow "silk" flower and leaf; ½ yd. red curling ribbon; paper for pattern; pencil; scissors; ruler.

DIRECTIONS:

1. Enlarge pattern of duck and wing from Fig. 9 onto paper, (*see* How To Enlarge Designs *on page 271*).

2. Fuse felt pieces according to directions with fusible web. Cut three of duck shape and two of wing from fused felt.
3. Glue two duck shapes together. Cut 6" piece chenille stem. Glue third duck shape to first two with 2" of chenille stem piece inserted between in position for leg. Dry well. Glue one wing to each side of body. Dry.
4. Make eye with dot of black paint. Paint bill and cut edges of bill yellow. Dry well.
5. Tie ribbon around duck's neck. Curl free ends of ribbon by pulling it firmly and quickly over dull knife blade.
6. Glue flower and leaf over knot. Fasten ornament to tree branch by twisting chenille stem around branch.

RAFFIA CONE WITH TASSEL

AVERAGE: For those with some perience in crafts.
MATERIALS: 4¼"-dia. round pla needlepoint canvas; 5 g natural ma artificial raffia; 5 g red artificial raf red sewing thread; tapestry and la sewing needles.

DIRECTIONS:

1. Hide all raffia ends by work stitches over the ends. Using doub red raffia, overcast edge of plastic c vas shape, inserting needle into sec

FIG. 9 DUCK

1 SQ. =

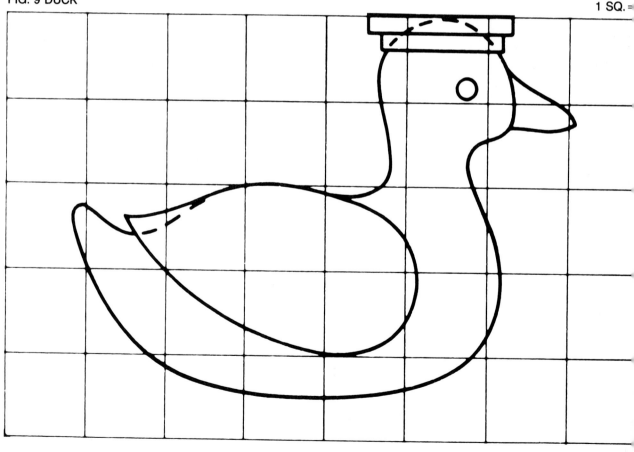

Watermelon Wedge Ornament

STENCILED RIBBON LOOP ORNAMENT

EASY: Achievable by anyone.
MATERIALS: 6″ piece 2½″-wide French blue burlap ribbon; 6″ piece 1¼″-wide terra cotta pineapple-motif ribbon; 12″ piece ⅛″-wide rust satin ribbon; dried statice and other small flowers; white craft glue; #28 wrapping wire; stapler; scissors.

Stenciled Ribbon Loop Ornament

DIRECTIONS:
1. Glue stenciled ribbon, centered, on burlap ribbon. Allow ¼″ border of burlap and cut off excess burlap ribbon and discard. Shape ribbon as loop with burlap sides together. Staple and glue loop at cut ends.
2. Cut two 6″ pieces satin ribbon. Make bow of one piece securing center with small piece of wire. Glue to loop over staple. Glue cut end of remaining piece over wire and opposite end of back of loop to make hanger.
3. Glue statice and flowers with stems inside loop.

WATERMELON WEDGE ORNAMENT

AVERAGE: For those with some experience in needlework.
MATERIALS: Two 4″-dia. plastic canvas circles; one 8 x 43″ mesh strip plastic needlepoint canvas; polyester rug yarn: 5 yds. bright pink, 3 yds. lime green, 3 yds. dark green; twelve 5mm black beads; black sewing thread; thread for hanger loop; tapestry needle; sewing needle; scissors; embroidery scissors.

DIRECTIONS:
1. Cut each circle in half along one side of center mesh. Retain halves with the center mesh, discard the others.
2. Cut canvas strip in shape with 25 *holes* in top row, centering count on the strip. Increase 3 on each end for next row (31 holes). Third row is 37 holes, 4th and 5th are each 43, 6th is 37, 7th is 31 and 8th is 25. Leave all edge meshes unworked.

ffia Cone with Tassel

of holes.
Using single strand of natural color
ia, overcast all interior rows work-
from left to right. This gives a
ating stitch on face of work and a
tical stitch on reverse side. Finish
iter with cross stitch.
Curl round into a cone. Fasten with
thread.
Make 2″-long tassel of ten 4″ lengths
red raffia which are tied at center,
ded at tie point and tied again ½″
ow fold. Sew tassel to point of cone.
Make 7½″ braid of three stands of
raffia. Knot at each end and leave
unbraided raffia extending to make
y tassel.
Sew knots to opposite side of cone
to make hanger.

3. Work half circles in gobelin stitch (*see Embroidery Stitch Guide on page 269*) over two meshes, using lime green in outermost row and bright pink in remaining rows. Compensate where necessary. Work centers in horizontal long stitches. Work strip of canvas in tent stitch using dark green. Back stitch between the three meshes at each end.

4. Evenly space and sew beads between third and fourth rows on half circles.

5. Join half circles along straight edges by overcasting with lime green and bright pink. Join rind strip to halves by overcasting with dark green.

6. Attach hanger.

DUCKY WREATH

EASY: Achievable by anyone.

MATERIALS: One 18″ outside dia. green wreath; 4 duck ornaments (*see Fig. 9, page 198*); 6 red chenille stems; red curling ribbon; $4\frac{1}{2}$ yds. $2\frac{1}{2}$″-wide striped craft ribbon (*see Materials Shopping Guide, page 272*); florist's wire; ruler.

DIRECTIONS:

1. Cut three 9″ pieces craft ribbon. Cut ends as shown. Hold pieces with ends even and slightly fanned and gather at center. Bind with chenille stem.

2. Cut three $11\frac{1}{2}$″ pieces. Repeat instructions. Place smaller group on larger and bind together with wire. Wrap small piece of craft ribbon around center and pin overlapping ends at back of bow.

3. Cut 32″ piece of same ribbon. Cut ends in same way. Fold crosswise slightly off center and wire to center bottom of wreath.

4. Wire bow over streamers. Cut eight $6\frac{1}{2}$″ pieces craft ribbon. Repeat instructions for bow but use only 2 pieces per bow. Wire bows as shown. Wire ducks over bows.

Ducky Wreath

5. Make fluffy piles of curled ribbon (pull ribbon over edge of dull knife); wire to wreath between the duck/bow trimming.

EARTS & CHECKERS UILT (about 46" x 64")

VERAGE: For those with some ex-
ience in quilting.

ATERIALS: 45"-wide small-print
ric, as follows: 5½ yds. white (in-
des quilt back), 1¼ yds. red and ½
green; 52 x 72" synthetic batting;
wn paper.

RECTIONS: (¼" *seams allowed*):
OTE: This quilt is assembled from 8
tchwork Blocks A and 7 appliquéd
art Blocks B (*see* Fig. 10). Borders
: added. A sawtooth border (of fold-
squares) is enclosed in outside seam.
ams are machine sewn; heart appli-
és and quilting are sewn by hand.

Pattern: Enlarge small and large
tterns for heart in Fig. 10a onto
wn paper, (*see How To Enlarge
esigns, on page 271*) placing broken
e on fold. Unfold for full pattern—
ger heart (solid line) is for quilting
otif; smaller heart (dotted line) is for
pliqué.
Cutting: *From white fabric,* cut two
x 52" pieces for quilt back, two
x 52" borders, one 7 x 49" border
d one 9 x 49" border, seven
0½ x 6½" and fourteen 2½ x 6½"
ctangles, thirty-two 2½" squares for
ilt blocks (A), and one hundred six-
2½" squares for sawtooth edge. *From
een fabric,* cut 72 patches 2½" square.
om red fabric, cut 124 patches 2½"
uare and, on the red fabric, trace
vithout cutting) 7 small (dotted line)
earts (*see* Fig. 10a) ½" apart.
Block A: Seam patches side by side
make 5 horizontal rows (*see* Fig. 10).
eam rows from top to bottom, seams
atching; to make the block. Make 8
locks.
Block B: Seam a red patch at each
nd of a white 2½ x 6½" strip. Seam
is to one long edge of a 10½ x 6½"
ctangle. Repeat at opposite edge.
lake 7 blocks.

FIG. 10 QUILT BLOCKS

BLOCK A

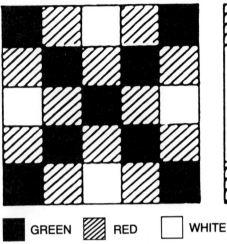

BLOCK B

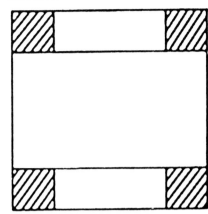

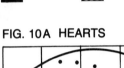

■ GREEN   ▨ RED   □ WHITE

FIG. 10A HEARTS

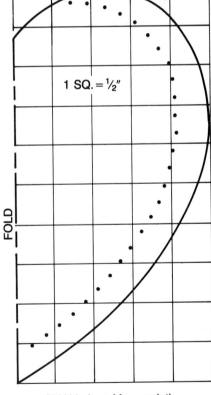

1 SQ. = ½"

FOLD

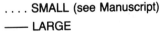

.... SMALL (see Manuscript)

—— LARGE

FIG. 10B

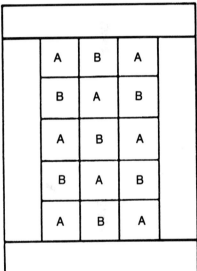

A	B	A
B	A	B
A	B	A
B	A	B
A	B	A

Hearts and Checkers Quilt

Assembly: Seam 5 horizontal rows [ ] blocks each (*see* Fig. 10b). Seam [ ]s one below another, seams match-[ ]

Borders: Seam a 52″ border at each [ ] of the assembly; trim ends flush [ ] fig. 10b). Seam 7″-wide border to [ ] and 9″-wide border to bottom of [ ]mbly.

[ ]. 10C

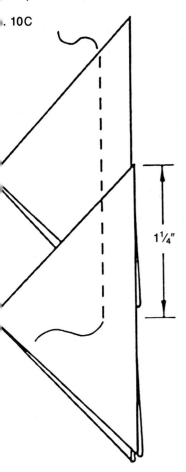

1¼″

7. Sawtooth Edge: Fold each 2½″ white square in half diagonally, then in half again, raw edges even, to make a "triangle"; press. Lap one tooth 1¼″ over another, single-fold at top, raw edges even (*see* Fig. 10c). Continue to make 33 points and stitch a scant ¼″ from raw edges for top border. Make a second row the same, for bottom border, then 2 more rows, each 47 points long for side borders. With right sides together and raw edges even, stitch the sawtooth strips to top and bottom edges of quilt top, then to each side edge (removing extra teeth if necessary). Press edging outward.

8. Quilt Back: Seam the 2 pieces together on a 52″ edge; press seam to one side. Spread out quilt, wrong side up, on a clean surface; tape down corners to prevent slipping. On top, spread same-size batting and then the quilt top, right side up and centered. With long stitches, baste from center diagonally outward to each corner and straight out to center of each edge. Add more basting rows about 6″ apart.

9. Quilting: Untape the quilt and place it in a frame or a quilting hoop (work from center outward if you use a hoop). Sew running stitches through all layers about ¼″ from each seam; at inner edge of the white borders, quilt ½″ outside the seam.

10. Appliqué: Over the back of the red fabric on which the 7 hearts are traced, spread a layer of batting. Machine-stitch on traced appliqué outlines. Cut out hearts ¼″ *outside the stitchlines.* Trim batting close to stitching. Pin a heart to center of each Block B, all points toward the bottom. Turn edges under on stitchline (clipping at top center) and slipstitch the heart in place through all layers. Quilt a smaller heart about an inch inside.

11. Border Quilting: With a hard pencil, trace a heart diagonally at each corner. Trace more hearts (points toward edges), spaced evenly in between. Quilt on traced lines and again about an inch inside for a smaller heart. Baste through quilt ½″ inside the sawtooth border.

12. Back Edges: Turn quilt wrong side up. Trim batting flush with the outside seamline. Trim quilt back ½″ outside the sawtooth seamline; turn under ½″ at each edge and slipstitch fold to the seamline all around quilt.

● **Country-Decorated Towels:** *Choose solid towels in holiday colors and washable ribbon in a complementary pattern. Measure the length of the woven band on every towel; add up the total for the yardage of ribbon needed. Edgestitch the ribbon to the towel band, turning cut edges under each end.*

● **Set up a "Toy Party"!** This is for adults and kids alike. Place a two-foot tree in a small red wagon and fill with brightly wrapped boxes (or real presents!). Use this as the focus of the table, set with plaid fabric and cover with stuffed animals and toys. To complete the theme, bake and decorate "toy" cookies—teddy bears, hobby horses, tin soldiers, etc.

Country Turkey Dinner, will all of the fixings.

COUNTRY TURKEY DINNER
(FOR 8)

*Hot Cider Punch**
Turkey with Cornbread Stuffing
*and Gravy**
*Collard Greens**
*Marinated Coleslaw**
*Spicy Red Pepper Relish**
*Sweet Potato Casserole**
*Buttermilk Biscuits**
*Chocolate Chess Pie**
*Pecan-Pumpkin Pie**
*Chocolate Pound Cake**
*Fresh Apple Fruitcake**

*Recipe follows

WORK PLAN

Up to two months ahead
● Make CHOCOLATE POUND CAKE, but do not glaze; freeze.
Up to one month ahead
● Prepare SPICY RED PEPPER RELISH; refrigerate.
Two days before
● Make cornbread for CORNBREAD STUFFING.
Day before
● Make CORNBREAD STUFFING; refrigerate. (Note: NEVER stuff a raw turkey with stuffing until just before you are ready to cook it.)
● Thaw CHOCOLATE POUND CAKE.
● Make FRESH APPLE FRUIT CAKE.
● Make MARINATED COLESLAW.
● Make CHOCOLATE CHESS PIE.
● Make unbaked pie shell, filling and topping for PECAN-PUMPKIN PIE; chill separately.

Early in the day
● Make PECAN-PUMPKIN PIE.
● Glaze CHOCOLATE POUND CAKE.
● Combine 1 cup of the cider with sugar, butter and spices, and heat, for HOT CIDER PUNCH.
● Cut COLLARD GREENS, but do not cook.
● Prepare SWEET POTATO CASSEROLE.
● Cut butter into dry ingredients for BUTTER-MILK BISCUITS, but do not add buttermilk yet!
Four to five hours before
● Stuff and begin roasting TURKEY.
Thirty minutes before
● Reheat SWEET POTATO CASSEROLE.
● Make COLLARD GREENS.
● Remove turkey from oven and let stand for 20 minutes before carving; meanwhile, make GRAVY. Make BUTTERMILK BISCUITS.
● Heat HOT CIDER PUNCH with remaining cider and applejack.
During dinner
● Whip cream, if desired, for CHOCOLATE CHESS PIE. If desired, warm up the pie.

Hot Cider Punch

Cider, combined with spices, butter and applejack, make a delicious warming punch.

Makes 20 servings.

1   bottle (½ gallon) apple cider
⅔   cup firmly packed light brown sugar
½   cup raw cranberries
¼   cup (½ stick) butter or margarine
1   tablespoon grated orange rind
1   tablespoon grated lemon rind
½   teaspoon ground cinnamon
¼   teaspoon ground nutmeg
1   cup applejack (apple brandy) or brandy
    Orange slices
    Cinnamon sticks

1. Combine the apple cider, brown sugar, cranberries, butter or margarine, orange and lemon rinds, cinnamon and nutmeg in a large saucepan. Heat slowly, stirring constantly, until the mixture comes just to boiling, but do not boil.
2. Carefully pour the mixture into a heatproof punch bowl; stir in the applejack. Garnish with the orange slices.
3. Serve in warmed punch cups or mugs with cinnamon sticks as stirrers.

Note: This punch can be made without the applejack. Increase cider by 1 cup. For a smaller party, halve the ingredients, if desired, or heat up half of mixture with ½ cup applejack and use the remainder another time, omitting the butter and applejack until ready to heat.

Turkey With Cornbread-Sausage Stuffing And Gravy

It's very important to have a roasting pan with a tight-fitting lid. Cooking the turkey covered for part of the time results in a very tender and juicy bird.

Roast at 400° for 15 minutes, then at 325° for 3¼ hours.
Makes 12 servings.

Cornbread-Sausage Stuffing:
½ pound bulk sausage, crumbled
2 cups chopped onion (2 large)
1 cup chopped celery
½ teaspoon sage
½ teaspoon leaf thyme, crumbled
½ cup chicken broth
¼ cup (½ stick) butter or margarine, melted
½ teaspoon salt
½ teaspoon pepper
Cornbread, crumbled (see recipe, page 210)

Turkey:
1 turkey (about 12 pounds), thawed if frozen
½ teaspoon salt
½ teaspoon pepper
2 cups water
1 carrot, pared and cut into 1-inch pieces
1 stalk celery, cut into 1-inch pieces
1 medium-size onion, peeled and quartered

Gravy:
2 cups defatted pan drippings
About 2 cups turkey broth made from giblets
OR: chicken broth
2 tablespoons butter or margarine
¼ cup unsifted all-purpose flour
Salt and pepper to taste

1. To prepare the Stuffing: Cook the sausage in a heavy skillet over low heat until well browned, stirring often. Drain on paper toweling. Discard all but 1 tablespoon fat from the skillet.
2. Sauté the onion and celery in the same skillet until tender, for about 10 minutes, stirring often. Stir in drained the sausage, sage and thyme. Cook for 1 minute. Add the chicken broth, butter, salt and pepper.
3. Crumble all of the Cornbread into a large bowl. Pour the sausage mixture over. Toss gently with a fork to moisten all the ingredients. Set aside until ready to stuff the turkey.
4. To prepare the Turkey: Preheat the oven to hot (400°). Remove the neck and giblets from the

turkey. Rinse the turkey well with cold water, inside and outside. Pat dry with paper toweling. Sprinkle the inside of body and neck cavities with ¼ teaspoon each of the salt and pepper. Spoon the stuffing loosely into both cavities. Tie the legs to the tail with string and skewer the neck skin to the back. Place the turkey on a rack in a roasting pan with a tight-fitting cover. Add the water, carrot, celery and onion. Sprinkle the turkey with the remaining salt and pepper.

5. Roast the turkey, uncovered, in the preheated hot oven (400°) for 15 minutes. Reduce the oven temperature to slow (325°). Cover the pan with the lid. Roast for 2½ hours. Uncover and roast for 45 minutes longer, or until the meat thermometer inserted in the thickest part of the thigh, without touching the bone, reaches 180°. Remove from the oven. Let stand at least 20 minutes before carving.
6. To prepare the Gravy: Strain the drippings from the roasting pan into a clear glass 4-cup measure. Skim off the fat and discard. You should have at least 2 cups of drippings without fat. Add enough broth to make a total of 4 cups. Melt the butter in a small saucepan. Stir in the flour and cook for 2 minutes. Gradually stir in the broth mixture. Cook over medium heat, stirring constantly, until the mixture thickens and boils. Lower the heat; simmer for 5 minutes. Season to taste with salt and pepper. Pour into a gravy boat.
7. To store any leftovers, remove the stuffing from the turkey and refrigerate separately.

Microwave Directions For Cornbread-Sausage Stuffing

650-Watt Variable Power Microwave Oven

DIRECTIONS:
Place a microwave-safe trivet in a 13 x 2-inch microwave-safe baking dish. Crumble the sausage onto the trivet. Microwave, uncovered, at full power for 3 minutes. Remove the trivet with the sausage from the baking dish. Drain the sausage on paper toweling. Pour off all but 1 tablespoon of the fat from the baking dish. Spread the onion, celery, sage, thyme, salt and pepper in the dish; add the butter, and microwave, uncovered, at full power for 6 minutes, stirring once. Crumble the cornbread into the vegetable mixture. Pour on the chicken broth; mix well.

TURKEY TALK

Storing

Fresh turkeys Refrigerate at all times. Cook within 1 to 2 days of purchase.

Frozen whole turkeys Store in original wrapper up to 12 months at 0^0 F or lower.

Thawing

Conventional (Long) Method

Thawing time: 3 to 4 days, about 24 hours for each 5 pounds of whole frozen turkey.

- Leave turkey in original wrapper.
- Place frozen turkey on tray in refrigerator.

Cold Water (Short) Method

Thawing time: About 30 minutes per pound of whole frozen turkey.

- Leave turkey in original wrapper.
- Place turkey in sink or large pan.

- Completely cover with cold water.
- Change water every 30 minutes.
- Keep immersed in cold water at all times.

Note: Never thaw at room temperature. Once thawed, cook or refrigerate immediately.

Stuffing

When? Just before you roast your turkey is the time to stuff it. You run the risk of food poisoning if you do this earlier.

How much? Allow $\frac{3}{4}$ cup stuffing per pound of bird for turkeys weighing more than 10 pounds; $\frac{1}{2}$ cup stuffing per pound for smaller birds.

Note: Never freeze cooked stuffing in a cooked bird or uncooked stuffing in a raw bird. Remove all stuffing from cooked bird; wrap separately and refrigerate.

MICROWAVE OVEN COOKING SCHEDULE
for Stuffed or Unstuffed Turkey
Approximate cooking time in 625- to 700-watt microwave ovens

Times		4lb.	5lb.	6lb.	7lb.	8lb.	9lb.	10lb.	11lb.	12lb.
		Weight								
		Part I—Breast down at Full Power (100%)								
	1	8 min.	10 min.	12 min.	14 min.	16 min.	18 min.	20 min.	22 min.	24 min.
	2	8 min.	10 min.	12 min.	14 min.	16 min.	18 min.	20 min.	22 min.	24 min.
		Part II—Breast up at Half Power (50%)								
	3	8 min.	10 min.	12 min.	14 min.	16 min.	18 min.	20 min.	22 min.	24 min.
	4	8 min.	10 min.	12 min.	14 min.	16 min.	18 min.	20 min.	22 min.	24 min.
	5*	8 min.	10 min.	12 min.	14 min.	16 min.	18 min.	20 min.	22 min.	24 min.
	6	8 min.	10 min.	12 min.	14 min.	16 min.	18 min.	20 min.	22 min.	24 min.
Total cook time:		48 min.	60 min.	72 min.	84 min.	96 min.	108 min.	120 min.	132 min.	144 min.

*Check for doneness after Time 5.

Testing for Doneness

- Meat thermometer inserted in meatiest part of thigh reads 180° F to 185° F.
- Turkey juices run clear.
- Drumsticks move up and down easily.

Resting Period

Let turkey stand at room temperature for 20 minutes. This allows juices to settle and meat to firm up for easier carving.

Got a Question?

- The U.S.D.A. Meat and Poultry Hotline at 800-535-4555 will answer questions about your holiday bird from 10 A.M. to 4 P.M. (EST), Monday-Friday, no weekends or holidays.
- The Butterball Turkey Talk-line at 800-323-4848 will answer any questions about preparing the holiday turkey and trimmings. The toll-free Talk-line will operate from November 2 through December 24, Monday-Friday, 8 A.M. to 8 P.M. (CST), Thanksgiving Day, 6 A.M. to 7 P.M. (CST), and Christmas Eve Day, 8 A.M. to 6 P.M. (CST).

Microwave Cooking Directions for Turkey
(625- to 700-Watt Microwave Oven)

If frozen, thaw turkey as directed, *at left.* Thawing a turkey in the microwave is not recommended.

First Steps

1. Free legs from tucked position. Do not cut band of skin.
2. Remove neck and giblets from neck and body cavities. To microwave, place 3 cups water, ½ teaspoon salt, neck, gizzard and heart in a 2-quart microwave-safe casserole and cover. Microwave at Half Power (50%) for 35 minutes. Add the liver, cover and microwave 10 minutes more. Cooked neck, giblets and stock may be used in making the turkey gravy or mixing with the stuffing.
3. Rinse the turkey and drain well.
4. If desired, stuff the neck and body cavities loosely. Cover any exposed stuffing with plastic wrap.
5. Turn the wings back to hold the neck skin in place. Return the legs to tucked position. No trussing is necessary.
6. Make a Browning Sauce: Microwave ½ stick butter in microwave-safe bowl at Full Power (100%) for 30 to 40 seconds, or until melted. Blend in ¼ teaspoon paprika and ⅛ teaspoon browning and seasoning sauce. Stir well before using.

To Cook

1. Place the turkey, breast down, in a microwave-safe dish. If turkey tips, level with microwave-safe item so turkey will cook evenly.
2. Brush the back of the turkey with 1 tablespoon of the Browning Sauce.
3. See Microwave Oven Cooking Schedule for cooking time. Use schedule closest to weight of turkey. Follow Part I and Part II Cook Times without any delaying interruptions.
4. Microwave at Full Power (100%) for Time 1. Rotate the turkey one-half turn. Microwave for Time 2. Remove and discard the drippings.
5. Turn the turkey, breast up. If stuffed, remove the plastic wrap. Brush with the Browning Sauce. Level if turkey tips.
6. Microwave at Half Power (50%) for Times 3, 4 and 5. At end of each Time, rotate the turkey one-quarter turn; discard drippings; brush the turkey with the Browning Sauce. If overbrowning occurs, shield with small pieces of foil. After Time 5, check for doneness. Meat thermometer inserted in the thickest part of thigh (not touching bone) should register 180° to 185° F; in thickest part of the breast, 170° F; in the center of the stuffing, 160° to 165° F. If any of these temperatures have not been reached, cook for Time 6. Recheck the temperature; cook longer if necessary.
7. Cover the turkey with aluminum foil. Let stand for 15 to 20 minutes before carving.

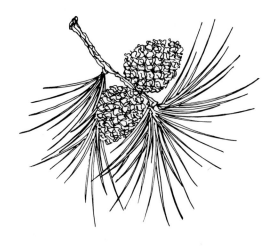

Cornbread

Bake at 425° for 20 to 25 minutes.
Makes 9 servings, or about 6 cups crumbled cornbread
for stuffing.

1   cup yellow cornmeal
1   cup unsifted all-purpose flour
1   tablespoon sugar
2   teaspoons baking powder
½   teaspoon salt
1¼   cups milk
¼   cup (½ stick) butter or margarine, melted

1. Preheat the oven to hot (425°). Grease a
   9 x 9 x 2-inch-square baking pan.
2. Combine the cornmeal, flour, sugar, baking
   powder and salt in a medium-size bowl; stir to mix
   well. Add the milk and melted butter; stir just
   until the dry ingredients are moistened. Pour the
   batter into the prepared pan.
3. Bake in the preheated hot oven (425°) for 20 to 25
   minutes, or until the center springs back when
   lightly pressed with fingertips. Cool in the pan on
   a wire rack.

Collard Greens

*Traditionally, greens are cooked for hours with slab bacon. This
is a lighter version.*

Makes 8 servings.

1¾   pounds trimmed collard greens (see Note below)
2   cups water
½   to 1 teaspoon salt, to taste
½   teaspoon pepper
3   to 4 tablespoons vinegar
     Chopped hard-cooked egg for garnish (optional)

1. Wash the collard leaves well under cold running
   water. Cut crosswise into ½-inch-wide strips.
   Place in a large pot with the water and salt. Bring
   to boiling. Lower heat to medium; cover and cook
   for 20 to 30 minutes until the greens are tender.
   (Cooking time will vary with the age and
   tenderness of the greens.)
2. Drain well; toss with the pepper and vinegar. Place
   in a serving bowl. Garnish with the chopped hard-
   cooked egg, if you wish.
Note: Two and three-quarters pounds of untrimmed
collard greens yield about 1¾ pounds trimmed leaves.

Marinated Coleslaw

A coleslaw that improves with standing.

Makes 8 servings.

8   cups shredded cabbage
       (about 1½ pounds)
1   large sweet green pepper, cut in thin strips
1   cup shredded carrot
¼   cup chopped pimiento
½   cup mayonnaise
¼   cup cider vinegar
2   to 4 tablespoons sugar
1   teaspoon celery seed
1   teaspoon prepared mustard
½   teaspoon salt
½   teaspoon pepper

1. Combine the cabbage, green pepper, carrot and
   pimiento in a large bowl. Stir together the
   mayonnaise, vinegar, sugar, celery seed, mustard,
   salt and pepper in a small bowl until well mixed.
   Pour over the vegetable mixture. Toss well to coat
   all the vegetables with the dressing.
2. Cover and refrigerate for at least 4 hours. Toss well
   before serving.

Spicy Red Pepper Relish

Make a day ahead for relish to mellow.

Makes 4 cups.

3   to 5 teaspoons finely chopped, seeded hot chili
       peppers
1½   cups distilled white vinegar
6   tablespoons water
6   tablespoons sugar
½   teaspoon salt
½   teaspoon dry mustard
4   cups chopped sweet red pepper
       (about 2 pounds)
2   cups chopped onion (2 large)

1. Combine the hot pepper, vinegar, water, sugar,
   salt and dry mustard in a large nonaluminum
   saucepan. Boil for 1 minute. Add the red pepper
   and onion. Boil for 5 to 7 minutes, or until the red
   pepper is cooked but still crunchy. Cool to room
   temperature.
2. Store, covered, in the refrigerator for up to 1
   month. Serve in hollowed-out pepper cups, if you
   wish.

Sweet Potato Casserole

This casserole improves with age, so it can be made 1 or 2 days in advance.

Bake at 400° for 1 hour.
Makes 8 servings.

3   *pounds sweet potatoes*
$1/2$ *cup raisins*
$1/4$ *cup ($1/2$ stick) butter or margarine, melted*
1   *cup apple cider*
2   *tablespoons firmly packed light brown sugar*
$1/2$ *teaspoon salt*
$1/2$ *teaspoon ground cinnamon*
$1/2$ *teaspoon vanilla*
$1/8$ *teaspoon ground nutmeg*

1. Preheat the oven to high (400°).
2. Butter a 10-inch iron skillet.
3. Peel the sweet potatoes; grate (you should have about 9 cups). Combine with the raisins and butter in the prepared skillet.
4. Combine the cider, brown sugar, salt, cinnamon, vanilla and nutmeg in a bowl; pour over the potatoes. Mix thoroughly. Cover tightly with aluminum foil.
5. Bake in the preheated hot oven (400°) for 30 minutes. Stir the potatoes. Bake, covered, for 30 minutes longer. Serve from the skillet or transfer to a serving bowl.

Microwave Directions For Sweet Potato Casserole

650-Watt Variable Power Microwave Oven

DIRECTIONS:
Place the butter in a 3-quart microwave-safe casserole. Microwave, uncovered, at full power for 1 minute to melt. Stir in the apple juice, brown sugar, salt, cinnamon, vanilla, nutmeg and raisins. Add the grated sweet potato; mix well. Microwave, covered, at full power for 18-20 minutes, or until the potatoes are cooked, stirring the potatoes halfway through the cooking time. Let stand, covered, for 5 minutes.

Buttermilk Biscuits

Try serving jellies and jams during the meal with the hot biscuits.

Bake at 500° for 10 to 12 minutes.
Makes 1 dozen biscuits.

2   *cups unsifted all-purpose flour (not unbleached)*
2   *teaspoons baking powder*
$1/2$ *teaspoon baking soda*
$1/2$ *teaspoon salt*
$1/4$ *cup well-chilled butter, margarine or vegetable shortening*
$3/4$ *to 1 cup buttermilk*

1. Preheat the oven to very hot (500°).
2. Sift together the flour, baking powder, baking soda and salt into a medium-size bowl. Cut in the butter with a pastry blender or 2 knives until the mixture resembles coarse meal. Stir in enough of the buttermilk to make a soft dough that leaves the side of the bowl; handle the dough as little as possible.
3. Turn the dough out onto a lightly floured surface. Knead gently about 5 times. Roll the dough out to $1/2$-inch thickness. Cut into 2-inch bisucits. Place on an ungreased baking sheet, leaving about 1 inch between biscuits.
4. Bake in the preheated very hot oven (500°) for 10 to 12 minutes, or until golden brown. Serve hot.

Chocolate Chess Pie

Typically very rich and sweet, but very good.

Bake at 350° for 45 to 50 minutes.
Makes 8 servings.

   Unbaked 9-inch Pie Shell (recipe follows)
$1^{1}/2$ *cups sugar*
$1/4$ *cup unsweetened cocoa powder*
1   *tablespoon unsifted all-purpose flour*
$1/2$ *cup (1 stick) butter or margarine, melted*
3   *eggs*
$1/4$ *cup milk*
2   *teaspoons vanilla*
   Unsweetened whipped cream for garnish

1. Prepare the Unbaked 9-inch Pie Shell.
2. Place the oven rack in its lowest position. Preheat the oven to moderate (350°).
3. Mix together the sugar, cocoa and flour in a large bowl until no lumps remain. Stir in the melted butter. Mix in the eggs, one at a time, until smooth. Stir in the milk and vanilla. Pour the mixture into the pie shell.
4. Bake on the lowest rack in the preheated moderate oven (350°) for 45 to 50 minutes. Cool on a wire rack. Serve at room temperature or chilled. Garnish with whipped cream.

Unbaked 9-Inch Pie Shell

1   cup unsifted all-purpose flour (not unbleached)
¼   teaspoon salt
¼   cup vegetable shortening
2   tablespoons well-chilled butter
3   tablespoons ice water

1. Stir the flour and salt in a bowl until mixed. Cut in the shortening and butter with a pastry blender until the mixture resembles coarse meal. Sprinkle the water over the mixture; stir with a fork until a dough forms. Shape into a ball; wrap in plastic wrap. Refrigerate for 1 hour.
2. Roll out the dough on a lightly floured surface into an 11-inch circle. Fit into a 9-inch pie plate. Roll up the pastry onto the rim of the plate; flute or shape as desired.

PERFECT PIECRUSTS

• *Avoid overhandling the dough.*
• *Only use as much flour as is needed to prevent sticking.*
• *Never pull or stretch the dough. Ease it into the pan.*
• *To minimize shrinking, chill the pastry shell before baking.*
• *To prevent soggy bottom crusts, pour your filling into the crust just before baking. Or, partially bake the empty crust and line it with aluminum foil. Fill it with raw beans or rice to weigh down the dough. Bake until partially set but not colored, then carefully remove the foil and beans. Fill and finish baking.*
• *If crust browns too fast, lightly cover it with aluminum foil, shiny-side up. Continue baking until the filling is set.*
• *If you like rolling pastry between sheets of wax paper, wipe the countertop with a damp cloth or sponge before placing the wax paper on it; the moisture will keep the paper flat and prevent it from sliding.*

Pecan-Pumpkin Pie

Bake at 425° for 15 minutes; then bake at 350° for 40 to 45 minutes.
Makes 8 servings.

Unbaked 9-inch Pie Shell (see recipe at left)
Pumpkin Filling:
½   cup firmly packed light brown sugar
1   tablespoon unsifted all-purpose flour
1   teaspoon ground cinnamon
½   teaspoon salt
½   teaspoon ground ginger
½   teaspoon ground nutmeg
     Pinch ground cloves
1   can (16 ounces) pumpkin purée
2   eggs
1   cup evaporated milk
2   teaspoons vanilla
Pecan Topping:
¼   cup firmly packed light brown sugar
¼   cup (½ stick) butter or margarine, softened
1   cup pecans, finely chopped

1. Prepare the Unbaked 9-inch Pie Shell.
2. Place the oven rack in its lowest position. Preheat the oven to hot (425°).
3. Prepare the Pumpkin Filling: Mix together the ½ cup brown sugar, flour, cinnamon, salt, ginger, nutmeg and cloves in a large bowl until well mixed. Add the pumpkin, eggs, milk and vanilla; stir with a whisk or beater until smooth. Pour into the pie shell.
4. Bake in the preheated hot oven (425°) for 15 minutes. Lower oven temperature to moderate (350°). Bake for 10 minutes longer. Leave the oven at 350°.
5. Meanwhile, prepare the Pecan Topping: Beat together the ¼ cup brown sugar and butter in a small bowl until well mixed. Stir in the pecans.
6. Sprinkle the Pecan Topping evenly over the top of the pie. Bake in the preheated moderate oven (350°) for 30 to 35 minutes, or until a knife inserted in the center comes out clean. Cool on a wire rack. Serve at room temperature with whipped cream and pecans, if you wish.

Did You Know...

Pies existed in Medieval times, with both savory fillings and fruit mixtures.

Chocolate Pound Cake

Be sure to start with a cold oven when you bake this cake.

Bake at 325° for $1\frac{1}{2}$ hours.
Makes 16 servings.

$1\frac{1}{2}$ cups (3 sticks) butter or margarine, softened
1 package (8 ounces) cream cheese, softened
3 cups sugar
2 teaspoons vanilla
$\frac{1}{2}$ teaspoon salt
3 squares (1 ounce each) unsweetened chocolate, melted
3 cups unsifted all-purpose flour
6 eggs, slightly beaten
Vanilla Glaze (recipe follows)

1. Do *not* preheat the oven. Grease and flour a 12-cup Bundt® pan.
2. Beat together the butter and cream cheese in a large mixer bowl until light and fluffy. Add the sugar, vanilla and salt; beat until well mixed. Stir in the melted chocolate until well mixed.
3. Mix in the flour and eggs alternately, beginning and ending with the flour, mixing well after each addition. Spoon the batter into the prepared pan.
4. Place the cake in the cold oven. Turn the oven on and set at low (325°). Bake for $1\frac{1}{2}$ hours, or until a wooden pick inserted in the center comes out clean. Cool the cake in the pan on a wire rack. Run a small flexible knife around the tube and edge of the pan. Invert onto a serving plate.
5. Spread with the Vanilla Glaze. Garnish with marzipan fruits, if you wish.

Vanilla Glaze: Place 1 cup *unsifted* 10X (confectioners') sugar in a small bowl. Gradually stir in $\frac{1}{2}$ teaspoon vanilla and up to 2 tablespoons of milk until the mixture is smooth and has a good glazing consistency.
Note: This cake freezes well, but do not glaze it until you are ready to serve it. Store leftover cake at room temperature.

Fresh Apple Fruitcake

Bake at 350° for $1\frac{1}{2}$ to $1\frac{3}{4}$ hours.
Makes 16 servings.

3 cups unsifted all-purpose flour
1 teaspoon baking soda
1 teaspoon salt
$2\frac{1}{2}$ teaspoons ground cinnamon
$\frac{1}{4}$ teaspoon ground mace
2 cups sugar
3 eggs
2 teaspoons vanilla
$1\frac{1}{2}$ cups vegetable oil
3 cups diced, pared apples (about 1 pound McIntosh or Stayman)
1 cup walnuts, chopped
1 cup chopped pitted dates

1. Preheat the oven to moderate (350°). Grease the bottom only of a 10 x 14-inch tube pan. Line the bottom with wax paper; grease the paper.
2. Sift together the flour, baking soda, salt, cinnamon and mace into a small bowl.
3. Beat together the sugar, eggs and vanilla in a large bowl until blended. Add the oil; beat until smooth. Stir in the flour mixture. Fold in the apples, nuts and dates. Spoon the batter into the prepared pan.
4. Bake in the preheated moderate oven (350°) for $1\frac{1}{2}$ to $1\frac{3}{4}$ hours, or until a wooden pick inserted into the center of the cake comes out clean. Cool the cake in the pan on a wire rack. Run a thin, sharp knife around the outer edge and inner tube of the pan to remove the cake. Invert onto the rack. Invert the cake again onto a serving plate. Dust the top with 10X (confectioners') sugar and garnish with alternating slices of red and green apple, if you wish.

Cookies for the Cookie Jar. (*See schematic on page 220.*)

Legend has it…Good King Wenceslaus, back in the 10th century, brought a feast to a poor family and started one of our most cherished Christmas traditions—sharing food with others. History reveals that on an icy winter's night, Wenceslaus spied a peasant from his palace window. Moved by the sight of the poor man trying to find firewood, the king packed up a basket of food and, with his servant, trudged through the snow to the peasant's home. Since then, baking cookies, giving care packages and cooking for others have become annual Christmas traditions enjoyed by all.

Chapter
VII
THE CHRISTMAS PANTRY

One of the best things about Christmas is home-made goodies—and lots of them! That's why we love this chapter: it's packed with a wonderful assortment of cakes and cookies, preserves and condiments, candies and treats. In short, everything you need to make sensational desserts, loving care packages and super cookie exchanges. But be warned: Once your family starts nibbling, there may not be anything left to give as gifts!

▌ *Low-Cost*

▌ *Make-Ahead*

▌ *Quick and Easy*

▌ *Low-Calorie*

▌ *Bazaar*

PUNCHES

Wine Cup Flambé

Wine Cup Flambé

Turn down the lights when you serve this dramatic punch of red and Port wines, flambéed with brandy.

Makes about 24 servings.

1/4	cup sugar
2	four-inch pieces stick cinnamon, broken
8	whole cardamom seeds, crushed
8	whole cloves
4	whole allspice
	Thin rind from 1 orange (no white)
1/2	cup water
1	bottle (2 liters) dry red wine
2	cups ruby Port wine
1	cup raisins
1	cup almonds
1	orange, sliced
20	tiny sugar cubes (1/2-inch size)
1	two-inch piece lemon rind studded with 3 whole cloves
1	cup brandy, warmed

1. Combine the sugar, cinnamon, cardamom, cloves, allspice, orange rind and water in a small saucepan; bring to boiling. Lower the heat; cover; simmer for 5 minutes. Let stand for several hours, or until ready to make the punch. Strain, discarding the spices and orange rind.
2. Combine the wine, Port, raisins and almonds in a large saucepan; add the strained spice mixture. Bring just to boiling. Pour into a warmed heatproof punch bowl; float the orange slices on top.
3. Place the sugar cubes and lemon rind in a large ladle; add about 1/4 cup of the warm brandy; carefully pour the remaining brandy over the surface of the punch bowl. Ignite the mixture in the ladle with a long match; rotate and shake the ladle until the sugar is almost dissolved.
4. Lower the ladle onto the punch to ignite the brandy floating on top; stir slowly a few times. When the flames have died, serve the punch in small mugs or cups with a few raisins and almonds in each serving.

Mocha Eggnog

A variation of the classic holiday drink.

Makes 1 1/2 quarts.

2	cups heavy cream
2	tablespoons instant coffee powder
5	tablespoons chocolate-flavored syrup
5	eggs, separated
1/3	cup sugar
3/4	cup bourbon whiskey
1/4	cup brandy

1. Stir together the cream, coffee and chocolate syrup in a 4-cup measure.
2. Beat together the egg yolks and sugar in a large bowl until the mixture is thick and lemon-colored. Stir in the whiskey, brandy and cream mixture. Chill.
3. Just before serving, beat the egg whites in a large bowl with an electric mixer at high speed until soft peaks form. Fold egg whites into the cream mixture.

Did You Know. . .

Christmas eggnog is one of the few native customs of the United States.

DECORATIVE ICE RING OR BLOCK

Fill a ring mold, metal pan or kugelhopf mold one-fourth full with water. Partially freeze. Add the fruit of your choice; citrus slices, strawberries, pineapple chunks, maraschino cherries, etc. Arrange in a decorative design. Freeze to anchor the fruit; fill with ice water and freeze again until solid.

● *It's always a good idea to make sure your ice mold will fit into the punch bowl! Invert the empty mold into the bowl, keeping in mind that the punch and garnishes will take up room, too. Then make the mold.*

HOLIDAY PARTY BAR

HOW TO CONVERT

Liquor and wine have gone metric. The following is a list of equivalents.

Metric measure replaces:	U.S. measure
500 milliliter or ½ liter (16.9 oz.)	the pint
750 milliliter (25.4 oz.)	the fifth
one liter (33.8 oz.)	the quart
two liters (67.6 oz.)	the ½ gallon
four liters (135.2 oz.)	the gallon

HOW MUCH TO BUY

Below is a chart indicating how many drinks you should get from bottles of liquor or wine. If serving wine with dinner, however, figure on fewer glasses to a bottle: 5-6 to a liter (quart); 3-4 to 750 milliliter (fifth).

	Number of drinks per bottle	
	liter	750 milliliter
whiskey, gin, vodka (mixed drinks, highballs—½-oz. servings)	22	17
table wines (red, white, rosé— 4.5 servings)	6-8	5-6
sherry (3-oz. servings)	11	8
cordials (1-oz. servings)	33	25
champagne, sparkling wine (4- or 5-oz. servings)	6-8	5-6

Be prepared for unexpected guests, as well as planned entertaining, with a well-stocked bar. To keep costs under control:

● Comparison shop when you're buying liquid refreshments for any gathering. Check ads and watch for specials.
● When purchasing sizeable quantities of beer, soda, wine, or liquor, ask the manager if he or she will sell to you at the case price.
● Save money by purchasing store brands and private-label liquors.
● Let the use of wine or liquor determine the price you pay for it. If you're mixing drinks where the liquor will be heavily masked by spices or fruit juices, buy an inexpensive brand. The same goes for wines. Buy nonvintage jug wines for punch bases and Sangria. You should, however, buy reputable brands of spirits such as Scotch or bourbon.

Spiced Peach Punch

A nonalcoholic punch for the whole family.

Makes about 2 quarts.

1	quart water
23	ounces peach nectar (half a 46-ounce can)
6	tea bags
12	whole allspice
4	whole cloves
4	cinnamon sticks
1	lemon, halved
1	cup firmly packed light brown sugar
2	tablespoons lemon juice

1. Combine water, nectar, tea bags, allspice, cloves, cinnamon sticks and lemon halves in a large saucepan. Bring to boiling; cover; steep for 5 minutes. Remove the tea bags; let remaining mixture steep for 10 minutes longer. Strain the punch; return to the saucepan.
2. Reheat; stir in the sugar until it dissolves. Add the lemon juice. Serve warm.

Champagne Punch

A sparkling punch that's right for the holiday season or any special occasion.

Makes 25 four-ounce servings.

½	cup light corn syrup
½	cup brandy
1	bottle (750 ml) sauterne wine, chilled
1	bottle (28 ounces) club soda, chilled
1	bottle (750 ml) champagne, chilled
	Ice ring (recipe follows)

1. Combine the corn syrup and brandy in a large punch bowl until well blended; stir in the sauterne.
2. Just before serving, stir in the club soda and champagne. Slide in the ICE RING and garnish with lemon slices, if you wish.

ICE RING: Pour water, club soda or mineral water into a decorative mold or container that will fit inside the punch bowl. Freeze for 8 hours, or overnight. To release, dip the mold or container quickly in and out of a pan of hot water, or allow to stand at room temperature for 5 minutes, then invert onto a cookie sheet. Slide the mold into the punch bowl.

Hot Mulled Cider

A spicy classic. Make up extra spice bags and sell them at bazaars with a copy of this recipe.

Makes 16 eight-ounce servings.

1	bottle (1 gallon) apple cider
1	cup firmly packed light brown sugar
9	whole cloves
9	whole allspice
4	three-inch pieces stick cinnamon, broken into 1-inch pieces
2	lemons, thinly sliced

1. Combine the apple cider and brown sugar in a large kettle.
2. Tie the cloves, allspice and cinnamon in a piece of cheesecloth; place in the kettle. Simmer the mixture for 5 minutes. Discard the spice bag.
3. Serve the cider in mugs, and float a lemon slice in each.

Cranberry Fizz Punch

Club soda adds sparkle to this nonalcoholic punch.

Makes 30 four-ounce servings.

2	bottles (32 ounces each) cranberry juice cocktail, chilled
2	bottles (28 ounces each) club soda, chilled
	Ice Ring recipe (see Champagne Punch)

1. Combine the well-chilled cranberry juice cocktail and the club soda in a large punch bowl.
2. Slide in the ICE RING. Garnish with mint sprigs, if you wish.

COOKIES

Remember: Cookies make wonderful bazaar treats, wrapped in baskets or decorative tins.

COOKIE SPECTACULAR

(Shown on page 214.)

1. *Oatmeal Sandwich Bars* **2.** *Tuiles Aux Amandes (Almond Tiles)* **3.** *Cherry-Pecan Balls* **4.** *Candy Canes* **5.** *Stained-Glass Cookies* **6.** *Pfeffernuss* **7.** *Choco-Nut Sandwiches* **8.** *Fruitcake Jewels* **9.** *Old-Fashioned Gingerbread* **10.** *English Toffee Drops* **11.** *Grace's Cookie Brittle* **12.** *Holiday Wreaths* **13.** *Two-Tone Slices*

$ ◄◄ ▶

Pfeffernuss

From Germany comes a cardamom-spiced cookie that gets better when aged a few weeks before serving.

Bake at 350° for 8 minutes.
Makes 6 dozen.

2¼ cups unsifted all-purpose flour
2 teaspoons pumpkin pie spice
½ teaspoon ground cardamom
¼ teaspoon baking soda
¼ teaspoon salt
⅛ teaspoon pepper
½ cup candied citron, finely chopped
2 tablespoons butter or margarine
1¼ cups sifted 10X (confectioners') sugar
2 eggs
Candied red and green cherries
1 teaspoon milk

1. Measure the flour, pumpkin pie spice, cardamom, baking soda, salt and pepper into a sifter; sift into a medium-size bowl; stir in the citron.
2. Beat the butter or margarine and 1 cup of the 10X sugar until well mixed in a medium-size bowl with an electric mixer at medium speed. Beat in the eggs, one at a time, then the flour mixture, just until blended. Refrigerate overnight, or until firm.
3. Preheat the oven to moderate (350°).
4. Roll the dough, about 1 teaspoonful at a time, into small balls; place, 2 inches apart, on cookie sheets. Top each with a piece of candied cherry.
5. In a small cup, stir the milk into the remaining ¼ cup 10X sugar until smooth. Drizzle very lightly over the top of each cookie.
6. Bake in the preheated moderate oven (350°) 8 minutes, or until very lightly browned. Remove from the cookie sheets at once with a spatula; cool completely. Store in a metal tin with a tight-fitting cover at least 4 weeks to mellow before serving.

BAKING BASICS

IF YOU'RE OUT OF SOMETHING

INSTEAD OF	USE
Baking powder (1 teaspoon)	¼ teaspoon baking soda and ⅝ teaspoon cream of tartar.
Buttermilk (1 cup)	1 tablespoon vinegar, mixed with milk to make 1 cup; let stand 5 minutes.
Chocolate, un-sweetened (1 ounce)	3 tablespoons cocoa and 1 tablespoon vegetable shortening.
Cornstarch (1½ teaspoons)	1 tablespoon flour.
Corn Syrup (1 cup)	1 cup sugar and ¼ cup liquid.
Cream of tarter (¼ teaspoon)	1 teaspoon lemon juice.
Egg (1, whole)	2 egg yolks.
Honey (1 cup)	1¼ cups sugar and ¼ cup liquid OR: 1 cup maple syrup OR: 1 cup light molasses.
Milk, whole (1 cup)	½ cup evaporated milk and ½ cup water.
Sour Cream (1 cup)	1 cup undiluted milk and 1 tablespoon vinegar or lemon juice.

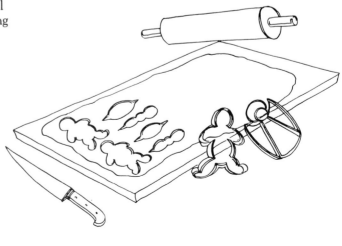

BAKING EQUIVALENT CHART

Ingredients	Equivalent

FLOUR

Regular, 1 pound . . . . 4 cups, sifted
     2 pounds . . . . 8 cups, sifted
     5 pounds . . . . 20 cups, sifted
     10 pounds . . . . 40 cups, sifted
     25 pounds . . . . 100 cups, sifted
Cake Flour, 1 pound . . . . 4½ cups, plus 2
     tablespoons, sifted

Graham crackers,
     11 squares . . . . 1 cup crumbs
Oatmeal, 18 oz., quick . . . . 7 cups
     ½ oz. packet, plain . . . . ½ cup

     SUGARS
     Granulated sugar, 1 pound . . . . 2 cups
       2 pounds . . . . 4 cups
       5 pounds . . . . 10 cups
Brown sugar, 1 pound . . . . 2¼ cups, packed
10X confectioners', 1 pound . . . . 4 cups

NUTS, shelled

Walnuts, 1 pound, whole . . . . 4 cups
     10-oz. pack, broken . . . . 2½ cups
     (ground by you . . . . 2⅔ cups)
Almonds, 1 pound, whole . . . . 3½ cups
     ¼ pound, whole . . . . 7 ounces
     6-oz. pack, sliced . . . . 2 cups
Filberts, 6-oz. pack, whole . . . . 1½ cups
     (ground by you . . . . 2 cups)
Pecans, 1 pound, whole . . . . 4 cups

FRUIT

Mixed, candied, 4 oz. chopped . . . . ½ cup
Citron, 4 oz. chopped . . . . ½ cup
Cherries, candied, 8 oz. whole . . . . 1 cup
Raisins, 15 oz . . . . 3 cups

NO-STICK CUT-UPS

● *To easily chop dried fruit, spray kitchen shears or chopping knife with non-stick cooking spray. Or, dredge the fruit in flour before cutting.*

Oatmeal Sandwich Bars

Filled with a lemon-scented date mixture, these bars keep well.

Bake at 400° for 25 minutes.
Makes about 30.

3   **cups cut-up pitted dates**
1½ cups water
¼   **cup granulated sugar**
    Grated rind and juice of 1 lemon
¾   **cup (1½ sticks) butter or margarine, softened**
1   **cup firmly packed light brown sugar**
1¾ cups sifted all-purpose flour
1   **teaspoon salt**
½   **teaspoon baking soda**
1½ cups quick-cooking rolled oats

1. Combine the dates, water, granulated sugar and lemon juice in a small heavy saucepan. Cook over low heat, stirring often until the mixture thickens. Remove the heat; stir in the lemon rind. Cool.
2. Preheat the oven to hot (400°).
3. Beat the butter or margarine and light brown sugar until fluffy in a large bowl with an electric mixer at high speed. Stir flour, salt and baking soda together; beat into butter mixture; beat in oats.
4. Press half of the oat mixture into a greased 9x13-inch baking pan, spreading evenly to cover the bottom of the pan. Spread the cooled date mixture in an even layer on top. Sprinkle the remaining oat mixture on top; pat down lightly.
5. Bake in the preheated hot oven (400°) for 25 minutes, or until the top is golden brown. Cool for 15 minutes in the pan on a wire rack. Cut into 2 x 1½-inch bars; cool completely in the pan on the wire rack. Store in an airtight container.

Tuiles Aux Amandes (Almond Tiles)

So named because they resemble French roof tiles, these buttery cookies are crisp and delicate.

Bake at 350° for 12 minutes.
Makes about 2 dozen cookies.

2¼ cups sliced almonds (8 ounces)
¾   **cup sugar**
¼   **cup unsifted all-purpose flour**
3   **egg whites**
¼   **cup (½ stick) butter or margarine, melted**

1   teaspoon vanilla
¼   teaspoon almond extract

1. Combine the almonds, sugar and flour in a large bowl until well blended; stir in the egg whites, melted butter or margarine, vanilla and almond extract. Cover with plastic wrap; refrigerate for at least 1 hour.
2. Preheat the oven to moderate (350°).
3. Line a cookie sheet with aluminum foil; grease generously.
4. Drop the batter, a level tablespoon at a time, 5 to 6 inches apart on the prepared cookie sheet; smooth the tops with a spoon or fork.
5. Bake in the preheated moderate oven (350°) for 12 minutes, or until the cookies are deep brown around the edges. Remove the sheet from the oven. Let stand for 30 seconds. Using a metal spatula, lift the cookies from the sheet; invert and curl around the rolling pin or bottle. If the cookies become too brittle to handle, return them to the oven for 30 seconds to 1 minute. Store in an airtight container in a cool spot.

NO-BAKE MINT JULEP CUPS:

Crush enough vanilla-type wafers to make 2½ cups crumbs. Combine with 1 cup sifted 10X (confectioners') sugar, 1 cup finely chopped walnuts or pecans, 3 T light corn syrup, 3 T bourbon and 1 T white crème de menthe in a large bowl; mix well. Drop with a measuring spoon (curved side up) into miniature (1¾-inch) muffin-pan liner cups. Drop another teaspoonful on top of the first. Mellow at room temperature for 24 hours. Store in airtight containers.

Fruity Chews

Moist squares filled with glacé fruit and pecans.

Bake at 350° for 45 minutes.
Makes 24 squares.

4   large egg whites, at room temperature
¼   teaspon salt
1¾ cups sugar
2   cups chopped pecans (8 ounces)
1   container (4 ounces) candied red cherries, chopped
1   container (4 ounces) mixed candied fruits
⅝   cup (1¼ sticks) butter or margarine, melted
2   teaspoons vanilla
1¾ cups unsifted cake flour
    Green decorating icing (from a 4¼-ounce tube)
    Candied red cherry halves

1. Preheat the oven to moderate (350°).
2. Line a 9x13-inch baking pan with wax paper; grease the paper.
3. Beat the egg whites and salt until foamy white and double in volume in a small bowl with an electric mixer at high speed; add the sugar, 1 tablespoon at a time; continue beating until the egg whites form stiff peaks.
4. Combine the pecans, cherries, candied fruits, butter or margarine and vanilla in a medium bowl. Alternately fold the flour and egg whites into the mixture with the wooden spoon, beginning and ending with the flour. Spread batter into the prepared pan.
5. Bake in the preheated moderate oven (350°) for 45 minutes, or until a skewer inserted in the middle comes out clean. Cool in the pan on a wire rack.
6. Cut into 24 squares (make 5 lengthwise cuts, 3 crosswise cuts). Decorate each square with a squiggle of the frosting and a halved candied cherry. When the frosting sets, layer in an airtight metal tin between the layers of wax paper.

◀◀◀

Choco-Nut Sandwiches

Filled with buttercream frosting, these chocolate drop cookies will remind you of fudgy brownies.

Bake at 350° for 10 minutes.
Makes about 20.

1   cup firmly packed brown sugar
½   cup vegetable shortening
1   egg
1   teaspoon vanilla
½   cup milk
2   teaspoons vinegar
1⅔ cups unsifted all-purpose flour
½   teaspoon salt
½   teaspoon baking soda
2   squares (1 ounce each) unsweetened chocolate, melted
½   cup chopped walnuts
     Vanilla Buttercream (recipe follows)
     Multicolored sprinkles

1. Preheat the oven to moderate (350°).
2. Beat the sugar and shortening until fluffy in a large bowl with an electric mixer at medium speed; add the egg and vanilla and beat well. Combine the milk and vinegar in a 1-cup measure to sour milk.
3. Sift the flour, salt and baking soda onto wax paper. Turn the mixer speed to low; add the soured milk and flour mixture, alternately, to make a smooth batter. Stir in the melted chocolate and walnuts.
4. Drop by teaspoonfuls, 2-inches apart, onto greased cookie sheets.
5. Bake in the preheated moderate oven (350°) for 10 minutes, or until the cookies are set when lightly touched with a fingertip. Remove from the cookie sheets with a metal spatula to wire racks. Cool completely.
6. Pair cookies, flat sides together, with the VANILLA BUTTERCREAM pressing lightly so the buttercream flows over the edge; roll in the sprinkles. Top with a dollop of the buttercream; decorate with more sprinkles.

Variation: For CHOCOLATE PEANUT DROPS, substitute ¼ teaspoon aromatic bitters for vanilla and 1 cup chopped peanuts for the walnuts. Do not pair with the buttercream.

VANILLA BUTTERCREAM: Makes enough to fill and decorate cookies. Beat 3 tablespoons softened butter or margarine until fluffy in a small bowl with the electric mixer at high speed. Add 1¾ cups 10X (confectioners') sugar alternately with ¾ teaspoon vanilla and 2 tablespoons milk, beating until creamy.

◀◀◀ ◣

Fruitcake Jewels

More like little cakes, these chewy delights are sweetened with honey.

Bake at 350° for 10 minutes.
Makes 4 dozen.

½   cup (1 stick) butter or margarine, softened
⅔   cup honey
4   eggs
3   tablespoons evaporated milk
2½ cups all-purpose flour
1   teaspoon salt
¼   teaspoon baking soda
2   teaspoons pumpkin pie spice
1   package (11 ounces) mixed dried fruit, chopped
2   cups chopped walnuts or almonds
     Candied red or green cherries

1. Preheat the oven to moderate (350°).
2. Beat the butter or margarine and honey until fluffy in a large bowl with an electric mixer at high speed. Add the eggs, one at a time, beating well; beat in the milk.
3. Sift the flour, salt, baking soda and pumpkin pie spice together onto wax paper. Fold into the creamed butter mixture; stir in the chopped fruit and walnuts or almonds. Drop by teaspoonfuls, 2 inches apart, on greased cookie sheets. Top with the candied cherry halves.
4. Bake in the preheated moderate oven (350°) for 10 minutes, or until golden brown and firm. Cool on the cookie sheets on wire racks for 3 minutes; remove to wire racks with a metal spatula; cool completely. Store in an airtight metal container.

Two-Tone Slices

A stacking technique creates these ribboned cookies.

Bake at 350 for 10 minutes.
Makes about 9 dozen.

4 cups unsifted all-purpose flour
1 teaspoon baking powder
1 teaspoon salt
$1/4$ teaspoon baking soda
$1\frac{1}{4}$ cups ($2\frac{1}{2}$ sticks) butter or margarine, softened
1 cup firmly packed brown sugar
$1/2$ cup granulated sugar
2 eggs
2 teaspoons vanilla
    Green food coloring
$1\frac{1}{2}$ squares ($1\frac{1}{2}$ ounces) unsweetened chocolate,
    melted and cooled

1. Sift the flour, baking powder, salt and baking soda together onto wax paper.
2. Beat the butter or margarine with the brown and granulated sugars until fluffy in a large bowl with an electric mixer at high speed. Beat in the eggs and vanilla until well blended. Stir in the flour mixture, a third at a time, to make a soft dough.
3. Divide the dough evenly into 4 parts. Leave 2 parts plain; tint one part green with a few drops of the green food coloring; mix melted chocolate into the remaining dough.
4. Roll out one plain piece of dough to a 14x3-inch rectangle between sheets of wax paper; repeat with the green dough.
5. Chill the doughs in the freezer for 10 minutes, or until firm. Halve each rectangle, lengthwise, cutting through wax paper; remove top sheets of paper. Lay one plain strip, paper-side up, on top of green strip and peel off paper; repeat with remaining strips, alternating colors to make 4 layers.
6. Repeat the process with the chocolate dough and the remaining plain dough. Wrap both stacks in wax paper. Refrigerate for at least 4 hours.
7. Preheat the oven to moderate (350°).
8. Slice the chilled dough $1/4$-inch thick. Place on greased cookie sheets.
9. Bake in the preheated moderate oven (350°) for 10 minutes, or until golden. Remove the cookies with a spatula to wire racks. Cool completely before packing between layers of wax paper in an airtight container.

TINTING COOKIES: IT'S IN THE BAG!

● *When tinting cookie dough with food coloring, knead it in a heavy-duty plastic bag to avoid staining hands and countertop.*

COOKIE BAKING TIPS

● *Use exact measurements and follow recipes to a "T."*
● *When working with a soft dough, try to avoid extremes in kitchen temperatures. Too cool a room and the dough becomes stiff; too hot, and the dough gets too soft.*
● *If the recipe calls for a firm, refrigerated dough, keep dough in refrigerator and remove only the amount you use at one time to roll or cut.*
● *Don't use extra-large cookie sheets that touch the sides of the oven. This prevents proper circulation of heat necessary for even cooking.*
● *Grease cookie sheets, if necessary, with vegetable cooking shortening or nonstick vegetable spray.*
● *Leave plenty of room between cookies so they won't spread and touch when baking.*
● *Check oven temperature with a thermometer before placing cookies in oven.*
● *Place racks in center slots of oven for evenly baked cookies.*
● *Check cookies at the minimum baking time for doneness. Waiting until the maximum time is sometimes too late.*

STORING COOKIES

● *To keep your cookies crisp, store between layers of wax paper in metal or glass container with a tight-fitting lid. Keep in a cool, dry place.*
● *To keep cookies soft, store in a tin with an apple wedge or a piece of soft white bread to add moisture, but be sure to replace it often.*
● *To freshen soft cookies, place them in a casserole, then cover and heat at 300° for 8 to 10 minutes.*
● *To freshen crisp cookies before serving them, place them on a baking sheet and heat at 300° for 3 to 5 minutes.*

🅂 🎨
Old-Fashioned Gingerbread

These spicy cut-out cookies make wonderful tree ornaments; or use as placecards for the holiday table.

Bake at 350° for 8 minutes.
Makes 6 dozen.

3³⁄₄ cups unsifted all-purpose flour
2   tablespoons cocoa powder
2¹⁄₂ teaspoons pumpkin pie spice
1   teaspoon baking soda
¹⁄₂ teaspoon salt
1   cup (2 sticks) butter or margarine, softened
1   cup sugar
1   egg
¹⁄₂ cup light molasses
    Red, white and green decorating icing (from
    4¹⁄₄-ounce tubes)
    Ornamental Frosting (recipe follows)
    Cinnamon red-hot candies

1. Sift the flour, cocoa powder, pumpkin pie spice, baking soda and salt together onto wax paper.
2. Beat the butter or margarine until fluffy in a large bowl with an electric mixer at high speed; gradually add the sugar, beating well after each addition. Add the egg and molasses; beat well. Stir in the flour mixture. Wrap in wax paper; refrigerate overnight.
3. Preheat the oven to moderate (350°).
4. Roll out the dough, one-quarter at a time, to ¹⁄₄-inch thickness on a floured pastry cloth or board. Cut, using your favorite 3-inch cookie cutters. Place on cookie sheets.
5. Bake in the preheated moderate oven (350°) for 8 minutes, or until edges are browned. Let the cookies cool for a few minutes on the cookie sheets on wire racks; remove to wire racks with a metal spatula; cool completely.
6. Decorate the cookies with the decorative icing for outlines, the ORNAMENTAL FROSTING for filling in areas, and the cinnamon red-hots. Let the frosting set completely. Store between layers of wax paper in airtight containers.

Tip: If you place a small, dry bean through the tops of these cookies before they go into the oven, they'll produce a hole for stringing a ribbon to hang them.

ORNAMENTAL FROSTING: Makes about 1 cup. Combine 1 cup 10X (confectioners') sugar, 1 tablespoon light cream or water and ¹⁄₂ teaspoon vanilla in a small bowl with a wire whisk; add 1 to 1¹⁄₂ teaspoons more liquid, if necessary, to make a spreadable frosting.

🎨
English Toffee Drops

Buttery, candylike cookies, combining almond brickle with semisweet chocolate.

Bake at 375° for 8 to 10 minutes.
Makes about 8 dozen.

2¹⁄₄ cups unsifted all-purpose flour
1   teaspoon baking soda
1   teaspoon salt
1   cup (2 sticks) butter or margarine, softened
³⁄₄ cup granulated sugar
³⁄₄ cup firmly packed brown sugar
1   teaspoon almond extract
2   eggs
1   package (12 ounces) miniature semisweet
    chocolate morsels
1   package (6 ounces) almond brickle chips

1. Preheat the oven to moderate (375°).
2. Sift the flour, baking soda and salt together on wax paper.
3. Beat the butter or margarine, granulated and brown sugars and almond extract in a large bowl with an electric mixer at high speed until creamy; beat in the eggs, one at a time. Stir in the flour mixture with a wooden spoon, mixing just until blended. Stir in chocolate pieces and almond brickle.
4. Drop the dough by rounded teaspoons, 2 inches apart, onto ungreased cookie sheets. (Do not crowd.)
5. Bake in the preheated moderate oven (375°) for 8 to 10 minutes, or until the edges are golden. Transfer to wire racks with a metal spatula; cool completely. Store in an airtight container.

Candy Canes

Simple to make, and a merry sight hanging on the Christmas tree.

Bake at 350° for 10 minutes.
Makes about 4 dozen.

3³⁄₄ cups unsifted all-purpose flour
1   teaspoon baking powder
1   teaspoon salt
¹⁄₂ cup (1 stick) butter or margarine, softened
1¹⁄₄ cups sugar
1   egg
¹⁄₂ teaspoon peppermint extract
¹⁄₄ cup milk
   Red and green food coloring

1. Preheat the oven to moderate (350°).
2. Sift the flour, baking powder and salt onto wax paper. Grease 2 or 3 cookie sheets.
3. Beat the butter or margarine and the sugar until fluffy in a large bowl with an electric mixer at high speed; beat in the egg and peppermint extract. Stir in the flour mixture alternately with the milk.
4. Spoon one quarter of the dough onto wax paper; knead in a few drops of red food coloring to tint pink. Repeat with another quarter of the dough and the green food coloring. Leave the remaining dough plain.
5. To form each candy cane: Pinch off about a teaspoonful each of the red or green dough and the plain dough; roll each into a pencil-thin strip 5 inches long. Place the strips side by side, pressing the ends together; twist to form a rope. Place the ropes on the prepared cookie sheet, 1 inch apart, bending into a cane shape.
6. Bake in the preheated moderate oven (350°) for 10 minutes or until firm. Cool a few minutes on the cookie sheets on wire racks. Carefully remove with a metal spatula to wire racks; cool completely. Use as tree decorations; store remainder in a metal tin.

Variations: To make **HOLIDAY WREATHS,** shown in photo, follow the above recipe, but bend the ropes into circles, pinching the ends together. After the cookies cool completely, decorate them with multicolored sprinkles and red-hot cinnamon candies, using dabs of decorative icing (from 4¹⁄₄-ounce tubes) to attach them.

   To make **CHERRY-PECAN BALLS,** roll 1-inch pieces of any color dough between palms of hands to form balls; roll the balls in multicolored sprinkles. Place the balls on the prepared cookie sheets; press a pecan half or a candied cherry half in the center. Bake as directed in the recipe above.

   To make **STAINED GLASS COOKIES,** make the recipe for CANDY CANES at left, reducing the milk to 2 tablespoons and substituting 1 teaspoon vanilla for the peppermint extract. Roll out on a lightly floured pastry cloth to ¹⁄₄-inch thickness. Cut out with assorted 3-inch cookie cutters; then cut out the centers with 1¹⁄₂-inch cookie cutters. Brush vegetable oil on cookie sheets. Place the cookies, no more than 6 at a time, on the cookie sheet. Center 1 sourball in each cutout. Bake in a preheated moderate oven (350°) for 10 minutes, or until cookies are golden and the candy is melted. Cool on the cookie sheet on a wire rack for 2 minutes. Gently loosen around each cookie with a long and wide spatula, then transfer to the wire rack to cool. (If the cookies stick to the sheet, return them to the oven for 2 to 3 minutes.)

Grace's Cookie Brittle

Cut into rectangles while still warm. Or cool and break into brittle-like pieces.

Bake at 375° for 25 minutes.
Makes 2 dozen.

1   cup (2 sticks) butter or margarine, softened
1   cup sugar
2   eggs
2   teaspoons vanilla
2   cups sifted all-purpose flour
¹⁄₂ teaspoon salt
4   bars (2.16 ounces each)
   chocolate-coated honeycomb peanut butter
   candy, chopped
   (2 cups)

1. Preheat the oven to moderate (375°).
2. Beat the butter or margarine with sugar until fluffy in a large bowl with an electric mixer at high speed; blend in the eggs and vanilla. Add the flour and salt, then the chopped candy with a wooden spoon; blend well.
3. Press mixture into an ungreased 15 x 10 x 1-inch jelly roll pan. Cover with wax paper; press flat and even; discard paper.
4. Bake in the preheated moderate oven (375°) 25 minutes, or until golden brown and firm when lightly pressed with a fingertip. Set pan on wire rack; cut while still warm, into 24 bars, making 4 crosswise cuts and 6 lengthwise cuts.
5. Cool unsliced dough in pan on rack; break into irregular pieces or cut into triangular shapes.

CAKES
AND
FRUITCAKES

Classic Cakes: Orange Hazelnut Loaf; Chocolate Raspberry Torte; Dobos Torte

Dobos Torte

Our crackle topping is a free-form version of the classic method.

Bake each layer at 375° for 5 minutes.
Makes one 8-inch cake.

1¼ cups unsifted all-purpose flour
    Pinch salt
4   eggs
¾   cups sugar
    Chocolate Buttercream (recipe follows)
    Crackle Topping (recipe follows)

1. Preheat the oven to moderate (375°).
2. Grease and flour 2 cookie sheets. Mark an 8-inch circle in the center of each sheet, using an 8-inch cake layer pan and a knife. Sift the flour with the salt.
3. Beat the eggs in the large bowl of an electric mixer at high speed; beat in the sugar gradually until the mixture is thick enough to form a ribbon. Fold in the flour, ⅓ at a time, just until blended.
4. Spoon ⅙ of the batter into each circle; spread out to the edge of the circle with a palette knife or a small spatula.
5. Bake in the preheated moderate oven (375°) for 5 minutes, or until the top springs back when lightly touched with a fingertip. Immediately remove from the oven; trim edges, if necessary, to form neat circles. Carefully transfer the layers with pancake turners to wire racks. Repeat this process to make 6 layers.
6. Sandwich the layers with part of the CHOCOLATE BUTTERCREAM. Frost the side and top with the remaining buttercream.
7. Top the cake with large pieces of the CRACKLE TOPPING. Crush the remainder; press around the side of the cake.

Chocolate Buttercream

Makes about 3 cups.

1   cup sugar
¼   teaspoon cream of tartar
½   cup water
7   egg yolks
1½ cups (3 sticks) butter, softened
3   squares (1 ounce each) unsweetened chocolate,
      melted and cooled
2   tablespoons rum

1. Combine the sugar, cream of tartar and water in a heavy saucepan. Cook over low heat, stirring, until the sugar dissolves completely.
2. Raise the heat to moderately high. Boil the syrup without stirring until the mixture reaches 238° on a candy thermometer (or until a few drops sprinkled in cold water form a soft ball).
3. Meanwhile, beat the egg yolks until very light and fluffy in a medium-size bowl with the electric mixer at high speed. Beat in the cooked syrup in a slow, steady stream, beating constantly.
4. Continue to beat the mixture for a few minutes after it thickens. Then set aside until it cools completely.
5. Beat in the softened butter, bit by bit, then the chocolate and rum, until the mixture is well blended and smooth. If too soft to spread, refrigerate for 2 hours, or place over ice and water for 15 minutes, until of spreading consistency.

Crackle Topping

Makes enough for 1 cake.

1½ cups sugar
1½ cups water

1. Combine the sugar and the water in a small, heavy saucepan. Cook over low heat until the sugar melts completely.
2. Raise the heat to moderate. Boil the syrup without stirring until it turns a rich golden brown. Do not overcook.
3. Immediately dip the base of the saucepan in cold water, to stop the cooking. After the bubbles subside, quickly pour the caramel onto a lightly oiled aluminum foil-lined cookie sheet, tipping the sheet back and forth to spread the caramel as thin as possible.
4. Cool until hardened.
5. Shatter into big pieces with a clean hammer or the back of a heavy skillet.

Chocolate Raspberry Torte

A super-rich layer cake with dark chocolate filling and raspberry buttercream frosting.

Bake at 350° for 25 minutes.
Makes one 9-inch cake.

³/₄	*unblanched almonds, toasted (see Note)*
1	*cup unsifted all-purpose flour*
6	*eggs*
1	*cup sugar*
	Pinch salt
½	*cup (1 stick) butter, melted*
¼	*cup crème de cassis liqueur*
1	*cup blanched whole almonds*
	Chocolate Fudge Filling (recipe follows)
	Raspberry Buttercream (recipe follows)
1	*cup sliced almonds, toasted*

1. Preheat the oven to moderate (350°).
2. Grease and flour two 9-inch square baking pans.
3. Grind the almonds and flour together in the container of the electric food processor, pulsing the machine on and off to prevent a paste from forming.
4. Place the eggs, sugar and salt in a large heatproof bowl; beat with a wire whisk until blended. Place the bowl over a saucepan of simmering water, stirring all the time with the whisk, until the mixture is lukewarm and the sugar dissolves. (Do not let the bottom of the bowl touch the water.) Remove the bowl from the saucepan.
5. Beat with the electric mixer at high speed until the mixture is cold and triple in volume. Quickly fold in the almond-flour mixture. Stir 1 cup of the batter into the melted and cooled butter in a small bowl, then fold this back into the remaining batter. Pour into the prepared pans, smoothing the batter into the corners.
6. Bake in the preheated moderate oven (350°) for 25 minutes, or until the top is golden brown and springs back when lightly pressed with a fingertip. Cool in the pans on wire racks for 10 minutes. Carefully loosen around the sides, invert onto the racks; cool completely.
7. Place one cake layer, bottom side up, on a serving platter. Sprinkle with half of the liqueur. Dip the whole almonds in part of the CHOCOLATE FUDGE FILLING; place on wax paper. Spread half of the remaining filling on the cake layer. Top with a second cake layer, bottom side up, then sprinkle with the remaining cassis and spread with the remaining filling. Refrigerate until the filling sets.
8. Spread the RASPBERRY BUTTERCREAM on the sides and top of the cake. Press the toasted, sliced almonds around the side of the cake. Decorate the top with the chocolate-dipped almonds.

Note: To toast the almonds, place them in one layer in a jellyroll pan. Bake in a preheated moderate oven (350°) for 20 minutes, or until golden. Cool.

CHOCOLATE FUDGE FILLING: Makes enough for 1 cake. Break 1 package (8 ounces) semisweet chocolate squares into half-squares. Heat 1 cup heavy cream to boiling in a medium saucepan over moderate heat; remove from the heat. Add the chocolate; stir with a wire whisk until melted. Let stand for 30 minutes before dipping the almonds or spreading on the cake.

Raspberry Buttercream

Makes enough for 1 cake.

1	*package (10 ounces) quick-thaw frozen raspberries in light syrup, thawed*
6	*egg yolks*
³/₄	*cup sugar*
2	*cups (4 sticks) butter, softened*

1. Purée the raspberries and their syrup in a food processor or blender; force through a fine sieve into a small bowl.
2. Combine the egg yolks, purée and sugar in a large heatproof mixing bowl. Place the bowl over a saucepan of simmering water (do not let the bottom touch the water). Beat constantly with a wire whisk until the mixture thickens and forms a ribbon when the whisk is lifted. Remove the bowl from the saucepan.
3. Beat with an electric mixer at high speed until the mixture is cold and thick. Beat in the butter, 1 stick at a time, beating well after each addition. Continue beating, scraping the sides of the bowl with a rubber spatula, until the buttercream is thick and fluffy.

Orange Hazelnut Loaf

Flavored with a hint of whiskey, this three-layer torte stays moist for several days.

Bake at 350° for 20 to 25 minutes.
Makes one 10-inch cake.

1   cup whole hazelnuts, toasted (see Note)
1   cup unsifted all-purpose flour
6   eggs
1   cup sugar
    Pinch salt
½   cup (1 stick) butter or margarine, melted and
        cooled
1   teaspoon grated orange rind
2   tablespoons orange juice
3   tablespoons American whiskey
    Orange Filling (recipe follows)
    Orange Buttercream (recipe follows)
1   cup hazelnuts, chopped
    Sugared Orange Shreds (recipe follows)

1. Preheat the oven to moderate (350°).
2. Grease and flour a 15 x 10 x 1" jellyroll pan.
3. Grind the toasted hazelnuts with the flour in the container of an electric food processor, pulsing the machine on and off.
4. Place the eggs, sugar and salt in a large heatproof bowl; beat with a wire whisk until blended. Place the bowl over a saucepan of simmering water, stirring constantly with the whisk until the mixture is lukewarm and the sugar dissolves. (Do not let the bottom of the bowl touch the water.)
5. Beat with an electric mixer at high speed until the mixture is cold and triple in volume. Quickly fold in the hazelnut-flour mixture. Stir 1 cup of the batter into the melted and cooled butter mixed the orange rind and juice in a small bowl, then fold this back into the remaining batter. Pour into the prepared pan, smoothing batter into the corners.
6. Bake in the preheated moderate oven (350°) for 20 minutes, or until the top springs back when lightly pressed with a fingertip. Cool in the pan on the wire rack for 10 minutes. Loosen around the side of the pan; invert onto a towel-lined wire rack; cool.
7. Cut the cake, lengthwise, into thirds carefully with a long serrated knife.
8. Place one layer, bottom side down, on a piece of cardboard cut to fit the cake and covered with aluminum foil; sprinkle cake with 1 tablespoon of the whiskey. Spread with half of the ORANGE FILLING and part of the ORANGE BUTTERCREAM.

Top with a second layer; sprinkle with 1 tablespoon of the whiskey and spread with the remaining ORANGE FILLING and part of the ORANGE BUTTERCREAM. Top with the remaining cake layer, bottom side up, and sprinkle with the remaining whiskey. Refrigerate until the filling is firm.

9. Spread the top and sides of the cake with the remaining ORANGE BUTTERCREAM. Using an icing comb (available at cake decorating stores) lightly swirl the frosting on top of the cake. Press the chopped nuts into the sides. Decorate the top with the SUGARED ORANGE SHREDS.

Note: To toast the hazelnuts, place them in a roasting pan. Bake in a preheated moderate oven (350°) for 15 minutes, or until the skins crack and the nuts are golden brown. Cool.

ORANGE FILLING: Makes enough to fill one 10-inch cake. Combine 5 egg yolks and ⅓ cup sugar in a small, heavy saucepan or the top of a double boiler. Place over low heat or over simmering water, stirring constantly, and adding grated rind and juice of 1 orange, and 2 tablespoons whiskey. Cook, stirring constantly and adding ¼ cup (½ stick) butter bit by bit. Continue cooking and stirring until the mixture thickens. Remove from the heat; pour into a small bowl. Cover the surface with wax paper. Let stand while preparing cake. Or, refrigerate up to 1 week.

STORING CAKES

- For cakes with a fluffy frosting, slip a knife under the cake carrier so it won't be airtight.
- For cakes with a whipped cream frosting, keep in the refrigerator or freezer, covered with an inverted bowl.
- Cakes with butter frostings may be loosely covered with foil or plastic wrap, or stored in a cake carrier. Refrigerate or freeze for long-term storage.

Orange Buttercream

Makes enough for one 10-inch cake.

5   large egg whites (about ⅔ cup)
1⅓ cups sugar
     Pinch salt
1¼ cups (2½ sticks) butter, softened

Grated rind of 1 orange
1/4 *cup strained fresh orange juice*

1. Place the egg whites, sugar and salt in a large heatproof bowl. Place the bowl over a saucepan of simmering water (do not let the bottom of the bowl touch the water).
2. Heat, stirring constantly with a wire whisk until the egg whites warm and the sugar dissolves; remove from the heat.
3. Beat with an electric mixer at high speed until the mixture is completely cold and forms a thick meringue.
4. Beat in the butter, bit by bit until it is incorporated. Add the orange rind and drizzle in the orange juice. Continue beating until the buttercream is smooth and thick enough to spread.

SUGARED ORANGE SHREDS: Combine 1/2 cup sugar and 1/4 cup water in a small heavy saucepan. Bring to boiling over moderate heat, stirring occasionally; let boil for 1 minute. Stir in the rind of 1 orange, cut into julienne strips, using a two-tined fork so the strips don't clump together. Continue boiling, stirring once or twice, until the syrup thickens and just begins to turn golden. (Do not let brown.) Quickly remove the orange rind from the syrup and drop onto a piece of wax paper sprinkled with 1/3 cup sugar. Toss to coat evenly, separating the pieces.

PAN SUBSTITUTION FOR BAKING FRUITCAKES

● *If you do not have the specific size of a baking pan or mold called for in a recipe, substitute a pan of equal volume from the list below.*
● *If the pan you are substituting is made of glass, reduce the baking temperature by 25°.*
● *If you are substituting a pan that is shallower than the pan in the recipe, reduce the baking time by about one-quarter.*
● *If you are substituting a pan that is deeper than the pan in the recipe, increase the baking time by one-quarter.*

4-cup mold:	**6-cup mold:**
9-inch pie plate	*10-inch pie plate*
8 x 1 1/4-inch cake pan	*9 x 1 1/2-inch cake pan*
7 x 3 x 2-inch loaf pan	*8 x 3 1/2 x 2 1/2-inch loaf pan*
8-cup mold:	**10-cup mold**
8 x 8 x 2-inch-square pan	*9 x 9 x 2-inch-square pan*
9 x 5 x 4-inch loaf pan	

Light Fruitcake

Bake at 300° for 1 hour, 15 minutes.
Makes 8 1/2 cups batter.

1 1/2 *cups (3 sticks) butter or margarine, softened*
3   *cups sugar*
6   *eggs*
1 1/2 *cups dairy sour cream*
1/4 *cup lemon juice*
5 1/2 *cups unsifted all-purpose flour*
2   *teaspoons ground spice* (see chart at right)*
     Nonstick vegetable spray
     Spirits *(see chart at right)
     Fruitcake Glaze (recipe follows)

1. Preheat oven to slow (300°).
2. Beat the butter or margarine and sugar in the large bowl of an electric mixer at high speed until fluffy. Beat in the eggs, one at a time, until well blended.
3. Combine the dairy sour cream and the lemon juice in a small bowl until well blended. Sift the flour, spice, baking soda and salt onto wax paper.
4. Turn the mixer speed to low and add the sifted dry ingredients alternately with the sour cream mixture, beginning and ending with the dry ingredients.
5. Measure the batter, 1 to 4 cups at a time, into a medium bowl. Add an equal total amount of candied and/or dried fruits and/or nuts. Spray molds liberally with nonstick vegetable spray. Spoon batter into molds that hold twice the volume of the batter. (For example, 2 cups batter in a 4 cup mold.) Continue until all the batter is used.
6. Arrange the molds on one shelf of the oven separating as much as possible.
7. Bake in the preheated slow oven (300°) for 1 hour, 15 minutes, or until a wooden skewer inserted near the center comes out clean. Cool in the molds on wire racks for 15 minutes. Loosen the cakes around the edges of the molds and invert onto the wire racks. Cool completely.
8. Drizzle with spirits; wrap each cake tightly in a plastic bag. Allow to mellow for at least 2 weeks at room temperature, or freeze for up to 1 year.

FRUITCAKE GLAZE: Makes enough to coat up to 6 cakes. Combine 2 cups honey, 1/2 cup lemon juice and 2 teaspoons lemon rind in a small saucepan. Heat to boiling; lower temperature and simmer for 5 minutes. Brush on the fruitcakes while still warm.

CUSTOMIZE YOUR FAVORITE FRUITCAKES

Bake a fruitcake with just the ingredients you prefer. Choose only your favorite spices, candied and/or dried fruits, nuts and spirits. Also, choose the pan size according to its intended use.

CANDIED FRUITS	DRIED FRUIT	NUTS	SPICES	SPIRITS
Mixed candied fruits	Apples	Almonds	Cinnamon	Cream Sherry
Candied cherries	Apricots	Pecans	Nutmeg	Brandy
Candied pineapple	Peaches	Walnuts	Ginger	Apricot brandy
Candied orange peel	Pears	Cashews	Cloves	Peach brandy
Candied citron	Prunes	Macadamia	Allspice	Bourbon
Candied lemon peel	Mixed dried fruits	Brazil nuts	Pumpkin pie spice	Canadian whiskey
Pickled watermelon rind	Raisins	Filberts	Apple pie spice	Raspberry liqueur
Pickled cantaloupe rind	Currants	Hazelnuts	Cardamom	Irish whiskey

Dark Fruitcake

Bake at 275° for 1 hour, 30 minutes.
Makes 9 cups batter.

1½ cups (3 sticks) butter or margarine
3 cups firmly packed light brown sugar
6 eggs
6 cups unsifted all-purpose flour
1 tablespoon baking powder
1 tablespoon spice (see chart above)
1 teaspoon salt
1 cup dry sherry, apple juice or orange juice
9 cups chopped candied or dried fruits
    or nuts (see chart above)
    Nonstick vegetable spray
    Spirits (see chart above)
    Dark Fruitcake Glaze (recipe follows)

1. Preheat the oven to slow (275°).
2. Beat the butter or margarine and the brown sugar at high speed in a large bowl of an electric mixer until light and fluffy. Beat in the eggs, one at a time, until well blended.
3. Sift the flour, baking powder, spice and salt onto wax paper.
4. Turn the mixer speed to low and add sifted dry ingredients alternately with sherry, apple juice or orange juice, beginning and ending with the dry ingredients.
5. Measure the batter, 1 to 3 cups at a time, into a medium bowl. Add an equal total amount of candied and/or dried fruits, and/or nuts. Spray the molds liberally with nonstick vegetable spray. Spoon the batter into molds that hold twice the volume of the batter. (For example, 2 cups batter in a 4-cup mold.) Continue until all the batter is used.
6. Arrange the molds on one shelf of the oven, separating as much as possible.
7. Bake in the preheated slow oven (275°) for 1 hour, 30 minutes, or until a skewer inserted near the center comes out clean. Cool in the molds on wire racks for 15 minutes. Loosen the cakes around the edges; invert onto the wire racks. Cool completely.
8. Drizzle each cake with ¼ cup spirits; wrap each cake tightly in a plastic bag. Allow to mellow for at least 2 weeks at room temperature, or freeze for up to 1 year.
9. Brush with DARK FRUITCAKE GLAZE and decorate as desired.

DARK FRUITCAKE GLAZE: Makes enough to coat up to 6 cakes. Combine 1 jar (2 pounds) strawberry jam and ½ cup brandy, sherry or apple juice in a small saucepan. Heat to boiling; lower temperature and simmer for 5 minutes. Brush on the fruitcakes while still warm.

TO FREEZE FRUITCAKES

- Do not brush the cakes with glaze.
- First, wrap the cakes in cheesecloth soaked in sherry or brandy.
- Next, wrap the cakes in heavy-duty aluminum foil, freezer-weight plastic wrap or large freezer bags.
- Seal the wrap around the cakes.
- Label, date and freeze for up to 1 year. Thaw before glazing and decorating.

HOW TO CANDY FRUITS
Add your personal touch to holiday baking and gift giving.

Elegant yet economical, candied fruit isn't just for fruit-cakes—it also makes splendid garnishes, delicate desserts, tasty additions to baked goods and welcome gifts.

Candied orange rind, for instance, will keep indefinitely in airtight containers. A ready garnish for puddings and ice cream, you can also add it to candied carrots, sweet potatoes or glazed chicken, as well as to muffins and breads.

Below, a step-by-step guide to candying fruits and citrus rinds, and making crystallized ginger. And don't forget to check out our serving suggestions for each!

CANDIED FRUIT
Fruits to Use
Firm fruits such as cherries, Golden Delicious apples, Red Flame seedless, Thompson seedless or other varieties of seedless grapes, crab apples, kumquats, whole figs and pears are among the best fruits for candying. Strawberries, raspberries, blackberries and peaches tend to lose their shape in the process.

How Candying Is Done
The candying method combines the process of preserving and drying fruit. The fruit is soaked in syrup, made heavier by daily additions of sugar, until gradually the moisture in the fruit is replaced with sugar. Finally, the fruit is dried, then rolled in sugar as crystallized fruit or dipped in syrup for glazed fruit. Allow two to three weeks to complete the process.

Basic Method For Candying Whole Fruit
● Pit small fruit (cherries or apricots) and prick larger fruit you intend to candy whole with a fork to allow the syrup to soak into the fruit. Large fruit—pears, apples—should be peeled and quartered. Candy different fruit separately so the natural flavors remain intact.

● Place 1 pound prepared fruit into enough boiling water in saucepan to cover, and boil rapidly for 3 minutes.
● Drain fruit but reserve the cooking liquid. Make a syrup of 1½ cups sugar and 1½ cups cooking liquid. Heat syrup, add fruit and heat just until syrup boils.
● Turn fruit and syrup into a china or glass container that has been rinsed in hot water. Fruit must be thoroughly covered with syrup. It will become hard and discolored if exposed to air. (Should you need more syrup to cover the fruit, combine equal parts sugar and water, boil for a minute and add to fruit.) Cover with plastic wrap or a large plate. Let fruit stand, covered, for 24 hours.
● Drain syrup into a saucepan and add ½ cup sugar and heat until sugar is dissolved. Add fruit, bring syrup to a boil, and pour syrup and fruit into a glass or china bowl and let stand another day.
● Repeat this process for 2 more days. On the 5th day, repeat the process, but allow the fruit to soak in syrup for 48 hours. Repeat this process, allowing the fruit to soak another 2 days.
● Check syrup; it should now have the consistency of honey. If not, drain it into a saucepan, bring to a boil until it is thick (approximately 228°F on a candy thermometer). Pour syrup over fruit. Let it stand 4 to 7 days (depending on size of fruit). Fruit should be saturated with syrup.
● Remove fruit from syrup, place in single layer on a cake rack. Set over a jelly roll pan to dry. Place racks in the sunshine, or in an oven that is off, but still warm from previous baking. The oven door should be left slightly open. Allow 10 hours to 3 days to dry fruit, depending on size, humidity and temperature. Fruit is dry when no longer sticky and syrup can't be squeezed from center.

Serving Suggestions
Candied fruit arranged in a china basket makes a lovely centerpiece for brunch or tea. Placed in a decorative jar, it makes a wonderful gift. Use candied fruit in such traditional baked goods as roly-poly pudding and Christmas cake. Dip in chocolate or fondant for a true "bon-bon." Candied fruit will keep three months in an airtight container.

CANDIED CITRUS RIND
Fruit Rinds To Use

Candied citrus rind is an easy, economical garnish that adds pizzazz to a variety of dishes. Once you develop the knack for making candied citrus rind, you may never toss out your grapefruit, lemon, lime, orange or tangerine peels again.

Note: Citrus rind may be candied using the Basic Method for Candying Whole Fruit, but this method is less time consuming and yields terrific results. Allow about one to two days, depending on the method you choose.

Basic Method for Candying Citrus Rind

● Choose brightly colored citrus fruit with thick rind, free of marks. Remove peel with a carrot scraper or sharp knife, and be careful to discard bitter white pith directly beneath skin.
● Cut peel into thin strips, place in saucepan and cover with cold water. Bring water to a boil and simmer 10 minutes. Repeat this process 3 to 5 times (6 for grapefruit) to remove the bitter taste. (Discard the water each time.)
● Make a syrup of $\frac{1}{2}$ cup water to 1 cup sugar for each 2 cups of peel. Boil peel in syrup until it is absorbed and the peel is transparent. Roll peel in sugar, allow to dry as described in Candied Fruit.

Serving Suggestions

Try sprinkling candied grapefruit peel over lettuce and avocado salads. Add candied orange rind to spinach salads, steamed carrots, curried dishes. Garnish fish with candied lemon rind and grilled pork with candied lime rind. All make tasty additions to muffins, quick breads and yeast breads, cookies, cakes and frostings. Sprinkle chopped candied rind over pudding, ice cream, sherbet. Use it to garnish cheesecake, pound cake, chiffon pies and mousses. Dip in chocolate or fondant. Candied rinds will keep in airtight containers at least a year.

CRYSTALLIZED GINGER
Method

● Allow approximately $1\frac{1}{2}$ cups water per 1 pound ginger root; cover ginger root with water. Simmer 20 minutes; add $\frac{1}{2}$ cup sugar; boil and stir until sugar dissolves. Remove from heat and let stand covered overnight.
● Return saucepan to heat; bring to boiling, simmer mixture 15 minutes. Add $\frac{1}{2}$ cup light corn syrup, bring to a boil, and simmer 30 minutes. Allow mixture to return to room temperature.
● Stir in one cup sugar, bring to a boil and simmer 30 minutes, stirring occasionally. Add $\frac{1}{2}$ cup sugar and simmer 10 minutes. Remove from heat and let stand in same saucepan, covered, 24 hours.
● Bring mixture to a boil, simmer until syrup is the consistency of honey (approximately 228°F on a candy thermometer). Drain ginger, reserving syrup. Dry slices on a rack set over a cookie tray overnight. Roll ginger in sugar. Store in tightly covered glass or metal containers (it will keep several years). Pour syrup into hot sterilized jars and seal, following manufacturer's directions. Use as a zesty topping for ice cream or sliced oranges.

Serving Suggestions

With the popularity of Oriental and Near Eastern cooking, crystallized ginger has become a staple in the well-stocked kitchen. Add it to stir-fried dishes, sprinkle on freshly steamed vegetables and try it on ice cream or lemon sorbet. Ginger syrup, a by-product of the candying process, makes a flavorful alternative to honey or maple syrup on pancakes or vanilla ice cream. Use ginger syrup in meat marinades or to glaze grilled poultry, sweet potatoes or acorn squash.

FREEZING CAKES

● Wrap unfrosted cakes in heavy-duty aluminum foil, plastic wrap or plastic bags. Label, date and freeze for up to 4 months. Thaw at room temperature for 1 hour.
● Freeze frosted cakes on a piece of heavy cardboard or a cookie sheet. When firm, wrap in heavy-duty aluminum foil, plastic wrap or plastic bag. Label, date and freeze for up to 3 months. Remove the wrapping while your cake is still frozen, so the frosting doesn't smear. Thaw at room temperature for 2 hours.

HOLIDAY YEAST BREADS

Holiday Yeast Breads: Santa Lucia Buns; California Apricot Braid; Panettone di Natale

QUICK & EASY DOUGH

Use this versatile dough as a foundation for many recipes.

Makes 2 yeast breads.

1½ cups milk
½ cup butter or margarine
½ cup sugar
1 teaspoon salt
2 envelopes fast-rising active dry yeast
½ cup very warm water
3 eggs
7 cups unsifted all-purpose flour
1 teaspoon ground pumpkin pie spice

1. Heat the milk, butter or margarine, sugar and salt in a saucepan; cool for 30 minutes.
2. Dissolve the yeast in the very warm water in the large bowl of an electric mixer (*see Yeast Basics, at right*). Add the cooled milk, eggs, 3 cups of the flour and the pumpkin pie spice.
3. Fit the electric mixer with the dough hook; beat at medium speed for 3 minutes, scraping the sides of the bowl several times.
4. Add enough of the remaining flour to make a soft dough.
5. Knead the dough for 5 minutes. Let rise in a warm place, away from drafts, for 1 hour, or until double in bulk.
6. Shape and bake the dough, following the individual recipes.

FREEZING BREADS AND MUFFINS

- *Cool before sealing in plastic freezing bags or wrapping in heavy-duty aluminum foil. Label, date and freeze.*
- *To serve: Remove bread from freezer and thaw 12 to 24 hours at room temperature. Remove wrappings and place on cookie sheet. Heat in slow oven (325°) 15 minutes, or until heated through.*
- *Glaze breads and muffins only after they have thawed.*

YEAST BASICS

- **To Dissolve Yeast:** *Combine yeast with 1 teaspoon sugar and very warm water. ("Very warm" water should feel warm when dropped on your wrist.)*
- **Substitute one cake (0.6 oz.) of compressed yeast** *for one envelope of active dry yeast in recipes. Use warm water to dissolve the fresh yeast. (Warm water will feel tepid when a few drops are sprinkled on the inside of your wrist.)*
- **To Heat Milk:** *Place milk with other ingredients in a small saucepan; heat slowly until the milk is hot, not boiling.*
- **To Knead Dough:** *Turn dough out onto a lightly floured pastry board; knead until smooth and elastic.*
- **To Let Rise:** *Pour dough in greased large bowl; turn to coat top; cover with plastic wrap; let rise in a warm place, away from drafts, until doubled.*
- **To determine when a dough has doubled in volume,** *press the dough flat in a greased bowl. Mark the dough's level, then remove it. Fill the bowl with water to double the first mark, then mark this second level. Return your dough to the bowl. OR: Dough has doubled in volume when a depression made with your fingertip remains.*
- **To Shape:** *Punch dough down on lightly floured pastry cloth or board; follow individual shaping.*
- **To Test for Doneness:** *Bake until bread is golden and gives a hollow sound when tapped with fingertip.*
- **To Cool:** *Cool bread in pan on wire rack 5 minutes; loosen around edges of pan; invert onto wire rack.*
- **For faster-rising active dry yeast,** *follow package directions. In general, water for dissolving yeast should be hotter; rising time is reduced.*

RASPBERRY ROYAL

Try this tall and handsome coffee cake from England.

Bake at 375° for 45 minutes.
Makes one 10-inch cake.

½ recipe Quick & Easy Dough (recipe, above)
¾ cup raspberry preserves
½ cup chopped pecans

1. Shape by rolling the QUICK & EASY DOUGH to a 16x12-inch rectangle; top with the preserves and the nuts.
2. Roll up jellyroll fashion, starting at a long end. Place, seam-side down, in a well-greased 10-inch tube pan; cut down into the top at 1-inch intervals. Let rise for 20 minutes.
3. Preheat the oven to moderate (375°).
4. Bake in the oven for 45 minutes, or until the top is golden. Top with white icing, if desired.

CALIFORNIA APRICOT BREAD

Almonds and apricots from California make this an All-American favorite.

Bake at 375° for 40 minutes.
Makes 1 large loaf.

½   recipe *Quick & Easy Dough (recipe, page 237)*
1   cup apricot preserves
1   egg
1   tablespoon water
¾   cup sliced almonds
    Granulated sugar

1. Roll out the QUICK & EASY DOUGH to a 16x12-inch rectangle on a lightly floured pastry cloth or board. Spoon the apricot preserves down the center of a long side of the dough. Spread to a 4-inch width.
2. Make cuts in the dough on either side of the center at 1-inch intervals; fold the strips over the preserves, alternating sides, to coat the preserves completely.
3. Place on a large greased cookie sheet; cover with plastic wrap. Let rise in a warm place, away from drafts, for 20 minutes, or until double in bulk.
4. Preheat the oven to moderate (375°).
5. Beat the egg with the water in a cup; brush over the dough; sprinkle with the almonds and sugar.
6. Bake in the preheated moderate oven (375°) for 35 minutes, or until golden. Loosen under the bread with a sharp knife; slide the bread onto a long wire rack to cool.

KUGELHUPH SQUARE

We use square pans rather than the traditional Kugelhuph pan for this German favorite.

Bake at 350° for 30 minutes.
Makes 3 small coffee cakes.

1   cup golden raisins
1   cup sliced natural almonds
¼   cup apricot or peach brandy
    or: ¼ cup orange or apple juice
1   cup milk
½   cup (1 stick) butter or margarine
4   cups unsifted all-purpose flour
2   envelopes faster-rising active dry yeast
½   cup sugar
½   teaspoon salt
3   eggs
    Whole almonds

1. Combine the raisins and the sliced almonds in a small bowl; add the brandy or juice and toss to coat evenly. Let stand for at least 30 minutes.
2. Heat the milk and butter or margarine in a small saucepan; cool.
3. Combine the flour, yeast, sugar and salt in the large bowl of an electric mixer; fit the mixer with the dough hooks.
4. Add the cooled milk mixture to the bowl and beat at low speed to blend; add the eggs, one at a time, beating well after each addition. Increase the speed to medium and beat for 5 minutes, or until the batter is elastic.
5. Stir the raisins and nuts into the batter with a wooden spoon. Butter three 4-cup baking pans and line with the whole almonds. Spoon the batter over, dividing evenly. Cover the pans with plastic wrap.
6. Let rise in a warm place, away from drafts, for 30 minutes, or until double in bulk.
7. Preheat the oven to moderate (350°).
8. Bake in the oven for 30 minutes, or until the tops are golden. Cool in the pans on wire racks for 5 minutes; loosen around the edges; invert onto wire racks and cool completely. Serve warm, or wrap and freeze.

SANTA LUCIA BUNS

Traditionally served in Sweden on December 13th.

Bake at 400° for 15 minutes.
Makes 2 dozen buns.

½   cup milk
    Pinch saffron, crushed (optional)
3   cups unsifted all-purpose flour
⅓   cup sugar
1   envelope fast-rising active dry yeast
½   teaspoon salt

¼ cup (½ stick) butter or margarine, softened
2 eggs, beaten
Raisins

1. Scald the milk with the saffron, if used, in a small saucepan; cool to lukewarm.
2. Combine the flour, sugar, yeast and salt in the large bowl of an electric mixer; add the cooled milk, softened butter or margarine. Reserve 2 tablespoons of the beaten egg and add the remainder to the bowl.
3. Fit the electric mixer with the dough hook and beat on medium speed for 5 minutes, or until the dough is smooth and elastic.
4. Turn the dough out into a greased bowl; turn the bottom to the top to coat the top of the dough. Cover with plastic wrap. Let rise in a warm place, away from draft for 40 minutes, or until double in bulk.
5. Turn the dough out onto a lightly floured pastry board and knead until smooth. Divide the dough into 24 pieces. Roll out each piece to an 8-inch rope.
6. Place each rope on a greased cookie sheet and turn one end of the rope to the left and the other end of the rope to the right, to make a curl. Insert a few raisins in each curl. Beat the reserved beaten egg with 1 tablespoon cold water; brush over the buns.
7. Cover with plastic wrap and let rise in a warm place, away from drafts for 20 minutes, or until double in bulk.
8. Preheat the oven to high (400°).
9. Bake in the oven for 15 minutes, or until golden brown. Transfer to wire racks with a spatula to cool.

PANETTONE DI NATALE

Italy's classic Christmas bread, rich with eggs and candied fruits.

Bake at 350° for 30 to 50 minutes.
Makes 2 coffee cakes.

¾ cup milk
½ cup sugar
⅓ cup butter or margarine
1 teaspoon anise seeds (optional)
2 envelopes faster-rising active dry yeast
½ cup very warm water
4½ cups unsifted all-purpose flour
½ teaspoon salt
3 eggs
2 teaspoons grated lemon rind

1 jar (8 ounces) candied mixed fruits
½ cup raisins
Creamy Frosting (recipe follows)
Natural whole almonds
Angelica and/or citron, cut into julienne pieces

1. Heat the milk, sugar, butter and anise seeds in a small saucepan over moderate heat. Dissolve the yeast in the very warm water (*see Yeast Basics on page 237*).
2. Strain the milk over the yeast in the large bowl of an electric mixer. Fit the mixer with the dough hooks. Add half of the flour and the salt.
3. Beat at medium speed for 3 minutes, scraping the sides of the bowl several times.
4. Beat in the eggs and lemon rind alternately with the remaining flour to make a soft dough. Increase the mixer speed to high and continue beating until the dough forms a ball.
5. Let rise in a warm place, away from drafts, for 40 minutes, or until double in bulk. Beat down; add the fruit and the raisins and beat together with a spoon.
6. Grease two 1-pound coffee cans or one 8-inch springform pan. Spoon in the dough; cover with plastic wrap. Let rise for 25 minutes, or until double in bulk.
7. Preheat the oven to moderate (350°).
8. Bake in the oven for 50 minutes for the coffee cans, 30 minutes for the springform pan. Let cool. Decorate with the CREAMY FROSTING, angelica, almonds and citron.

CREAMY FROSTING: Makes about 1½ cups. Combine 2 tablespoons butter or margarine and 1 cup 10X (confectioners') sugar in a bowl with an electric mixer. Beat at low speed. Add 1 tablespoon cream and ½ teaspoon almond extract; beat until creamy and smooth.

Did You Know. . .

In Sweden, the Christmas season begins on Dec. 13 with the Feast of Santa Lucia. Each community chooses a Lucia Queen to represent a girl martyred for her religion in ancient Rome. In families with daughters, the youngest usually plays Lucia. Her privilege is to wait on everyone else during the day.

CONDIMENTS AND PRESERVES

Pear and Pineapple Marmalade

Pickled Mushrooms

A tempting appetizer to serve at holiday parties.

Makes 5 cups.

2　cups water
³⁄₄　cup vegetable oil
¹⁄₂　cup lemon juice
3　ribs celery, cut into 3-inch pieces
1　clove garlic, halved
¹⁄₂　teaspoon ground coriander
¹⁄₄　teaspoon leaf thyme, crumbled
¹⁄₈　teaspoon fennel seeds
¹⁄₂　teaspoon salt
8　peppercorns
1¹⁄₂　pounds small mushrooms
1　jar (4 ounces) pimientos, drained and sliced

1. Combine the water, oil, lemon juice, celery, garlic, coriander, thyme, fennel, salt and peppercorns in a medium-size saucepan; bring to boiling. Lower the heat; add mushrooms; simmer for 5 minutes.
2. Remove from the heat and turn into a large bowl. Cool.
3. Add the pimientos. Pack the mushrooms, celery and pimientos into sterilized jars; pour the liquid over the mushrooms to within ¹⁄₄-inch of the jar tops. Cover; refrigerate. Will keep for up to 1 week.

Pear And Pineapple Marmalade

This big batch of tangy marmalade will make enough for family and friends.

Makes 10 half-pints.

5　pounds slightly underripe pears (about 11 medium-size)
1　small pineapple
2　teaspoons grated lemon rind
2　tablespoons lemon juice
¹⁄₂　pound crystallized ginger, finely chopped
5　cups granulated sugar

1. Pare, core and quarter pears; cut the quarters into slices. Pare the pineapple; cut into lengthwise quarters; core and chop coarsely.
2. Combine the pears, pineapple, lemon rind, lemon juice, ginger and sugar in a kettle. Bring to boiling, stirring constantly, until the sugar dissolves. Lower the heat slightly; cook, uncovered, until the mixture is thickened and will sheet from a cold metal spoon, about 1¹⁄₂ hours. As the mixture thickens, stir occasionally to prevent sticking.
3. Ladle, hot, into hot half-pint preserving jars; wipe the rims; seal. Process for 15 minutes at simmering (180° to 185°) in a Hot Water Bath, following the directions on page 242. Cool; label and store in a cool, dry place.

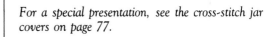

For a special presentation, see the cross-stitch jar covers on page 77.

HOW TO CAN

1. Wash your jars in hot, sudsy water and rinse them well. Leave the jars in hot water until you're ready to use them.
2. Place new domed lids in a bowl and cover them with boiling water. Keep them in the water until ready to use.
3. Follow the individual recipe directions to make the preserves.
4. Remove the jars from the water, one at a time. Place them on paper towels or a clean cloth. Pack and/or ladle food into the jars, leaving the headroom called for in the individual recipe.
5. Wipe the top and outside rim of the jar with a clean cloth. Place a domed lid on top and screw the metal rings on tightly, but do not force them.

HOW TO MAKE A HOT WATER BATH

1. Place your hot-water-bath canner onto a burner, then add enough water to half-fill the canner (a tea kettle does this job easily.) Cover the canner and bring the water to boiling.
2. Place your filled and covered jars in the canner rack and lower into the rapidly boiling water, adding more boiling water to the kettle if the level of the water is not two inches above the jars. Cover the kettle and allow the water to return to a full boil.
3. Process, following the times given the individual recipes and calculated from the time the water comes to the second boil.
4. Remove the jars from the canner and place them, at least three inches apart, on wire racks on a cloth-lined surface. Allow them to stand for 12 hours, or until cool.
5. Test all your jars to be sure they are sealed, by tapping the top with a spoon. (A clear ringing sound means a good seal. A hollow sound means the jar is *not* sealed properly. Improperly sealed jars should be stored in your refrigerator and used within a month. You may also freeze unsealed jars for up to one year.)
6. If you wish, remove the metal rings, then wipe the jars with a clean, damp cloth. Label, date and store the jars in a cool, dark, dry place for up to one year.

Note: For altitudes above sea level, add one minute for each 1,000 feet when the recipe processes under 20 minutes. When you're processing jars for more than 20 minutes, add two minutes for each additional 1,000 feet above sea level.

Dilled Mushrooms And Carrots

Colorful pickled vegetables with dill flavor to serve with sandwiches or include in an hors d'oeuvre platter.

Makes 6 pint jars.

3	pounds small fresh mushrooms
1	pound carrots, peeled and cut into 1-inch chunks
6	cloves garlic
4	tablespoons salt
2	cups water
2	cups white vinegar
¼	cup dillweed
½	cup sugar
1½	teaspoons whole peppercorns

1. Simmer the mushrooms and the carrots in boiling water for 5 minutes. Drain well. Pack into clean hot pint canning jars.
2. Place 1 clove garlic in each jar. Combine the salt, water, vinegar, dillweed, sugar and peppercorns in a saucepan. Bring to boiling; pour over the vegetables. Wipe the rims; seal. Process for 20 minutes in a Hot Water Bath, following the directions on page 242. Cool; label and store in a cool, dry place.

Brandied Apple Slices

Makes 5 cups (10 to 12 servings).

6	Golden Delicious apples
1	cup orange juice
2	cinnamon sticks
¾	cup sugar
½	cup brandy

1. Peel, core and slice the apples into eighths. Place in a large saucepan; add the orange juice and the cinnamon sticks. Bring to boiling; lower the heat and simmer, covered, for 10 minutes, or until the apples are tender but still firm.
2. Remove from the heat; stir in the sugar and brandy. Cool; spoon into a gift container. Keeps in the refrigerator for up to 1 month.

Your Own Mustard

A French-style mustard that complements cold meat platters or sandwiches. Add different herbs and spices for variety.

Makes 3 half-pint jars.

2	large onions, chopped (2 cups)
2	cloves garlic, chopped
2	cups dry white wine
1	can (4 ounces) dry mustard
2	tablespoons honey
2	tablespoons vegetable oil
2	teaspoons salt
¼	teaspoon seasoned pepper

1. Combine the onion, garlic and wine in a large saucepan; bring to boiling. Lower heat; simmer for 15 minutes; remove from the heat; allow to stand for 15 minutes.
2. Pour the mixture, half at a time, into the container of an electric food processor or blender; cover; process on high until smooth; pour into a large bowl.
3. Combine the dry mustard, honey and oil in the same saucepan until smooth; blend in the onion pureé, salt and pepper.
4. Bring to boiling, stirring constantly; lower the heat. Cook, stirring constantly for 5 minutes, or until the mixture thickens; ladle into three hot sterilized half-pint jars; seal, and process, following the directions in How To Can on page 242.

💲 🎚
Mint Jelly

A natural with leg of lamb and cold sliced meats. Or use to sandwich holiday cookies.

Makes 6 half-pints.

3   **tablespoons diced mint leaves**
1   **cup boiling water**
1½ **cups apple juice**
¼   **cup cider vinegar**
1   **box (1½ ounces) powdered pectin**
4½ **cups sugar**
     Few drops green food coloring

1. Combine the mint leaves and boiling water in a small ceramic bowl; cover and let stand for 15 minutes.
2. Strain the liquid into a large heavy kettle; stir in the apple juice, vinegar and powdered pectin. Bring to boiling over high heat.
3. Stir in the sugar until well blended. Bring to a full rolling boil; allow to boil for 1 minute, stirring constantly.
4. Remove the kettle from the heat and stir in the green food coloring to tint green.
5. Skim the foam from the top of the jelly and ladle into hot sterilized ½-pint canning jars to within ½ inch of top. Seal the jars, following the directions in How To Can on page 242.

💲 🎚 ◗
Corn Relish

This recipe simplifies matters by using canned corn. Make it in the fall or early winter for your holiday bazaar.

Makes 6 half-pint jars.

1   **cup sugar**
¼   **cup sifted all-purpose flour**
1½ **teaspoons turmeric**
1   **teaspoon salt**
2   **cups cider vinegar**
2   **cans (12 or 16 ounces each) whole-kernel corn, drained**
2   **cups finely shredded cabbage**
2   **medium-size sweet red peppers, quartered, seeded and chopped**

1. Combine the sugar, flour, turmeric and salt in a large saucepan; stir in the vinegar, corn, cabbage and red peppers.
2. Bring to boiling over low heat; continue cooking, stirring often for 10 minutes, or until the mixture thickens.
3. Ladle into six hot sterilized half-pint jars; seal, following the directions in How To Can on page 242. Cool; label; date.

💲 🎚
Pickled Watermelon Rind

A great way to use the part usually thrown away. Plan ahead and make extra for the holidays.

Makes 6 half-pint jars.

     Rind from half of a large watermelon (about 2 pounds)
8   **cups water**
½   **cup salt**
4   **cups sugar**
1   **lemon, thinly sliced**
1   **tablespoon whole cloves**
1   **tablespoon whole allspice**
6   **one-inch sticks of cinnamon**
2   **cups cider vinegar**
2   **cups water**

1. Pare the green skin from the watermelon; cut the rind into 1-inch cubes. (There should be about 8 cups.) Soak overnight in the 8 cups water and the salt in a large bowl.
2. Drain; place in a large kettle; cover with fresh water. Heat to boiling; lower heat; simmer for 10 minutes, or just until the cubes are tender but still firm; drain.
3. While the rind drains, combine the sugar, lemon, cloves, allspice, cinnamon, vinegar and the 2 cups water in the same pan; heat to boiling; stir in the drained rind. Simmer, stirring often for 1 hour, or until the rind is clear and the syrup is thick.
4. Ladle the rind and spices evenly into six hot sterilized half-pint jars; fill to within $\frac{1}{2}$-inch of rim with remaining hot syrup. Seal, following the directions in How To Can on page 242. Label, date and store in a cool place.

Cucumber Conserve

Use your food processor to get cucumber slices of uniform size.

Makes 6 half-pint jars.

3   *medium-size cucumbers, trimmed and sliced thin (4 cups)*
$\frac{1}{2}$ *cup golden raisins*
$\frac{3}{4}$ *cup water*
$\frac{1}{2}$ *cup lime juice*
1   *package (about 2 ounces) powdered fruit pectin*
5   *cups sugar*
    Green food coloring

1. Combine the cucumbers, raisins, water, lime juice and pectin in a large saucepan. Bring to boiling, stirring often.
2. Stir in the sugar, then add a few drops of the food coloring to tint a pale green. Bring to a full boil, stirring constantly. Cook, stirring constantly for 1 minute; remove from the heat.
3. Ladle into six hot sterilized half-pint jars, seal following the directions in How To Can on page 242. Label, date and store in a cool, dry place.

Orange Marmalade

Here's a fruit spread like grandma used to make.

Makes 7 half-pint jars.

4   *medium-size navel oranges*
4   *medium-size lemons*
2   *cups light corn syrup*
4   *cups sugar*

1. Wash the oranges and the lemons. Remove the peel from the oranges; scrape off most of the white pith and discard. Pare the thick yellow rind (zest) of the lemons. Slice the rind of both fruits into paper-thin slivers; place the rind in a medium saucepan; cover with water. Simmer for 20 minutes; drain.
2. Section and seed the oranges and lemons, reserving their juices; chop the pulp coarsely. (You should have about $3\frac{1}{2}$ cups.)
3. Place the pulp and the rind in a large saucepan. Measure the juices; add enough water to make 4 cups; stir into the fruit. Bring to boiling; lower heat; cover. Simmer for 20 minutes, stirring occasionally.
4. Stir in the corn syrup. Bring to boiling; boil, uncovered for 5 minutes. Add the sugar, stirring constantly until dissolved. Continue boiling, stirring occasionally, about 1 hour, or until syrup sheets from a spoon and the mixture thickens.
5. Ladle into 7 hot sterilized half-pint jars. Seal, following directions in How To Can on page 242. Label, date and store in a cool, dry place.

CANDIES & CONFECTIONS

Always welcome around the holidays, these treats are excellent
money-makers at bazaars, if you have any left!

Candies *(clockwise from foreground)*: Bon Bons, Fondant-Stuffed Fruits, Chocolate
Divinity, Caramels, Chocolate Coconut Almond Drops, Cherry Divinity and Chocolate Caramels.

Caramels

Here's a caramel recipe that's unsurpassed in quality and versatility. Serve this candy to confirmed caramel cravers or use it to make the variations.

Makes about 1¾ pounds.

2   cups sugar
1¼ cups light corn syrup
¼   teaspoon salt
1½ cups light cream
1   teaspoon vanilla

1. Butter an 8 x 8 x 2-inch pan.
2. Combine the sugar, corn syrup, salt and ½ cup of the cream in a large saucepan. Clip a candy thermometer to the side of the pan. Cook, stirring constantly, until the mixture reaches 236° (soft ball stage).
3. Stir in another ½ cup of the cream. Cook, stirring constantly, until the mixture again reaches 236°.
4. Stir in the remaining cream; cook, stirring constantly, until the mixture reaches 242° (firm ball stage). Stir in the vanilla.
5. Pour into the prepared pan (do not scrape the saucepan clean); cool. Turn out onto a cutting board. Cut into squares; wrap each in wax paper or foil.

Variations

Turtles: Place small clusters of walnuts, pecans or peanuts on a buttered cookie sheet. Prepare the recipe through Step 4. Spoon the caramel over the clusters to cover. When set, dip in melted semisweet chocolate. Place on wax paper until set. Makes 24.
Nut Caramels: Add 1 cup chopped nuts to the mixture after it reaches 242°. Pour into prepared pan; cool. Cut into squares. Makes about 2 pounds.
Chocolate Caramels: Add 1 square semisweet chocolate to the mixture (1 ounce) with the last addition of the cream. Makes about 1¾ pounds.

Divinity

Tender airy confections of whipped egg white and sugar.

Makes about 1½ pounds.

2½ cups sugar
½   cup light corn syrup
½   cup hot water
¼   teaspoon salt
2   egg whites
1   teaspoon vanilla
1   cup chopped nuts

1. Combine the sugar, corn syrup, water and salt in a large saucepan. Cook, stirring just until the sugar dissolves, but *not* after the mixture begins to boil. Cover the pan for 3 minutes to let the steam dissolve the sugar crystals on the side of the pan. This will prevent graininess in the Divinity. Clip a candy thermometer to the side of the pan.
2. Cook the mixture, uncovered, to 238° on the candy thermometer (soft ball stage). While the syrup is cooking to temperature, beat the egg whites in a medium-size bowl until stiff. When the syrup reaches the temperature, slowly pour ½ of the hot syrup in a slow but steady stream into the beaten whites, while beating continuously. Place the remainder back on the stove to cook to 258° (hard ball stage). Continue beating the egg white-syrup mixture while adding the remaining syrup and the vanilla, until the mixture forms stiff peaks. Stir in the nuts. Drop the mixture by teaspoonfuls onto wax paper. Let cool; store in airtight containers.

Variations

Chocolate Divinity: Stir ½ cup semisweet chocolate pieces into the mixture until melted, just before spooning onto the wax paper. Makes about 1¾ pounds.
Cherry Divinity: Substitute ¼ cup maraschino cherry juice for ¼ cup of the water in the recipe. Stir in ¼ cup chopped maraschino cherries just before spooning out. Makes about 1¾ pounds.
Cinnamon Divinity: Add ½ cup cinnamon candy red hots with the syrup mixture in the recipe. Makes about 1¾ pounds.

Butter Fondant

Fondant is the basis for cream centers in most chocolate-covered candy assortments. Unlike Divinity, it is kneaded, then ripened before using. It can be finger molded into desired shapes or used to complement dried fruit. Many flavored cream centers can be made from one batch of basic fondant then disguised in melted chocolate.

Makes about 1 pound.

2   **cups sugar**
2   **tablespoons light corn syrup**
³/₄   **cup water**
¹/₈   **teaspoon salt**
2   **tablespoons butter**
1   **teaspoon vanilla**

1. Combine the sugar, corn syrup, water, salt and butter in a large saucepan. Cook, stirring constantly, just until the sugar dissolves, but not after the mixture begins to boil. Cover the pan for 3 minutes to let the steam dissolve the sugar crystals on the side of the pan. This will prevent graininess in the fondant. Wipe any crystals that may remain on the side of the pan with a damp cloth wrapped around the tines of the fork. Clip a candy thermometer to the side of the pan.

2. Cook the mixture, uncovered, to 238° on the candy thermometer (soft ball stage). When the syrup reaches the temperature, pour it into a chilled metal bowl or pan, and let cool without disturbing.

3. When the bottom of the bowl is lukewarm to the touch (110°), add the vanilla and beat with an electric mixer until the mixture becomes creamy, then stiffens. This will take several minutes. Knead the fondant by hand, working out any lumps, until it softens. Wrap in plastic wrap or foil; refrigerate for 24 hours to allow it to ripen.

Variations

Bonbons: Melt the butter Fondant in the top of a double boiler over hot, not boiling, water. Divide into 3 portions, tinting green, pink and yellow. Prepare the Maple Nut Creams (*recipe follows*), rolling the mixture into ½-inch balls. Dip in the melted fondant; place on wax paper to set. Store in an airtight container. Makes about 2 pounds.

Maple Nut Creams: Prepare the Butter Fondant, working in 1 teaspoon of maple flavoring and ½ cup finely chopped walnuts into the ripened fondant. Makes about 1 pound.

Stuffed Fruits: Stuff pitted dates or apricots with a small ball of the Butter or Maple Nut Fondant.

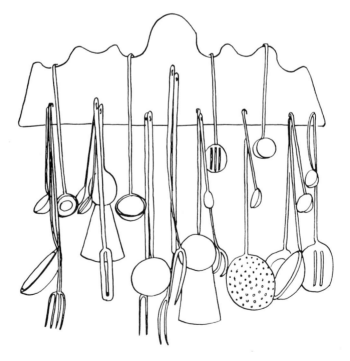

Coconut Candy

Coconut is one of nature's sweetest, most versatile fruit. Try this moist coconut candy recipe and all its variations.

Makes about 1½ pounds.

1   *cup sugar*
1½ *cups light corn syrup*
½   *cup water*
1   *package (14 ounces) flaked coconut*
½   *teaspoon almond or vanilla extract*

1. Combine the sugar, corn syrup and water in a large saucepan. Cook, stirring constantly, just until the sugars dissolve. Clip a candy thermometer to the side of the pan.
2. Cook without stirring to 236° (soft ball stage) on the candy thermometer. Remove from the heat. Stir in the coconut and the almond or vanilla extract; cool.

Chocolate Coconut Almond Drops: Shape the cooled coconut mixture into 1-inch balls, flattening the bottoms. Top each with a toasted almond. Chill for at least 1 hour. Dip in melted chocolate. Makes about 2 pounds.

Acorns: Shape the cooled coconut mixture into 1-inch balls; then taper balls to a cone shape to resemble an acorn; chill for at least 1 hour. Dip the large end of the cone into melted chocolate. Makes about 1¾ pounds.

Coconut Ribbon: Cook the coconut mixture to 240° on the candy thermometer. Divide into 3 parts. Tint parts pink, green and yellow with food coloring. Pour into a buttered 8 x 8 x 2-inch pan in layers; cool. Cut into bars or squares.

DIPPING CANDIES

For easy candy-dipping, follow this simple procedure:
1. Keep all utensils dry—moisture causes the chocolate to bloom, or acquire gray streaks.
2. Use a double boiler, placing only 1 inch of water in the bottom pan so that it does not touch the upper pan when in place.
3. Heat the water, but do not boil—steam can affect the chocolate.
4. Add the cut-up unsweetened chocolate, semisweet squares, semisweet chocolate pieces or milk chocolate. Stir only to melt—beating causes bubbles to form.

5. Add a small amount of shortening to thin the chocolate, if needed.
6. Dip the candies. Drain slightly; place on wax paper.
7. When the candies are set, pack in inexpensive candy dishes, fancy tins or boxes lined and covered with gold foil or Christmas wrap.

Chocolate Rum Raisin Mounds

Makes 4 dozen.

1   *box (15 ounces) seedless raisins (3 cups)*
1   *cup light or dark rum*
1   *package (12 ounces) semisweet chocolate pieces*
1   *tablespoon light corn syrup*

1. Place the raisins in a large plastic food bag; add the rum; secure the bag. Let the raisins soak for 3 hours. Drain the raisins by putting in a sieve; do not press. Use the liquid in fruit compote or spoon over ice cream.
2. Combine the chocolate pieces and the corn syrup in the top of a double boiler. Place over hot, not boiling, water until the chocolate melts; stir occasionally. Remove from the heat.
3. Fold the raisins into the melted chocolate, coating well. Drop by heaping teaspoonfuls onto wax paper. Chill until firm. Store in the refrigerator. When packing for gift giving, place wax paper between the layers to prevent sticking.

EASY SPREAD

When butter or margarine is too firm to cut, use a potato peeler to cut thin slices from a stick. It will soften in minutes.

SAVORY NIBBLES

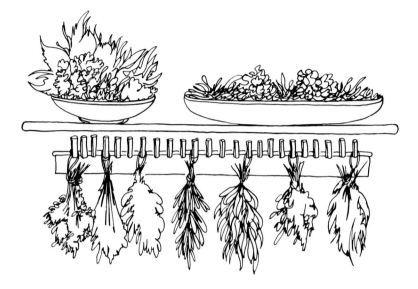

Cheese Twists

Bake at 400° for 10 to 12 minutes.
Makes 4½ dozen.

1   cup unsifted all-purpose flour
¼   teaspoon salt
¼   teaspoon cayenne pepper
5   tablespoons butter, well chilled (margarine
      won't work)
4   ounces Cheddar cheese, shredded (about 1 cup)
2   tablespoons ice water
1   teaspoon lemon juice

1. Preheat the oven to hot (400°).
2. Sift together the flour, salt and cayenne into a
   large bowl. Cut in the butter with a pastry blender
   until coarse crumbs are formed. Add the cheese;
   toss to combine.
3. Combine the water and lemon juice in a small
   bowl. Add to the flour mixture, stirring with a fork
   until the mixture forms a dough and comes
   together. Add another 1 teaspoon of water, if
   necessary.
4. Divide the dough in half. Keep one-half covered.
   Roll the other half out on a lightly floured surface
   into a 10 x 7-inch rectangle. Cut the dough in

half to form two 7 x 5-inch rectangles. Cut each
into fourteen 5 x ½-inch strips. Twist each strip 3
or 4 times. Place on an ungreased baking sheet.
5. Bake in the preheated hot oven (400°) for 10 to 12
   minutes, or until golden brown. Cool on the wire
   rack. Repeat with the remaining dough.
6. The twists can be stored in an airtight container at
   room temperature for up to 1 week.

Chili Cheese Spread

This zesty gift has a fiery Tex-Mex flavor. Good with taco chips.

Makes about 3 cups.

1   can (15 ounces) chili con carne with beans
1   package (8 ounces) cream cheese, softened
½   pound sharp Cheddar cheese, shredded (2 cups)
1   tablespoon chili powder
½   cup chopped parsley

1. Combine the chili con carne, cream cheese,
   shredded Cheddar cheese and chili powder in a
   large bowl. Blend well.
2. Turn into a crock; chill until firm, at least 6 hours
   or overnight. Garnish with the chopped parsley.

Cheddar And Ale Spread

You can shape this savory mixture into two parsley-nut-coated spheres.

Make about 6 cups.

6 cups shredded Cheddar cheese (about 1½ pounds)
1 package (3 ounces) cream cheese
¼ cup (½ stick) butter, softened
¾ cup ale or beer
1 teaspoon dry mustard
¼ teaspoon crushed red pepper flakes
½ cup finely chopped pistachio nuts
½ cup chopped parsley

1. Beat the Cheddar, cream cheese and butter in a large bowl with an electric mixer on high speed until smooth. Lower the mixer speed.
2. Gradually beat in the ale, mustard and red pepper flakes. Refrigerate the mixture until it is stiff enough to hold its shape, about 2 hours.
3. Line two small bowls (about 3 cups each) with plastic wrap. Divide the mixture equally between the bowls, smoothing tops. Cover; refrigerate for 4 hours or overnight.
4. Combine the pistachios and the parsley on wax paper. Unmold the cheese from the bowls; peel off the plastic wrap. Press the pistachio-parsley mixture over the balls to cover completely. Or, center a star-shaped cookie cutter on top of one ball; sprinkle the pistachio mixture outside, leaving the center of the cutter uncoated. Repeat with the second ball. The spread will keep in the refrigerator for up to 3 days.

SHORTENING KNOW-HOW

- *To measure shortening, pack into dry measuring cup, making sure all air pockets are gone; level off at top with knife or spatula.*
- *Shortening can be measured before or after it is melted.*
- *One stick of butter or margarine equals 4 ounces; 4 sticks equal 1 pound, or 2 cups.*
- *Vegetable shortening is not a substitute for butter or margarine, unless called for in a recipe.*
- *To ease removing packed shortening from a measuring cup, run hot water over it and immediately unmold it.*

Spiced Walnuts

Bake at 300° for 10 minutes.
Makes 3 cups.

¼ cup vegetable oil
2 teaspoons chili powder
½ teaspoon ground cumin
½ teaspoon ground turmeric
    Pinch cayenne
3 cups walnuts
½ teaspoon salt

1. Preheat the oven to slow (300°).
2. Combine the oil, chili powder, cumin, turmeric and cayenne in a large skillet. Heat over low heat until the oil is quite hot (do not let the oil smoke). Remove from the heat.
3. Add the walnuts to the oil; stir until coated. Spread the walnuts in a paper towel-lined shallow baking pan.
4. Bake in the preheated slow oven (300°) for 10 minutes, or until crisp. Sprinkle with the salt. Cool before storing in a covered container. The walnuts can be stored for up to a month.

Olivade

This pungent olive sauce goes well with hot or cold pasta, steamed or sautéed vegetables and broiled chicken or fish.

Makes 5 cups.

2 pounds large Kalamata olives in brine*, pitted
1½ cups extra-virgin olive oil
1¼ cups walnuts
2 small cloves garlic
2 teaspoons leaf basil, crumbled
½ teaspoon pepper
1 cup grated Parmesan cheese
2 to 4 teaspoons red wine vinegar, to taste

1. Combine the olives, olive oil, walnuts, garlic, basil and pepper in the bowl of a food processor or, working in batches, in a blender. Chop finely with several on-off pulses; do not over process; mixture should still be coarsely textured. Transfer to a bowl.
2. Stir in, by hand, the Parmesan cheese and the vinegar. The Olivade can be stored, tightly covered, in the refrigerator for up to 2 months.

*Note: Sold in the gourmet section of your supermarket or in specialty food shops.

FOOD
WRAP-UPS

Once you've baked your cookies, glazed the fruitcakes and prepared the snack mix, it's important to wrap your food attractively and safely.

● Wrap nuts or candy in glitter-sprinkled plastic wrap; tie up with narrow ribbon and attach to bow on a package.

● Give a fragrant clue to what's inside! Tie a cluster of cinnamon sticks to sprigs of greenery; wrap pickling spices or herbs in muslin, or tie up whole nutmeg in colorful red or green net and attach a mini-grater to it.

● Pair up your gift with something to eat it with—fancy toothpicks, a pickle fork, jam or relish spoon, demitasse spoons.

● Giving cheese? A cheese board, knife or box of imported crackers makes a happy addition!

● Fill a tissue-lined flower pot with cakes or cookies; tie up with a big cheerful bow.

● Make a cluster of small jingle bells and tiny tree ornaments or miniature candy canes; secure with a pretty bow. Fill out with sprigs of greenery.

● Tie together extra boughs from your tree; wire on two or three small pine cones and finish off with a velvet bow.

● Let your gift shine through—put special popcorn or nuts in inexpensive see-through canisters or tall glasses.

● Use wine glasses as containers for wine jellies. Cover tops of glasses with foil, then with a square of fabric tied around glass.

● Line a cake or cookie box with red and green tissue, fold over food, close with a gold seal.

● Place miniature cakes or pastries on individual doilies.

● Make your own elegant liqueur decanter from an old whiskey or liqueur bottle. Remove original label, paste on a pretty blank one and write the contents and the year and sign it. If the cap has a brand name on it, paint over with bright red nail polish. Tie a big bow around the neck and it's ready to give!

● Look for decorative bottles and decanters to hold flavored vinegars, oils and homemade liqueurs.

● For jams and jellies, look for jars with tight-fitting lids. If desired, top with a Decorative Jar Cover (explained below), a doily or a round piece of fabric cut with pinking shears and tied around the top with ribbon or yarn. For thick spreads, try attaching a small wooden spoon or spreader to the lid.

● *Decorative Jar Cover:* Using pinking shears, cut a circle one-inch wider than the top of your jar out of a piece of lightweight fabric. Sew some lace trim around the edge of the round. Sew $\frac{1}{4}$-inch elastic $\frac{1}{2}$ inch from the outer edge. (*See also our Cross-Stitch Jar Covers in Chapter V.*)

● For both jars and bottles, you can tie a piece of one of the ingredients (such as a whole chili pepper or a knob of fresh gingerroot) around the lid, using a piece of yarn or ribbon.

● Use large mugs to hold snack mixes and hors d'oeuvre straws. Tie with ribbon and wrap in heavy cellophane.

● Place fruitcakes and breads on top of a breadboard that is big enough to hold the food. Then wrap it all in heavy cellophane and tie it with a ribbon.

● Give cookies in baskets lined with doilies and threaded with grosgrain ribbon. Wrap with colored cellophane.

● Present cakes and cupcakes in the pans in which they were baked. This way, it's a double gift.

● Use fragrant herbs and greens to decorate the tops of jars and baskets.

● Wrap cookies and confections in colored tissue and twist the ends. Pile wrapped nibbles in a decorative tin or basket.

● Make homemade jams extra special by giving them in crystal jars.

● Small, plastic-wrapped loaves of bread look even more tantalizing when wrapped in colorful fabric. Try adding some ribbon, too.

● Sew sacks that are large enough to hold jars or bottles, then thread the tops with some decorative ribbon.

PACKING SHIPPING AND FOOD

Be sure to choose the right cakes, breads and cookies for mailing. Foods to be mailed must be sturdy and should keep well. Soft drop, bar and fruit cookies are good travelers, as are fruitcakes and pound cakes, and all kinds of breads. Give your crisper cookies and tender pies to neighbors and family nearby.

● Cylindrical containers in quart and half-gallon sizes are good choices for packing nuts, candies and cookies. Many come printed with holiday designs.

For Cookies: Use empty metal coffee or shortening tins for packing. Wrap two drop cookies back to back but wrap bar cookies individually with foil, and then seal using cellophane tape.

For Breads and Cakes: These should be sent in strong cardboard boxes, after you've wrapped your delicacies first in plastic wrap or strong plastic bags, and then again in aluminum foil.

To Pack:
● Line your containers with waterproof plastic wrap, wax paper or aluminum foil As filler, use crumpled foil, tissue paper or wax paper. Do *not* pack unsalted popcorn this way; it can become moldy, especially if the package is sent overseas.

● Pack cookies close together in order to leave as little empty space as possible. Shifting will cause them to break. If you're sending a variety of cookies, place the heaviest ones on the bottom. Place wrapped cakes and breads in a filler-lined box.

● Add more filler to the container, packing it down to minimize shifting and breakage. The box should be so full that you have to use pressure to tape it shut.

● If you can, wrap your package in corrugated cardboard, then a double layer of brown paper.

● Label only the top with the address of your friend or family member. Write "Fragile—Handle with Care" and "Perishable—Keep from Heat" on the top and on the sides of your package.

● Send overseas packages by air whenever possible to avoid spoilage.

QUICK, LAST-MINUTE FOOD TREATS

Simple-to-prepare goodies to serve or give as gifts.

Cheddar-Port Spread: Shred 1½ pounds sharp Cheddar cheese in the container of an electric food processor. Add 2 sticks butter, cut into pieces; process on high speed until blended. Pour ¼ cup Port wine, part at a time, through the feed tube. Process until smooth. Add 1 cup chopped, toasted walnuts and process 15 seconds longer. Spoon mixture into glass or ceramic bowls; cover with plastic wrap; chill up to 1 week. Decorate with whole pecans. Makes 4 cups.

Peanut Butter "Truffles": In a medium-size bowl, combine 1¼ cups graham cracker crumbs, 1 cup unsifted 10X (confectioners') sugar, 1 cup peanut butter and ¼ cup (½ stick) butter or margarine, softened.

Beat with a wooden spoon until well blended. Roll into walnut-size balls between palms, then roll in 1 cup chopped peanuts or chocolate jimmies. Makes about 3 dozen.

Pizza Popcorn: Melt ¼ cup (½ stick) butter or margarine in a small saucepan; stir in ½ teaspoon *each* leaf oregano and basil, crumbled, ½ teaspoon garlic salt and ⅛ teaspoon crushed red pepper flakes. Heat slowly for 1 minute, stirring. Pour mixture over 12 cups freshly prepared popcorn in a large bowl; sprinkle with 2 tablespoons grated Parmesan Cheese. Toss gently until coated. Makes 12 cups.

Pineapple Topping: Combine ½ cup firmly packed brown sugar and 1 tablespoon cornstarch in a medium-size saucepan; stir in 1 can (20 ounces) crushed pineapple in syrup. Cook, stirring constantly, until mixture thickens and boils for 3 minutes. Remove from heat; stir in 4 tablespoons (½ stick) butter or margarine just until melted. Serve warm or chilled over ice cream or steamed pudding. Makes 3 cups.

Mocha Fudge Sauce: Melt one 6-ounce package semisweet chocolate pieces in the top of a double boiler over hot, not boiling, water. Stir in 1 can (14 ounces) sweetened condensed milk, 1 teaspoon vanilla and a pinch of salt and continue cooking, stirring constantly, until mixture thickens slightly. Stir in 2 teaspoons instant espresso powder dissolved in ¼ cup hot water, and 2 tablespoons coffee liqueur. Let cool; pour into jar. Cover and refrigerate. If necessary, sauce may be thinned with some additional hot water. Makes about 1½ cups.

Quick Dilled Mushrooms: Place one jar (4½ ounces) whole mushrooms and their liquid in a small bowl. Stir in ¼ cup white vinegar, 1 to 2 tablespoons sugar, ¼ teaspoon salt and 2 tablespoons chopped fresh dill OR: ¾ teaspoon dried dillweed. Return mixture to jar; cover and refrigerate. (Or transfer to decorative container.) Makes 1 cup.

Chocolate-Covered Pretzels: Melt one 6-ounce package semisweet chocolate pieces with 1 tablespoon vegetable shortening in a small heatproof bowl over simmering water. Remove from heat, but keep bowl over water. Drop small pretzels, one at a time, into chocolate. Lift out with a fork, lightly tapping fork against side of bowl so excess chocolate drips back into bowl. Place dipped pretzels on wire rack over wax paper-lined cookie sheet. Allow to dry before packing between layers of wax paper in a container. Makes about 2 dozen.

Herb-Marinated Goat Cheese: Place small, round goat cheeses in wide-mouthed canning jars. Scatter hot red and green pickled peppers, cut into julienne pieces, over tops, then sprinkle with cracked pepper and thyme. Place a peeled garlic clove in each jar, then pour in enough fruity olive oil to cover cheese completely. Seal each jar well. Let stand in refrigerator for up to 2 weeks.

Honeyed Walnuts: Combine 1 cup light corn syrup with 2 cups honey, 1 cup orange juice, 1 tablespoon grated orange rind in a large saucepan. Bring mixture just to boiling. Remove from heat; stir in 1 pound walnut pieces, until well blended. Refrigerate and use as a topping for ice cream, cakes and steamed puddings.

Fresh Cranberry Sauce: Combine 2 cups fresh cranberries with 1 cup each sugar and orange juice in a medium-size saucepan. Cook over low heat until the sugar dissolves. Cover; bring to boiling. Continue cooking until the berries pop, about 10 minutes. Remove from heat; cool. Refrigerate. Makes 2 cups.

Herb Vinegar: Heat red or white wine vinegar slightly in a saucepan over low heat. Pour over a handful of fresh herbs packed in a decorative jar or cruet. Let stand, covered, at least 2 weeks.

Raspberry Butter: Blend ½ cup (1 stick) unsalted butter with ⅓ cup raspberry preserves and 2 teaspoons lemon juice in a small bowl until creamy. Place in a crock. Cover and refrigerate or freeze. Makes about ¾ cup.

CRAFTS BASICS
AND
ABBREVIATIONS

It doesn't matter if you've never picked up a knitting needle or crochet hook before. This primer will show you the basics of knitting and crocheting and embroidery stitches. With these skills, you can create virtually all our projects. We also explain the abbreviations used for the crafts in this book, as well as how to enlarge our designs.

So learn these basics, and get crafting. You'll be surprised how simple our projects really are when you go back through your Christmas Treasury and begin making all the wonderful gifts that are as much a joy to give as they are to receive.

HOW TO KNIT

KNITTING ABBREVIATIONS AND SYMBOLS

Knitting directions are always written in standard abbreviations. They look mysterious at first, but you'll soon know them: **beg** — beginning; **bet** — between; **bl** — block; **ch** — chain; **CC** — contrasting color; **dec(s)** — decrease(s); **dp** — double-pointed; " or **in(s)** — inch(es); **incl** — inclusive; **inc(s)** — increase(s); **k** — knit; **lp(s)** — loop(s); **MC** — main color; **oz(s)** — ounces(s); **psso** — pass slipped stitch over last stitch worked; **pat(s)** — pattern(s); **p** — purl; **rem** — remaining; **rpt** — repeat; **rnd(s)** — round(s); **sc** — single crochet; **sk** — skip; **sl** — slip; **sl st** — slip stitch; **sp(s),** — space(s); **st(s)** — stitch(es); **st st** — stockinette stitch; **tog** — together; **yo** — yarn over; **pc** — popcorn stitch.

* (asterisk) — directions immediately following * are to be repeated the specified number of times indicated in addition to the first time — i.e. "repeat from * 3 times more" means 4 times in all.

() (parentheses) — directions should be worked as often as specified — i.e., "(k 1, k 2 tog, k 3) 5 times" means to work what is in () 5 times in all.

THE BASIC STITCHES

Get out your needles and yarn, and slowly read your way through this special section. Practice the basic stitches illustrated here as you go along. Once you know them, you're ready to start knitting.

CASTING ON: This puts the first row of stitches on the needle. Measure off about two yards of yarn (or about an inch for each stitch you are going to cast on). Make a slip knot at this point by making a medium-size loop of yarn; then pull another small loop through it. Place the slip knot on one needle and pull on end gently to tighten (FIG. 1).

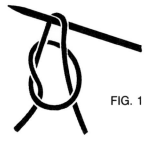

FIG. 1

● Hold the needle in your right hand. Hold both strands of yarn in the palm of your left hand securely but not rigidly. Slide your left thumb and forefinger between the two strands and spread these two fingers out so that you have formed a triangle of yarn.

Your left thumb should hold the free end of yarn, your forefinger the yarn from the ball, while the needle in your right hand holds the first stitch (FIG. 2).

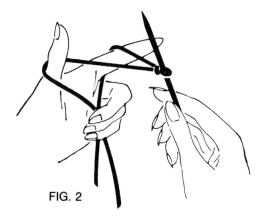

FIG. 2

You are now in position to cast on. See ABBREVIATIONS for explanations of asterisk (*).

● * Bring the needles in your right hand toward you; slip the tip of the needle under the front strand of the loop on left thumb (FIG. 3).

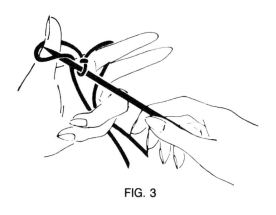

FIG. 3

• Now, with the needle, catch the strand of yarn that is on your left forefinger. (FIG. 4).

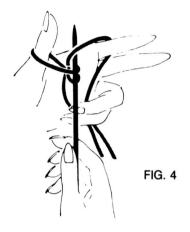

FIG. 4

• Draw it through the thumb loop to form a stitch on the needle (FIG. 5).

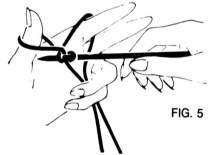

FIG. 5

• Holding the stitch on the needle with the right index finger, slip loop off your left thumb (FIG. 6). Tighten up the stitch on the needle by pulling the freed strand back with your left thumb, bringing the yarn back into position for casting on more stitches (FIG. 2 again).

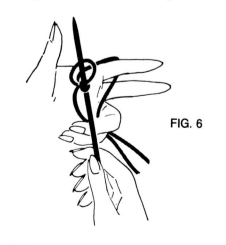

FIG. 6

• **Do not cast on too tightly.** Stitches should slide easily on the needle. Repeat from * until you have cast on the number of stitches specified in your instructions.

KNIT STITCH (k): Hold the needle with the cast-on stitches in your left hand (FIG. 7).

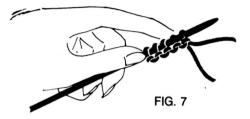

FIG. 7

• Pick up the other needle in your right hand. With yarn from the ball in **back** of the work, insert the tip of the right-hand needle from **left to right** through the front loop of the first stitch on the left-hand needle (FIG. 8).

FIG. 8

• Holding both needles in this position with your left hand, wrap the yarn over your little finger, under your two middle fingers and over the forefingers of your right hand. Hold the yarn firmly, but loosely enough so that it will slide through your fingers as you knit. Return the right-hand needle to your right hand.
• With your right forefinger, pass the yarn under (from right to left) and then over (from left to right) the tip of the right-hand needle, forming a loop on the needle (FIG. 9).

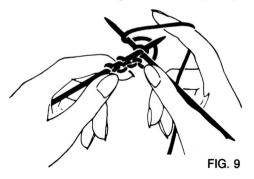

FIG. 9

● Now draw this loop through the stitch on the left-hand needle (FIG. 10).

FIG. 10

● Slip the original stitch off the left-hand needle, leaving the new stitch on right-hand needle (FIG. 11).

FIG. 11

Keep stitches loose enough so that you can slide them along the needles, but firm enough so they do not slide when you don't want them to. Continue until you have knitted all the stitches from the left-hand needle onto the right-hand needle.

● To start the next row, pass the needle with stitches on it to the left hand, reversing it, so that it now becomes the left-hand needle.

PURL STICH (p): Purling is the reverse of knitting. Again, keep the stitches loose enough to slide, but firm enough to work with. To purl, hold the needle with the stitches in your left hand, with the yarn in **front** of your work. Insert the tip of the right-hand needle from **right to left** through the front loop of the first stitch on the left-hand needle (FIG. 12).

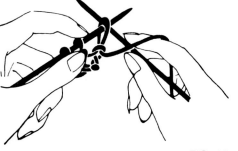

FIG. 12

● With your right hand holding the yarn in the same manner as to knit, but in **front** of the needles, pass the yarn over the tip of the right-hand needle, then under it, forming a loop on the needle. (FIG. 13).

FIG. 13

● Holding the yarn firmly so that it won't slip off, draw this loop through the stitch on the left-hand needle (FIG. 14).

FIG. 14

● Slip the original stitch off the left-hand needle, leaving the new stitch on the right-hand needle. (FIG. 15).

FIG. 15

SLIP STITCH (sl st): Insert the tip of the right-hand needle into the next stitch on the left-hand needle, as if to purl, unless otherwise directed. Slip this stitch off the left-hand needle onto the right, **without working it** (FIG. 16).

FIG. 16

BINDING OFF: This makes a finished edge and locks the stitches securely in place. Knit (or purl) two stitches. Then, with the tip of the left-hand needle, lift the first of these two stitches over the second stitch and drop it off the tip of the right-hand needle (FIG. 17).

FIG. 17

One stitch remains on the right-hand needle, and one stitch has been bound off.
● Knit (or purl) the next stitch; lift the first stitch over the last stitch and off the tip of the needle. Again, one stitch remains on the right-hand needle, and another stitch has been bound off. Repeat from * until the required number of stitches has been bound off.
● Remember that you work **two** stitches to bind off one stitch. If, for example, the directions read, "k 6, bind off the next 4 sts, k 6..." you must knit six stitches, then knit **two more** stitches before starting to bind off. Bind off four times. After the four stitches have been bound off, count the last stitch remaining on the right-hand needle as the first stitch of the next six stitches. When binding off, always knit the knitted stitches and purl the purled stitches.

● Be careful not to bind off too tightly or too loosely. The tension should be the same as the rest of the knitting.
● To end off the last stitch on the bound-off edge, if you are ending this piece of work here, cut the yarn leaving a six-inch end; pass the cut end through the remaining loop on the right-hand needle and pull snugly (FIG. 18).

FIG. 18

SHAPING TECHNIQUES

Now that you know the basics, all that's left to learn are a few techniques which will help shape whatever it is you are making.

Increasing (inc): This means adding stitches in a given area to shape your work. There are several ways to increase.

1. To increase by knitting twice into the same stitch: Knit the stitch in the usual way through the front loop (FIG. 19),

FIG. 19

but **before** dropping the stitch from the left-hand needle, knit **another** stitch on the same loop by placing the needle into the back of the stitch. (FIG. 20).
Slip the original stitch off your left-hand needle. You have made two stitches from one stitch.

2. To increase by knitting between stitches: Insert the tip of the right-hand needle under the strand of yarn **between** the stitch you've just worked and the following stitch; slip it onto the tip of the left-hand needle (FIG. 21).

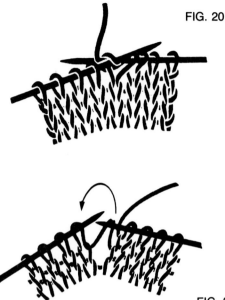

FIG. 20

FIG. 23

FIG. 21

Now knit into the back of the loop (FIG. 22).

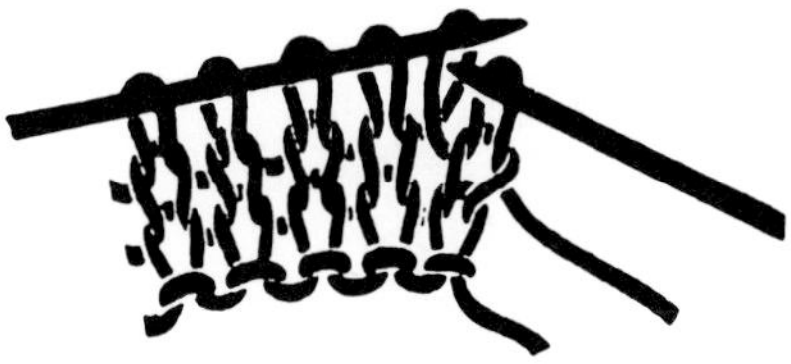

Decreasing (dec): This means reducing the number of stitches in a given area to shape your work. Two methods for decreasing are:

1. To decrease by knitting (FIG. 24) or purling (FIG. 25) two stitches together:

FIG. 24

FIG. 22

3. To increase by "yarn-over" (yo): Pass the yarn over the right-hand needle after finishing one stitch and before starting the next stitch, **making an extra stitch (arrow in FIG. 23). If you are knitting,** bring the yarn under the needle to the back. **If you are purling,** wind the yarn around the needle once. On the next row, work all yarn-overs as stitches.

FIG. 25

Insert the right-hand needle through the loops of two stitches on the left-hand needle at the same time, complete the stitch. This is written as "k 2 tog" or "p 2 tog."
● If you work through the **front** loops of the stitches in the usual way, your decreasing stitch will slant to the right. If you work through the **back** loops of the stitches, your decreasing stitch will slant to the left.

2. Slip 1 stitch, knit 1 and psso: Insert the right-hand needle through the stitch on the left-hand needle, but instead of working it, just slip if off onto the right-hand needle (go back to FIG. 16). Work the next stitch in the usual way. With the tip of the left-hand needle, lift the slipped stitch over the last stitch worked and off the tip of the right-hand needle (FIG. 26).

FIG. 26

Your decreasing stitch will slant to the left. This is written as "sl 1, k 1, psso."

Pass Slipped Stitch Over (psso): Slip one stitch from the left-hand needle to the right-hand needle and, being careful to keep it in position, work the next stitch. Then, with the tip of the left-hand needle, lift the slipped stitch over the last stitch and off the tip of the needle (FIG. 26).

ATTACHING THE YARN

When you end one ball of yarn or wish to change colors, begin at the start of a row and tie the new yarn with the previous yarn, making a secure joining. Continue to knit or purl (FIG. 27).

FIG. 27

HOW TO CROCHET

CROCHET ABBREVIATIONS

Following is a crochet abbreviations listing, with definitions of the terms given. To help you become accustomed to abbreviations used, we have repeated them through our stitch instructions.

beg — begin, beginning; **ch** — chain; **dc** —double crochet; **dec** — decrease; **dtr** — double treble crochet; **hdc** — half double crochet; **in(s)** or **"** — inch(es); **inc** — increase; **oz(s)** — ounce(s); **pat** — pattern; **pc** — picot; **rem** — remaining; **rnd** — round; **rpt** — repeat; **sc** — single crochet; **skn(s)** — skein(s); **sk** — skip, **sl st** — slip stitch; **sp** — space; **st(s)** — stitch(es); **tog** — together; **tr** — triple crochet; **work even** — continue without further increase or decrease; **yo** — yarn over; **'** — repeat whatever follows **'** as many times as indicated; () — do what is in parentheses as many times as indicated.

Directions for right-handed and left-handed crocheters
Most crochet stitches are started from a base of chain stitches. However, our stitches are started from a row of single crochet stitches which gives body to the sample swatches and makes practice work easier to handle. When making a specific item, follow the stitch directions as given.

Holding the crochet hook properly (see FIG. 1), start by practicing the slip knot (see FIG. 2) and base chain (see FIG. 3, page 264).

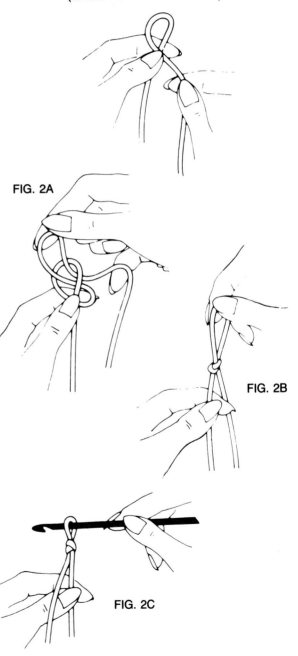

FIG. 2 THE SLIP KNOT (BASIS FOR CHAIN STITCH)

FIG. 2A

FIG. 2B

FIG. 2C

FIG. 1 HOLDING THE HOOK

Chain Stitch (ch): Follow the steps in FIG. 3. As you make the chain stitch loops, the yarn should slide eaily between your index and middle fingers. Make about 15 loops. If they are all the same size, you have maintained even tension. If uneven, rip them out by pulling on the long end of the yarn. Practice making chains and ripping out until you have a perfect chain.

For Left-handed Crocheters
FIGS. 1 to 3 are for right-handed crocheters and are repeated in FIGS. 1 Left to 3 Left for left-handed crocheters.

**LEFT-HANDED CROCHETERS
FIGS. 1 LEFT TO 3 LEFT**

FIG. 3 CHAIN STITCH (CH)

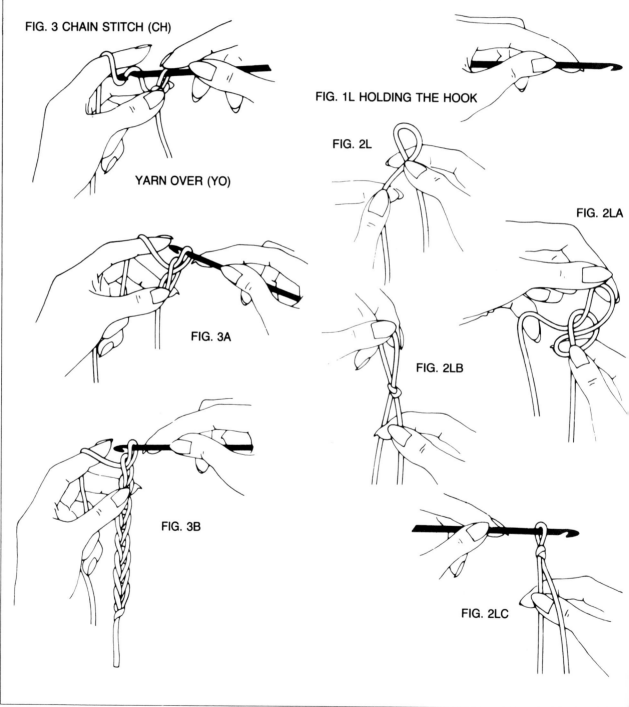

YARN OVER (YO)

FIG. 3A

FIG. 3B

FIG. 1L HOLDING THE HOOK

FIG. 2L

FIG. 2LA

FIG. 2LB

FIG. 2LC

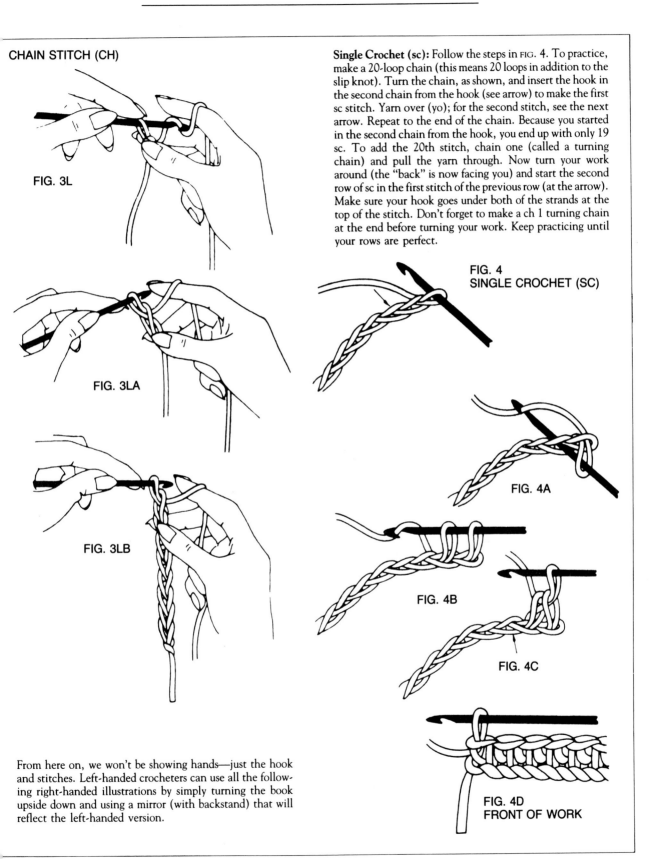

CHAIN STITCH (CH)

FIG. 3L

FIG. 3LA

FIG. 3LB

Single Crochet (sc): Follow the steps in FIG. 4. To practice, make a 20-loop chain (this means 20 loops in addition to the slip knot). Turn the chain, as shown, and insert the hook in the second chain from the hook (see arrow) to make the first sc stitch. Yarn over (yo); for the second stitch, see the next arrow. Repeat to the end of the chain. Because you started in the second chain from the hook, you end up with only 19 sc. To add the 20th stitch, chain one (called a turning chain) and pull the yarn through. Now turn your work around (the "back" is now facing you) and start the second row of sc in the first stitch of the previous row (at the arrow). Make sure your hook goes under both of the strands at the top of the stitch. Don't forget to make a ch 1 turning chain at the end before turning your work. Keep practicing until your rows are perfect.

FIG. 4
SINGLE CROCHET (SC)

FIG. 4A

FIG. 4B

FIG. 4C

FIG. 4D
FRONT OF WORK

From here on, we won't be showing hands—just the hook and stitches. Left-handed crocheters can use all the following right-handed illustrations by simply turning the book upside down and using a mirror (with backstand) that will reflect the left-handed version.

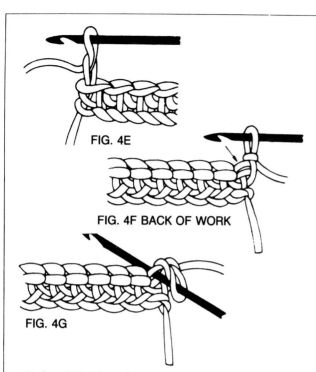

FIG. 4E

FIG. 4F BACK OF WORK

FIG. 4G

Ending Off: Follow the steps in FIG. 5. To finish off your crochet, cut off all but 6" of yarn and end off as shown. (To "break off and fasten," follow the same procedure.)

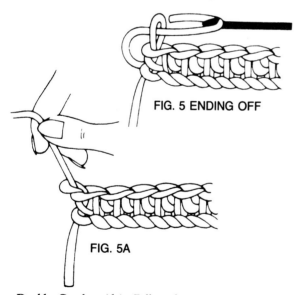

FIG. 5 ENDING OFF

FIG. 5A

Double Crochet (dc): Follow the steps in FIG. 6. To practice, ch 20, then make a row of 20 sc. Now, instead of a ch 1, you will make a ch 3. Turn your work, yo and insert the hook in the second stitch of the previous row (at the arrow), going under both strands at the top of the stitch. Pull the yarn through. You now have three loops on the hook. Yo and pull through the first two, then yo and pull

through the remaining two—one double crochet (dc) made. Continue across the row, making a dc in each stitch (st) across. Dc in the top of the turning chain (see arrow in FIG. 7). Ch 3. Turn work. Dc in second stitch on the previous row and continue as before.

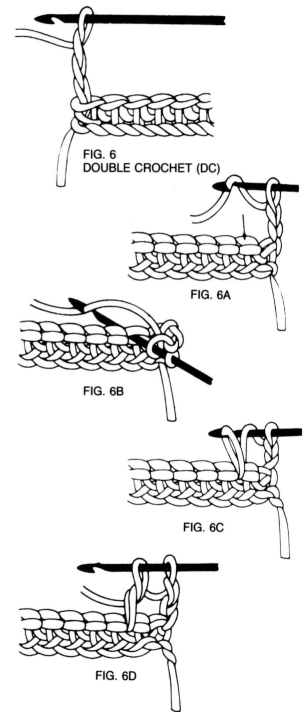

FIG. 6
DOUBLE CROCHET (DC)

FIG. 6A

FIG. 6B

FIG. 6C

FIG. 6D

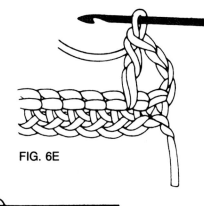

FIG. 6E

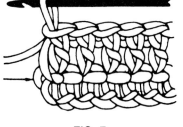

FIG. 7

Note: You may also start a row of dc on a base chain (omitting the sc row). In this case, insert the hook in the fourth chain from the hook, instead of the second (see FIG. 8).

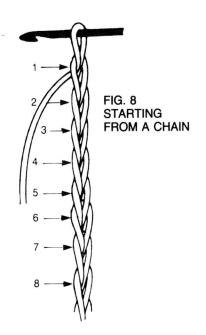

FIG. 8
STARTING
FROM A CHAIN

Slip Stitch (sl st): Follow the steps in FIG. 9. This is a utility stitch you will use for joining, shaping and ending off. After you chain and turn, *do not yo.* Just insert the hook into the *first* stitch of the previous row (see FIG. 9A), and pull the yarn through the stitch, then right through the loop on the hook—sl st made.

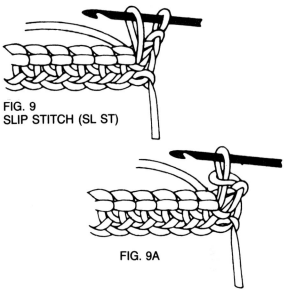

FIG. 9
SLIP STITCH (SL ST)

FIG. 9A

Half Double Crochet (hdc): Follow the steps in FIG. 10 and 10A. To practice, make a chain and a row of sc. Ch 2 and turn; yo. Insert the hook in the second stitch, as shown; yo and pull through to make three loops on the hook. Yo and pull the yarn through *all* three loops at the same time—hdc made. This stitch is used primarily as a transitional stitch from an sc to a dc. Try it and see—starting with sc's, then an hdc and then dc's.

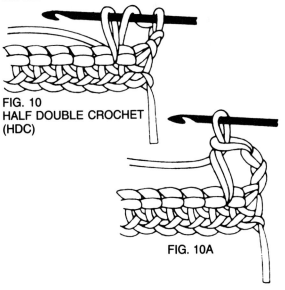

FIG. 10
HALF DOUBLE CROCHET
(HDC)

FIG. 10A

Techniques of Crocheting: Now that you have practiced and made sample squares of all the basic stitches, you are ready to learn about adding and subtracting stitches to change the length of a row whenever it's called for. This is achieved by increasing (inc) and decreasing (dec).

To increase (inc): Just make two stitches in the same stitch in the previous row (see arrow in FIG. 11). The technique is the same for any kind of stitch.

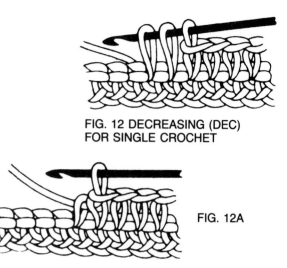

FIG. 12 DECREASING (DEC) FOR SINGLE CROCHET

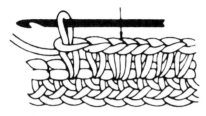

FIG. 11 INCREASING (INC) FOR SINGLE CROCHET

FIG. 12A

To decrease (dec) for single-crochet (sc): Yo and pull the yarn through two stitches to make three loops on the hook (see steps in FIG. 12). Pull the yarn through all the loops at once—dec made. Continue in regular stitches.

To decrease for double crochet (dc): In a dc row, make the next stitch and stop when you have two loops on the hook. Now yo and make a dc in the next stitch. At the point where you have three loops on the hook, pull yarn through all loops at the same time. Finish the row with regular dc.

EMBROIDERY STITCH GUIDE

Blanket Stitch

Work from left to right, with the point of the needle and the edge of the work toward you. The edge of the fabric can be folded under or left raw. Secure the thread and bring out below the edge. For the first and each succeeding stitch, insert the needle through the fabric from the right side and bring it out at the edge. Keeping the thread from the previous stitch *under* the point of the needle, draw the needle and thread through, forming a stitch over the edge. The stitch size and spacing can be the same or varied.

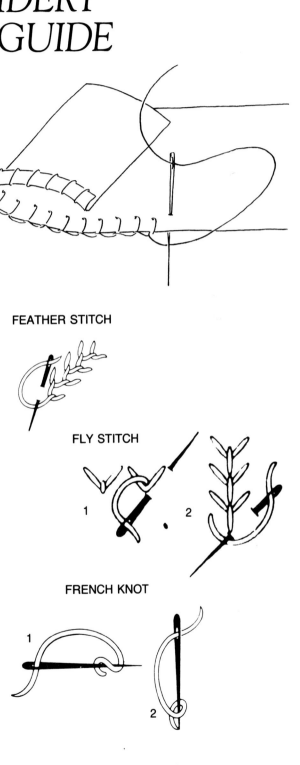

CHAIN STITCH

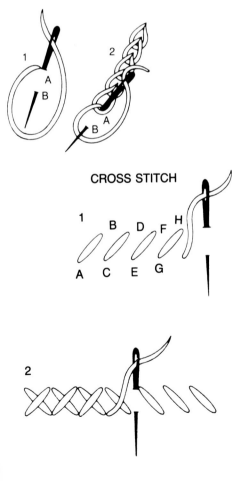

CROSS STITCH

FEATHER STITCH

FLY STITCH

FRENCH KNOT

INTERLOCKING GOBELIN STITCH

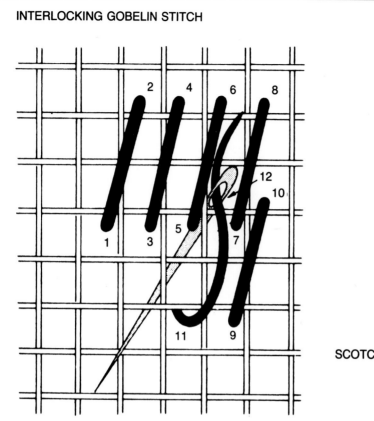

LONG AND SHORT

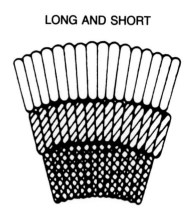

SCOTCH STITCH

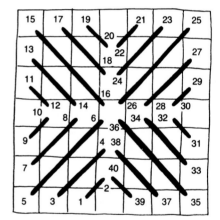

MOSAIC STITCH

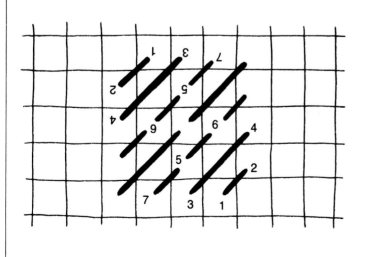

SCOTCH STITCH VARIATION

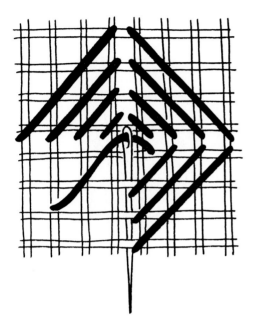

STRAIGHT STITCH

TENT OR CONTINENTAL STITCH OR PETIT POINT

SLANTED GOBELIN STITCH (worked vertically)

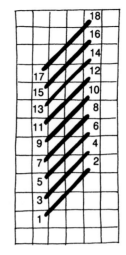

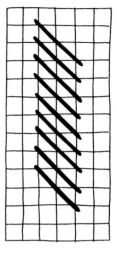

HOW TO ENLARGE DESIGNS

If the design is not already marked off in squares, make a tracing of it. Mark the tracing off in squares: For a small design, make squares ¼"; for larger designs, use ½" or 2" squares, or the size indicated in the directions. Decide the size of enlargement. On another sheet of tracing paper, mark off the same number of squares that are on the design or original tracing. For example, to make your design, each new square must be 6 times larger than the original. Copy the outline from your original tracing to the new one, square by square. Use dressmaker's carbon and a tracing wheel to transfer the design onto the material you are decorating.

MATERIALS SHOPPING GUIDE

The following page lists the projects that suggest using specific manufacturers' products. Next, you'll find an alphabetized list of these manufacturers, along with their mailing addresses. All items were available at press time.

PROJECTS AND PRODUCTS

Stencilled Gifts (*page 92*)—Self-adhesive stencils and fabric-painting dyes: Accent Country Color Fabric Painting Dyes (2-ounce squeeze bottle) in colors #2421 Holiday Red; #2448 Apricot Stone; #2428 Off-White; #2451 Village Green; Accent Country Colors Acrylic (2-ounce squeeze bottle) in colors in #2448 Apricot Stone; #2451 Village Greene; #2450 Roseberry, #2428 Off White. Accent Clear Acrylic Spray Sealer #173 Clear Acrylic. Accent Designer Spray (8 oz.) #150 Soft White. Accent Instant Finish Alkyd Varnish #191 Clear Gloss. All products by Illinois Bronze Paint Co.

Patchwork Clock (*page 104*)—Craft Ribbon: "Country Cottage Collection" by Offray-Gear®.

Satin Stocking, Nosegay Ornaments, Satin-Covered Balls and Lace Wreath (*pages 132-3*)—Ribbon for flowers, picot-edge taffeta (Style #7411, ½" and 1½" wide); by C.M. Offray & Son, Inc.; gift-wrap lace, "Realace" (1" and 2½" wide, Color White) and white floral ribbon, "Stem-tex," by Lion Ribbon Co.; pearl stamens available at LeeWards Retail Stores: fabric for balls and stockings, "Bridal Slipper" satin (Style 800, 100% Eastmans Estron® acetate, 45" wide, Colors Shocking Pink, Lilac) by Pago

Fabrics Corp.; Styrofoam® balls and wreath from Modern-Miltex Corp.; narrow lace on balls (Style #L1524, Color White) and ruffled lace on stocking by Hirschberg, Schutz & Co., Inc.; clear acrylic spray for sizing, "Krylon" Crystal Clear by Borden® Consumer Products Div.

Star Ornaments (*page 151*)—Chenille and Gold Tinsel-Tex stem from D. Jay Products.

Pine Cone Wreath (*page 166*)—Wire star bases available from floral supply shops.

Ducky Wreath (*page 200*)—Striped craft ribbon: "Kerry" ribbon from Lion Ribbon Co.

MANUFACTURERS AND ADDRESSES

Borden Consumer Products, Div., Borden Chemical Inc., 180 East Broad Street, Columbus, OH 43215

D. Jay Products, 138 Washington St., Newark, NJ 07102

Gear Licensee, C.M. Offray and Son, Route 24, P.O. Box 601, Chester, NJ 07930-0601

Hirschberg, Schutz and Co., Inc. 317 St. Pauls Ave., Jersey City, NJ 07306

Illinois Bronze Paint Co., 300 East Main Street Lake Zurich, IL 60047

Lace Country, H.K. Company (Emil Katz) 21 West 38 St., New York, NY 10018

Lion Ribbon Co., 100 Metro Way, Secaucus, NJ 07094

Modern-Miltex Corp., 280 East 134th St., Bronx, NY 10454

Pago Fabrics Corp., 48 W. 38 St. New York, NY 10018

Springs Industry, 104 West 40th St., New York, NY 10018

INDEX

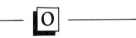